COMPENSATION MANAGEMENT

Dr. Kanchan Bhatia

Himalaya Publishing House
ISO 9001:2015 CERTIFIED

First Edition : 2009
Reprint : 2010, 2011, 2012, 2015
Reprint 2016, 2017, 2019, 2021
Reprint : 2022, 2023, 2024
Reprint : 2026

Published by : Mrs. Meena Pandey
for **HIMALAYA PUBLISHING HOUSE PVT. LTD.,**
Vishal Industrial Estate, 1st Floor, Office No. 63/64,
Bhandup Village Road, Subhash Nagar (Opp. CEAT Tyres),
Nahur (W), Mumbai - 400 078. **Phone:** 022-35131464/65/66/67
E-mail: himpub@bharatmail.co.in; **Website:** www.himpub.com

Branch Offices :

New Delhi : "Pooja Apartments", 4-B, Murari Lal Street, Ansari Road, Darya Ganj, New Delhi - 110 002. Phone: 011-23270392, 23278631; Fax: 011-23256286

Nagpur : Kundanlal Chandak Industrial Estate, Ghat Road, Nagpur - 440 018. Phone: 0712-2738731, 2721216

Bengaluru : Plot No. 91-33, 2nd Main Road, Seshadripuram, Behind Nataraja Theatre, Bengaluru - 560 020. Phone: 080-41138821; Mobile: 09379847017, 09379847005

Hyderabad : No. 3-4-184, Lingampally, Besides Raghavendra Swamy Matham, Kachiguda, Hyderabad - 500 027. Phone: 040-27560041, 27550139

Chennai : No. 34/44, Motilal Street, T. Nagar, Chennai - 600 017. Mobile: 09380460419

Pune : First Floor, "Laksha" Apartment, No. 527, Mehunpura, Shaniwarpeth (Near Prabhat Theatre), Pune - 411 030. Phone: 020-24496323, 24496333; Mobile: 09370579333

Cuttack : Plot No 5F-755/4, Sector-9, CDA Markat Nagar, Cuttack - 753 014, Odisha. Mobile: 09338746007

Kolkata : 3, S.M. Bose Road, Near Gate No. 5, Agarpara Railway Station, North 24 Parganas, West Bengal - 700 109. Mobile: 09674536325

DTP by : Rajani Tambe

Printed by : Trinity Academy, Delhi. On behalf of HPH.

Dedicated To,

God Almighty

PREFACE

This book recognizes the important role played by compensation in modern organization. An organization understands that effective compensation and benefit plans are critical to success in today's highly competitive business environment. A shortage of qualified talent and demands for more stringent executive accountability and long term commitment.

Conventional compensation has quickly become obsolete, requiring a more creative approach as well as new compensation techniques and vehicles.

Compensation is the cornerstone of every organization's talent management strategy. It drives the long term planning for a company and effects key performance drivers for the workforce. Compensation is a key issue for the high performance organization, as the employee and management systems utilized by the organizations must be reinforced through the reward structure.

This book integrates the theories, principles and applications of specific behavioural disciplines to provide an in-depth understanding of the subject and incorporates the invaluable practical experiences of practicing managers. Specifically, an attempt has been made to clarify, enhance and update the information to truly reflect the emerging perspective in the field of compensation.. Appropriate modifications have been made in the various topics covered and the numerous research studies published during the preceding years have been included.

A special feature of this book is that, it provides a basic purpose for establishment of a sound compensation and reward administration and aligns compensation strategy with business strategy. This book adapts a system viewpoint, thereby projecting cohesive, organic "whole" consisting of interrelated and interdependent facets examined through Twelve chapters. Each chapter is relevant for achieving sustainable competitive advantage. Chapter 1 initiates the discussion on concept and objectives of compensation. It also focusses on components and dimensions of compensation and non-compensation system. Compensation is defined as money received in performance of work and many kinds of services and benefits that organization's provide to their employees. It is a systematic approach of providing monetary value to employees in exchange of work performed. Chapter 2 focusses on strategic perspectives in compensation and aligning compensation strategy with business strategy. It also reflects trends in compensation, diagnosis and benchmarking.

Chapter 3 tells us how to design a compensation system and internal & external equity in compensation. Chapter 4 focusses on performance based compensation system. It covers issues like pay related performance, performance linked incentives, and relationship of performances, compensation and motivation. Chapter 5 explains the concept of wages, wage determination process and wage policy in India.

Chapter 6 throws light on basic concept of incentives, types of wage incentive plan and suggest measures to make incentive system effective.

Chapter 7 discusses the nature. significance and need for job analysis and also discusses job design and its approaches. Chapter 8 introduces job evaluation which is a systematic technique determining the worth of a job in relation to other jobs. It also explains the prerequisite for successful job evaluation program.

Chapter 9 explains the concept of benefits. It is defined as any wage cost not directly connected with employees productive, effort , performance service or sacrifies. It includes legally required benefits retirement, medical and employee stock option plan.

Chapter 10 discusses various statutory provisions related to compensation. Chapter 11 discusses special features and components and compensation for CEO's and top executives.

Chapter 12 explains the objectives of international compensation, compensation practices of MNCs, strategic choice in global compensation and focusses on emerging trends in global compensation. An attempt has been made to clarify and update various concepts, practices and present emerging perspectives abroad and in India, which provides the student with the opportunity to solve real world problems.

Comments and suggestions for the improvement of the book shall be highly appreciated and duly acknowledged.

Dr. Kanchan Bhatia

ACKNOWLEDGEMENT

I wish to express my sincere thanks to many people who have contributed to my understanding of compensation and to the preparation of this textbook. It is a combined contribution of the writings of so many scholars, authors and the publishers.

I express my immense gratitude to them for their ideas and valuable contribution.

I am also appreciative to my family members who helped me in the completion of this book.I owe a special, continuing depth of gratitude to my studends, staff of my college and my colleagues who motivated me to complete this book.

I am thankful to the Managing Director, Himalaya Publications and his committed team for expediting and the nice getup of the book.

I will be failing in my duty if do not acknowledge the assistance of my institute people for their kind support.

My thanks to Dr. P.K. Mishra, Dean & Director CRIM, Bhopal, Prof. V.P. Singh Director, SIRT, Dr. S. K. Govil, Director, LNCT, Dr. R.S. Tiwari Director, Bansal College, Prof. P. K. Chopra, Director VNS College, col. Kundalkar

Dr. Kanchan Bhatia

CONTENTS

INTRODUCTION TO COMPENSATION

1

LEARNING OBJECTIVES

After reading this chapter, you should be able to understand —

- ➯ Concept of compensation
- ➯ Objectives and importance of compensation
- ➯ Understand the components and dimensions of compensation
- ➯ The dimensions of non-compensation system
- ➯ Factor's effecting employee compensation

CONCEPT OF COMPENSATION

Compensation is a systematic approach to providing monetary value to employees in exchange for work performed. It is a tool used by management for a variety of purposes to further the existence of the company.

It may be adjusted according to the business needs, goals and available resources.

Definition

Compensation may be defined as money received in performance of work and many kinds of services and benefits that an organization provides to their employees.

Compensation is a systematic approach of providing monetary value to employees in exchange for work performed. It may help to achieve several purposes, such as recruitment, job performance and job satisfaction. It is also defined as the package of quantifiable rewards an employee receives for her or his labour. It represents both, the intrinsic (psychological mindsets resulting from job performance) and extrinsic (including both monetary and non-monetary) rewards. The term, compensation, refers to all forms of financial returns and tangible benefits that an employee receives as a part of employment relationship. In the globalization era, where the business environment has become increasingly complex and challenging, designing an effective compensation program to attract and retain talent is an important function of organizational effectiveness.

OBJECTIVES OF COMPENSATION

- To recruit and retain qualified employees.
- To increase or maintain morale/satisfaction.
- To motivate employees for better performance.
- To attract and retain skilled and talented workforce.
- To determine basic wages and salary administration.
- To achieve internal and external equity.
- To ensure equal pay for equal work, that is, each individual's pay is fair in comparison to that of another person doing a similar job.
- To support, communicate and reinforce an organization's culture, value and competitive strategy.
- To reduce turnover and encourage company loyalty.
- To reward for exceptional job performance with plans including bonuses, commissions, profit sharing, stocks, gain sharing etc.
- To control cost - A rational compensation system helps the organization to obtain and retain workers at a reasonable cost.
- Comply with legal regulation - A sound wage and salary system consider the legal challenges imposed by the government and ensures the employees compliance.

Morale and job satisfaction is affected by compensation. Often there is a balance (equity) that must be reached between the monetary value the employer is willing to pay and the sentiments of worth felt by the employee. In an attempt to save money, employers may opt to freeze salaries or salary levels at the expense of satisfaction and morale. Conversely, an employer willing to reduce employee turnover may seek to increase salaries and salary levels.

IMPORTANCE OF COMPENSATION PROGRAM

Compensation represents by far the most important element in the employment relationship and is of equal interest to the employer, employee and government.

To the employer; because it represents a significant part of his cost, is increasingly important to his employee's performance and to competitiveness and affects his ability to recruit and retain a labour force of quality.

To the employee because it is fundamental to his standard of living and is a measure of the value of his services or performance.

To the government; because it affects the aspects of macroeconomics, stability such as employment, inflation, purchasing power and socio-economic development in general.

Compensation will be perceived by employees as fair if based on systematic components. Various compensation systems have developed to determine the value of positions. These systems utilize many similar components including job description, salary ranges/structure and written procedures.

Job description: A critical component of both compensation and selection systems, job description define in writing the responsibilities, requirements, functions, duties, location, environment, conditions and other aspects of the job. Description may be developed for job individually or for entire families.

Job analysis: The procedure of analyzing jobs from which job description is developed. Job analysis techniques include the use of interviews, questionnaires and observations.

Job evaluation: A system for comparing jobs for the purpose of determining compensation levels for individual jobs or job elements.

Pay structure: It is useful for standardizing compensation practices. Most pay structures include several grades with each grade containing a minimum salary/wage and either step increments or grade range. Step increments are common with union positions where the pay for each job is predetermined through collective bargaining.

Salary surveys: Collections of salary and market data. It includes average salaries, inflation indicators, cost of living indicators and salary budget averages. Companies may purchase result of surveys conducted by salary vendors or may conduct their own salary surveys.

Policies and regulations: It includes fair policies of compensation, which is comprised of a system of components developed to maintain internal and external equity.

Total compensation package

Compensation or rewards (incentives) can be classified into:

(a) Direct compensation

(b) Indirect compensation

(c) Non-monetary compensation

Direct compensation includes money, popularly known as basic salary or wage, (gross pay) where the individual is entitled for his job, overtime work and holiday premiums, bonuses based on performance, profit sharing and opportunities to purchase stock option.

Indirect compensation includes benefits that may consist of life, accident, health insurance, the employers contribution to retirement (pension), pay for vacation or illness and employers are required to make payments for employees welfare as social security.

Non-monetary compensation can include any benefits an employee receives from an employer or job that does not involve tangible value. This includes career and social rewards such as job security, flexible hours and opportunity for growth, praise and recognition, task enjoyment, friendships etc.

CORE COMPONENTS OF COMPENSATION (ELEMENTS OF SUCCESSFUL COMPENSATION PACKAGE)

Compensation is one of the most important human resource functions in an organization. For many organizations, compensation is the biggest single cost of doing business. An organization's compensation system can help to reinforce the key corporate values and facilitate the achievement of organizational objective.

The total compensation package may be described in many ways, but is basically classified into various components.

Direct Compensation

(1) Base pay — It is the first component of executive remuneration. It is determined through job evaluation i.e., according to level of skill, effort and responsibility required to perform the jobs and the severity of the working conditions. Because paying a wage is a standard practice, the competitive advantage can only come by paying a higher amount.

(2) Bonus — It is mainly a gift given occasionally to reward exceptional performance or for special occasions. It plays an important role in today's competitive executive payment program. Bonuses can show an employer appreciating his/her employees and ensure that good performance or special events are rewarded. This type of incentive is usually short-term (annual) and is based on performance or profit sharing.

New English Dictionary defines Bonus as, A boon or gift over and above what is normally due as remuneration to the receiver and which is therefore, something wholly to be good.

There are basically four types of bonuses namely:

(1) Production bonus,

(2) Bonus as an implied term of contract between the parties,

(3) Customary bonus in connection with some festival, and

(4) Profit bonus.

Profit bonus has been given statutory recognition in the Payment of Bonus Act. Under this, the quantum of bonus depends on the extent of profit obtained in the relevant year. Executives deserve bonus because they have much more opportunity to influence organizational success than non-managerial staff.

(3) Long-term incentives or stock options — It is defined as a right to buy a piece of the business, which may be given to an employee to reward excellent service. If bonus constitutes short-term benefit, stock options are long-term benefits offered to executives.

An executive is given the right to purchase the company's share at afixed price. Stock option is valuable as long as the price of share keeps increasing. An employee, who owns a share of the business, or just a few acres, is far more likely to go an extra mile for the operation.

(4) Perks or perquisites — Perks constitute a major source of income for executives. In addition, to the normally allowed perks like provident fund, gratuity executives enjoy perks such as vacation travel, membership in club and well-furnished houses. In many cases, companies take care of servants, telephone bills and even car fuel.

While monetary incentives often appear as important motivators, many factors unrelated to money can also serve as, " attention-getters" and " encouragers of action". The classification of such non-financial incentives tends to a source of desirable 'things' that are potentially at disposal of the organization.

The creation of such rewards is only limited by manager's ingenuity and ability to assess payroll's that individuals within the organization find desirable and which are within the manager's jurisdiction".

Indirect Compensation

In a tight labour market, indirect compensation becomes increasingly important. Businesses that cannot compete with high cash wages can offer very individualized alternatives that meet the needs of the employee. Some of the indirect compensation alternatives are:

- Flexible working schedules.
- Elder care
- Retirement programs
- Moving expenses
- Insurance (health, eye, dental)
- Subsidized housing
- Paid leaves (sick/holiday/personal days)
- Subsidized utilities
- Tickets to events (ball games, concerts)
- Magazines subscriptions
- Boots and clothing
- Laundry services
- Company parties
- Use of machinery, farm produce goods/meals
- Cellular phones/pagers
- Child care.

Non-monetary benefits: These includes challenging job responsibilities, competent supervision, offer supportive leadership and management, comfortable working conditions etc.

DIMENSIONS OF NON-COMPENSATION SYSTEM

Non-compensation rewards: These rewards have an indefinite number of components that relate to the work situation and to the physical and psychological well-being of each worker. (Richard Henderson).

The model of non-compensation system is mentioned in the figure below:

Dimension of Non-compensation System

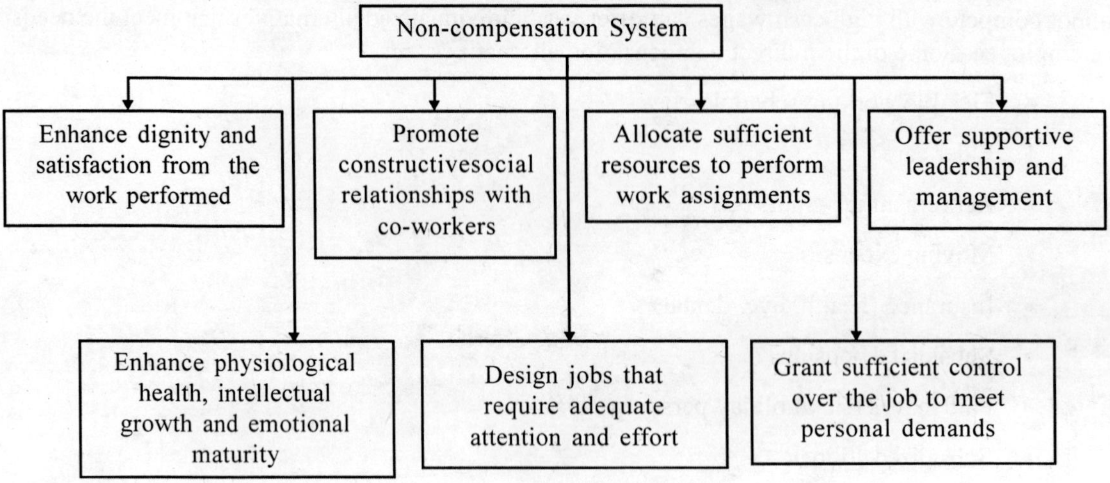

Fig. 1.1

Source: Henderson Richard 1, "Compensation Management in Knowledge Based World" , p.-23."

(1) Enhance dignity and satisfaction from work performed

It is the most powerful and motivating reward by an organization to an employee to recognize the person as valuable asset of that particular organization. It is less costly and enhances the feeling of pride and satisfaction among the members. Every compensation and non-compensation reward component should carry with it the message, "we need you and appreciate your efforts."

(2) Promote constructive social relationships with co-workers

It is a valued reward for an employee to get an opportunity to interact and communicate with other people. A work place environment where trust, fellowship, loyalty and love emanate from the top level of management to the lowest level of the organization promotes the kinds of social interaction most people need in order to thrive. Any feeling of jealously, conflict and discontent destroys constructive relationship and decreases the level of productivity. Therefore, it is necessary for an organization to improve social relationships among employees and encourages team-based approach.

(3) Allocate sufficient resources to perform work assignments

It is essential to allocate sufficient resources to an employee for the accomplishment of the goal. If employees do not have knowledge or skills for certain assignments than this is a failure or dissatisfaction for not only the organization but also for employers. It decreases morale and motivation level of an individual. An organization must do everything possible to assist the employee in completing missions successfully. It is necessary for an organization to offer sufficient time to accomplish an assignment along with necessary human, technical, or physical resources and some degree of challenge and assurance.

(4) Offer supportive leadership and management

This dimension is recognized as unique dimension of the non-compensation reward. All individuals require guidance and support of those who help them in achieving their goals. They look to managers who have influence and can bring about desired changes. Employees faith and trust in management assist in establishing workplace environment where job security becomes accepted, social interaction thrives, and where work satisfaction is possible. Supportive leadership includes skill and interest in coaching and counselling, appreciation, recognition, constructive feedback leading to improvement of job performance.

(5) Enhance physiological health, intellectual growth, and emotional maturity

There is always a necessity of safe working environment, as any health related problem effects intellectual growth and emotional maturity of an employee. Provision of safe equipment i.e., a work environment that is risk free, minimization of noxious fumes, avoidance of extreme heat, cold and humidity conditions, elimination of carcinogens and other disease related material and substances is expectation of all employees. Additional stress is caused by technological advancement that requires rapid changes in the knowledge and skills of workers. Although these problems are universal and almost impossible to overcome, management can recognize their existence and can take action to limit their negative influence on the performance of each employee.

(6) Design jobs that require adequate attention and effort

When an activity is no longer challenging, innovative and the employee feels boredom and discontented, special attention has been focused on scientific management efforts to specialize work assignments where workers were required to perform these few tasks for as long as they remained on the job. This leads to employee frustration, absenteeism, job turnover and declining performance. To overcome this problem, behavioural scientists and managers at all levels have been searching for and implementing new approaches to improve the quality of work life. Restructuring of job tasks, job redesigning and job responsibilities are receiving top attention. Diversification and flexibility in job requirement is being provided by rotating jobs and by giving employees more opportunities to schedule work days and work weeks.

(7) Grant sufficient control over the job to meet personal demands

The decision of granting greater opportunity for the employees to participate in decision making process of the organization is gaining more importance. One of the most important decisions being made by more and more workers is that of scheduling work activities, and in some cases, of choosing the location of assignments. With the advent of the personal computer and networking, more employees are allowed to work at home or at a worksite of their choice.

Like many other non-compensation rewards, the benefits gained by granting such privileges frequently outweigh the costs of having an additional employee on the payroll. Also an option of casual dress wear makes life easier.

Some examples of non-monetary incentives

The need-motives for affiliation, power and recognition in particular, can be appealed by such incentives.

- A person with strong need for affiliation may respond readily to job assignments, that provide with opportunities to relate to socially attractive and satisfying individuals or groups.
- The opportunity to communicate with and relate to others is a factor many workers emphasize and seek.

- Persons who are very status conscious, can be motivated with the ability of a panelled office or various kinds of status symbols.
- An employee with high level desires for power may respond easily to opportunity, whereby he can gain leadership and administration responsibilities.
- The use of job enlargement provide added incentives to some employees because they feel capable of controlling wider sets of activities than they previously performed.
- Workers in safety minded organization are often attracted by competition on awards for best safety performance records.
- Individuals proud of their past accomplishments may feel recognized and rewarded if their superiors extend opportunities for participation on more complex and more important job assignments.

FACTORS EFFECTING EMPLOYEE'S COMPENSATION

There are number of factors influencing the compensation package payable to employees. They can be categorized into

(1) External factor

(2) Internal factor.

External factors

These are demand and supply of labour, cost of living, society, labour unions, legislation, economy and compensation survey.

(1) Demand and supply of labour: Even in times of high employment, individuals with certain skills or abilities are in demand. This demand and supply of labour influences wage and salary fixation. Jobs in high demand frequently will receive premium wages, as in case of skilled labour. However, if supply of labour exceeds the demand, then employers are willing to pay less. High remuneration to skilled labour is necessary to attract and retain it. But exploitation of unskilled labour, like, for instance, paying less wages because it is available in plenty, is unjustifiable. The Minimum Wages Act, 1948, is precisely meant to prevent this kind of exploitation.

The basic point of this approach is that firm pays its employees the "going rate" for the type of work they do. Going rate analysis is done by reviewing all job description and then collecting relevant salary market data through participating in national, regional, and local salary surveys and by third party survey administrators (generally human resources consulting firms).

Going rates are those that are paid by different units of an industry in a locality and by comparable units of the same industry located elsewhere. If the firm offers pay much below the going rate, it may be unable to attract and retain qualified workers. If it pays much more than the going rate, it may be unable to charge comparative prices for its product because its labour costs are too high.

Productivity of labour also influences wage fixation in labour market. Productivity can arise due to increased effort of the worker, or as a result of the factors beyond the control of the worker such as improved technology, better management etc. Greater effort of the worker is rewarded through piece – rate or other forms of incentive payments.

Productivity is the relationship between the input of labour measured in man-hours and its output in the form of money or physical terms. Productivity linked wages may help utilize human resources better and help determine fair wages.

(2) Cost of living: The logic for using cost of living as a pay determinant is both simple and important. A pay increase must be roughly equivalent to the increased cost of living, if a person is to maintain a precious level of real wages. A rise in the cost of living is sought to be compensated by payment of dearness allowance, basic pay to remain undisturbed. Some firms even index pay increases to the inflation rate and sacrifice merit pay to provide across the board increases designed to offset the results of inflation.

(3) Society: Compensation paid to employees often affects pricing of the firms goods or services. For this reason, consumers may also become interested in compensation decisions. Businesses in a local labour market are also concerned with the pay practices of new firms locating in their area. The Supreme Court has been keeping social and ethical considerations in adjusting wage and salary disputes. It was also considered to keep the company wages in line with other wages in the community.

(4) Labour unions: The presence or absence of labour organizations often determine the quantum of wages paid to employees. When union uses comparable pay as a standard in making compensation demands, the employer needs accurate labour market data. When a union emphasizes cost of living, it may pressure management into including a cost of living allowance. The employees of strongly unionized companies too, have no freedom in wage and salary fixation. They are forced to yield to the pressure of labour representation in determining and revising pay scales.

(5) Legislation: There are numerous Legislation Acts which affect the compensation system. Equal employment legislation, including The Civil Rights Act, Family and Medical Leave Act, Payment of Wages Act, 1948; The Payment of Bonus Act, 1965; Equal Remuneration Act, 1976; Payment of Gratuity Act, 1972 etc. The Payment of Wages Act seeks to protect workers against irregularities in payment of wages and unauthorized deductions by the employer. The Minimum Wages Act enables the Central and State Governments to fix minimum rates of wages payable to employees in sweated industries. The Equal Remuneration Act provides for payment of equal remuneration to men and women workers for same or similar work. The Equal Pay Act, 1963 prohibits an employer from paying an employee of one gender less money than an employee of the opposite gender, if both employees are performing same nature of job. (same skill, effort and responsibility).

In addition to legal enactment's, there are wage boards, tribunals and fair wages committees which aim at providing a minimal standard of living to workers. Also there is the Companies Act, 1956, which checks the managerial remuneration.

(6) The economy: The economy definitely affects financial compensation decisions. For example, a depressed economy generally increases the labour supply and lowers the market rate. On the other hand, a booming economy results in greater competition for workers and price of labour is driven upward.

Since the cost of living is commonly used as pay standard, the economy's health exerts a major impact upon pay decisions. Cost of living typically rises as the economy expands.

(7) Compensation survey: A compensation survey strives to obtain data regarding what other firms are paying for specific jobs within a given labour market. The surveys may be either outsource to a consulting firm or conducted by the organization itself. In this, market rates remain the most important standard for determining pay.

Most big organizations provides low, high and average salary for a given position with the help of compensation survey. It provides information for establishing both direct and indirect compensation. A firm should take the determinants such as the geographical area of the survey and the specific firms to contact before conducting a compensation survey.

Internal Factors

Among the internal factors that affect pay structure are the compensation policies, organizational ability to pay, job analysis, and job descriptions, employee, trade union's bargaining power.

(1) Compensation policies: It provides general guidelines for making compensation decisions. The first thing employers should consider when developing compensation package is fairness. It should be vital and maintain internal and external equity. The policy should include the company's philosophy related to the major components of incentive compensation, including the strengths and weaknesses of each and how the overall plan provides optional alignment of interest with shareowners.

The policy should provide broad guidelines by which the company will use alternative forms of compensation, and the relative weight in relation to overall compensation if "others" form of compensation will be utilized. An organization often, formally or informally, establishes compensation policies that determine whether it will be a pay leader, a pay follower, or strive for an average position in the labour market.

(*Source:* R. Wayne Mondy and Robern M. Noe)

(i) Pay leaders: They are organizations that pay higher wages and salaries than competing firms. This helps to retain and attract high quality and productive employees.

(ii) The market rate: These are the average pay that most employers provide for a similar job in a particular area or industry, it is also known as going rate.

(iii) Pay followers: These are companies that choose to pay below the market rate because of poor financial condition or a belief that they simply do not require highly capable employees.

(2) The organizational ability to pay: An organization's ability to pay is also an important factor in determining compensation package. Companies that have good sales and, therefore, high profits tend to pay higher wages than those which running at a loss or earning low profits because of the high cost of production or low sales. However all employers, irrespective of their profits or losses, must pay no less than their competitors to attract and retain potential employees.

(3) Job analysis and job description: It is found that the more difficult and challenging a job, the higher are the wages. For this, the particular job is analyzed and then the relative value of a job is determined. Job analysis is the systematic process of determining the skills and knowledge required for performing job.

(i) Determine what tasks must be accomplished by whom.

(ii) Decide which job classifications should be exempt and which should be non-exempt.

(iii) Develop model job descriptions for exempt and non-exempt positions and distribute the models to incumbents for reviews and comment; adjust job descriptions if necessary.

(iv) Finalize and document all job descriptions.

(v) Evaluate jobs.

(vi) Also a general task analysis is conducted by major departments to the jobs within each senior,s, vice president's and manager's department and then rank jobs between and among departments.

(vii) Verify ranking by comparing it to industry market data concerning the ranking and adjust if necessary.

(viii) Prepare a matrix organizational review.

(ix) Determine grades.

(x) Establish the number of levels – senior, junior, intermediate and beginner for each job family and assign a grade to each level.

(xi) Determine the number of pay grades, or monetary range of position at particular level and establish the salary range.

(4) Employee: In addition to all the above factors, employee related factors are also important in determining wage structure. These factors include performing on the job, seniority experience, and membership in the organization and their potential.

Trade union's bargaining power

The stronger and more powerful the trade union in any organization, the higher the wages. Trade union's bargaining powers are often measured in terms of its membership, its financial strength and the nature of its leadership.

KEY TERMS	
Compensation	Cost of living
Base pay	Pay followers
Perquisite	Going rate
Non-monetary incentives	

SUMMARY

This chapter identifies and briefly describes the concept of compensation, its objectives and importance. The various objectives of compensation are to recruit and retain qualified employees, to increase morale of employees, reduce absenteeism, job turnover and mainly to determine basic wages and salary administration,

Total compensation package or rewards (incentives) can be classified into:

(a) Direct compensation

(b) Indirect compensation

(c) Non-monetary compensation.

Direct compensation includes money, popularly known as basic salary or wage, (gross pay) where the individual is entitled for his job, overtime work and holiday premiums, bonuses based on performance, profit sharing and opportunities to purchase stock option. Indirect compensation includes benefits that may consist of life, accident, health insurance, the employers, contribution to retirement (pension), pay for vacation or illness and employers are required to make payments for employees welfare as social security.

Non-monetary compensation can include any benefits an employee receives from an employer or job that does not involve tangible value. There are number of factors influencing the compensation package payable to employees. They can be categorized into:

(1) External factor

(2) Internal factors

External factors: These are demand and supply of labour, cost of living, society, labour unions, legislation, economy and compensation survey. Among the internal factors that affect pay structure are the compensation policies, organizational ability to pay, job analysis, and job descriptions, employee, trade union's bargaining power.

To operate within a competitive environment, organizations must understand how to correlate and influence their compensation practices and make the kinds of reasoned decisions that permit them to function effectively and efficiently.

REVIEW QUESTIONS

1. Define the term compensation.
2. Identify the major parts of the compensation program.
3. Distinguish between monetary and non-monetary compensation .
4. Bring out the components of employee remuneration.
5. Outline the various factors that effect compensation.
6. What differences can an employer's philosophy have on rates of pay?

References

Armstrong, M. and H. Murlis (1991) Reward Management, 2nd ed., *Kogan Page/IPM,* London.

Dessler Gary, Human Resource Management, 9th ed, *Prentice Hall of India,* New Delhi, 2003.

Dowling, P. J. and R. S. Schuler (1990), International Dimensions of Human Resource Management, *PWS-Kent, Boston, Mass.*

Henderson Richard, Compensation Management, *Prentice Hall,* NJ,1994.

K. Asahwathappa, Human Resource Management, 4th ed., *Tata McGraw-Hills,* New Delhi, 2005.

Mejia Gomez, and Cardy Robert, Managing Human Resources, *Pearson Education,* New Delhi, 2001.

Milkovich, G.T, and Newman J. M, Compensation, (4th ed.). *Homewood,* ILL: Irwin.

Wallace M.J, and Fay C. H., Compensation Theory and Practice, 1st ed. *Tata McGraw-Hill.*

STRATEGIC PERSPECTIVES IN COMPENSATION

2

LEARNING OBJECTIVES

After reading this chapter, you should be able to understand —

- ➪ Aligning compensation strategy with business strategy
- ➪ Strategic pay decisions
- ➪ Trends in compensation
- ➪ Competency based compensation programme
- ➪ Diagnosis and benchmarking
- ➪ Influence of pay on employee attitude and behaviour

ALIGNING COMPENSATION STRATEGY WITH BUSINESS STRATEGY

In recent years, the necessity for organizations to control labour costs, while at the same time increasing productivity and enhancing quality and customer service, has never been more urgent. Although, many companies have become acutely aware of this problem, few companies have yet to fully address this issue. The present competitive environment requires new strategies toward employee compensation, new management and employee practices, and new methods of educating employees to the shifting competitive environment that has brought about the necessity for these changes.

At the same time that companies are examining the method and basis for compensating employees, there has been a growth in the number of companies seeking to develop high performance and high commitment work systems. These systems, based upon expanded roles for employees, requires the employees to accept more responsibility and accountability.

Other organizational initiatives, such as flatter organization structure; more fluid organization design; and faster-paced, quicker-response customer focus have driven sweeping changes. Often it has been difficult for compensation systems to keep pace and support these changes. Additionally, employee compensation is a critical component to financial success. Careful attention must be placed on the development of reward systems that reflect the financial capability of the company, as well as reinforce the new directions associated with contemporary organizational strategies. Compounding all of these problems are the recent dynamics of the labour market. In contrast to the period 1985-1995, when wages and salaries grew only modestly, the period 1996-1997 has been marked by an increasingly dynamic labour market in which wages and salaries are beginning to grow at a pace not seen in many years. The tightened labour market has meant that, for the first time in many years, greater attention must be given to the traditional role of compensation, i.e., attraction and retention.

Changing compensation systems is a difficult task for any organization. Employee and management perceptions of organizational compensation systems are typically well-formed. Concerns and skepticism over how they will be affected by any new system are natural. It is difficult for organizations to achieve compensation driven changes in behaviour if their compensation plans have not been adequately communicated, employee understanding and trust established, and new expectations firmly "seated" and accepted. It goes without saying that communications, training and execution are critical.

Compensation in the high performance organization needs to reinforce the directions set by the leadership. We under score the word reinforce as efforts to make compensation too great a driver for change, may lead to unintended consequences. That is, if the organization becomes too heavily compensation driven, the focus may be lost on the factors leading to successful high performance organization and instead toward short-term compensation goals.

Compensation philosophy is the set of values and beliefs that an organization has in regards to compensation decision-making. This often is combined with a set of guiding principles that further assist in compensation administration. Many firms report that they have no formal compensation philosophy and this would certainly be true of many we have worked with over the years. However, we would argue very strongly that the collection of decisions that the firm has made over a period of time constitutes a compensation set of beliefs and values — a compensation philosophy —regardless of whether or not the firm has actually committed those ideas to a formal document.

Compensation strategy issued to guide the design of specific compensation decisions.

Differences in compensation philosophies are widespread. Thus, some organizations believe in the widespread use of incentive compensation, while others only apply incentive compensation to a very narrow group of employees who are believed to affect the bottom-line. This represents a significant philosophical difference between the firms. Another illustration may be found in the examination of the behaviour of firms who seek to apply compensation levels "at the mid-point." These firms differ philosophically from those firms that seek to pay at the top of the market, thus enabling them to attract the highest calibre employees that they can find. Business settings often explain these differences. Somefirms are proportionally more generous to certain levels to exempt employees, while others believe in principles of achieving widespread equity across all employees. The openness with which compensation decisions are made, and the degree of stakeholder involvement in those decisions, is yet another example of philosophical differences that may exist between organizations.

Needless to say, compensation is a key issue for the high performance organization, as the employee and management systems utilized by the organization must be reinforced through the rewards structure. Again, our experience is telling in avoiding making compensation unduly controversial, thus adversely affecting the very heart of the high performance system.

It is important to approach compensation strategically by developing a philosophy toward compensation, along with a set of objectives. Three factors are employed:

(1) business and operating inputs;

(2) industry and labour market practices and trends; and

(3) employee inputs and preferences.

Once a philosophy and objectives are developed, the four elements of compensation can be determined. Base pay structures deliver to employees their wage or salary, Employees typically receive 90-100% of the cash compensation and two-thirds of their total compensation from their base pay.

Variable pay plans are organizational systems for sharing the economic benefits of improved productivity, cost reductions, quality, and overall business performance in the form of regular cash bonuses. Most variable pay plans incorporate existing, or develop enhanced systems of employee involvement. To develop a variable pay plan system requires examination of existing management and compensation practices. In most cases, fringe benefit structures are set at a corporate level and are highly influenced by legal requirements.

From the point of view of compensation strategy, fringes represent a substantial cost of total compensation and therefore must be considered as a strategic cost. Organizations derive little if any behavioural change from this portion of compensation. Fringes can influence attraction and retention.

Compensation administration includes a collection of activities required to sustain the effectiveness of a compensation strategy. Thus, issues ranging from labour market surveying to performance management to skill certification and peer review come under this umbrella. Involving stakeholders in compensation administration can reinforce the values and beliefs underlying the compensation philosophy and strategy.

Thus compensation decisions should be fully integrated into the organization's business and operations strategy, through its compensation philosophy. The design of compensation systems should be subsequent to, and not precede, this key analysis and decision point. For the high performance firm, an appropriate level of employee involvement can further reinforce the organization's general beliefs and values.

Below we provide a checklist of key compensation questions.

➢ Base Pay Delivery

- Method of delivery — Job-based *vs.* individual-based
- Number of levels
- Structure of levels
- Pricing strategies
- Adjustment method
- Weighting of individual performance.

➢ Organization Performance or Variable Pay

- Role in total compensation strategy
- Structure
- Measures

- Targets
- Tolerance for pay at risk
- Risk - reward ratios
- Use of other monetary rewards
- Use of non-monetary rewards
- Individual performance recognition.

➢ Fringe Benefits

- Usually determined at corporate level; limited scope at other levels
- Tie to business and human resource objectives
- Coverage
- Cost
- Communications (purpose-coverage-value)

➢ Compensation Administration

- Stakeholder role in compensation administration
- Performance management and evaluation
- Overtime policy (exempt and non-exempt)
- Shift differentials
- Attendance policy
- Role of seniority.

➢ Employee Inputs and Preferences

- Perceptions of external pay equity
- Perceptions of internal pay equity
- Pay delivery beliefs
- Form (cash, gainsharing, benefits)
- Method (individual, small group, large group)
- Risk tolerance
- Trust in management

➢ Business and Operating Inputs

- Operations and manufacturing strategy
- Sales development strategy

- Percentage of compensation costs to total product/service costs
- Percentage of compensation costs to controllable product/service cost
- Existing markets/products
- Potential markets/products
- Anticipated volume
- Reinforce/enhance work design
- Maintain cultural change processes
- Other operating issues.

➤Industry and Labour Market Practices and Trends

- Availability and quality of work force
- Industry practices
- Retention of work force
- Retention of key contributors
- Wage/salary levels and movement
- Wage/salary delivery charges

➤ Compensation Philosophy and Objectives

- How much emphasis should be placed on rewards to drive organization
- What issues are to be driven by compensation as opposed to management practices
- Market definition (exempt and non-exempt)
- Method of delivery
- Targeted position in labour market
- Targeted position in product market
- Relationship within total company
- Relationship to selection and retention
- Portion of pay guaranteed and at risk
- Percentage of workforce bonus eligible.

STRATEGIC PAY

"Pay structure has strategic value that assigns different pay rates for jobs of different values which differentiate individual employee contributions. A well designed pay structure is one which attract and retain potential employees.

A company's pay structure is the method of administering its pay philosophy. The two leading types of pay structures are the internal equity method, which uses a tightly constructed grid to ensure that each job is compensated according to the jobs above and below it in a hierarchy, and market pricing, where each job in an organization is tied to the prevailing market rate.

A company needs job descriptions for all its positions so that people know where they fall within the organization. A pay structure helps answer questions about who's who, what each person's role is, and why people are compensated differently. It also helps human resources personnel to fairly administer any given pay philosophy. For example, a company might want to pay everyone at market; or pay some people at market and some above it. Opportunities for incentives are also dealt with in the pay structure. For example, people with strategic roles will likely have opportunities for higher incentives.

Out Source if Necessary

Many firms have one or more in-house compensation consultants who can set up a pay structure consistent with the company's pay philosophy. Small organizations and other companies without the resources to hire a compensation consultant can either train someone in how to set up a pay philosophy, or outsource this service.

How to construct a pay structure

Compensation specialist develop pay structure based on five steps:

(i) Deciding on how many pay structure to construct

(ii) Determining a market pay line

(iii) Defining pay grades

(iv) Calculating pay ranges for each pay grade

(v) Evaluating the results.

Effective administration of pay structure requires a balance between the pay levels for employees inside the company (internal equity) and the pay level those employees could command in the company's recruiting markets (external equity).

Business considerations for pay structure design include strategic issues, competitive practices, the organizational culture, and the affordability of pay. The key strategic issues to consider are the objectives of the company and the extent to which salary will be used to attract and retain employees capable of achieving business success. Also the salary practice of competition in consideration, surveys that report data regarding how they structure their salary administration program organization with a dynamic culture tend to place less emphases on basic pay in favor of variable pay, which has greater impact on employee's behaviour for achieving business objectives.

Whereas organization with states cultures, place emphases on base pay because they can reasonably predict business performance and employee behaviours.

Technical considerations for pay structure design include the number of range levels, width of the ranges from minimum to maximum values (i.e., range spreads), the distance between adjacent range midpoint values (i.e., midpoint differentials), and the degree of overlap between adjacent ranges. The number of ranges in a salary structure is a characteristic that describes the number of hierarchical levels needed to distinguish the value of jobs in the organization. The number of ranges required to compose a complete structure is determined by the following considerations:

- The number of skill and/or responsibility distinctions evident in the organization's job worth hierarchy.
- The number of supervisor-subordinate relationships in the company's organizational structure.
- The degree of emphasis on career development and progression.
- The resources available to administer the pay program.

Generally, the more range levels, the more administration required.

The "range spread" is a characteristic of salary structures that describes the distance between the minimum and the maximum salary range values. The degree of range spread is dependent on a balance between the internal value a company places on the job and the range of salaries paid to comparable jobs in the relevant recruiting markets. Essentially, spread reflects the range of salary opportunity for the jobs that are assigned to the range, from a minimum to maximum salary values.

To calculate range spread, divide the difference between the maximum and minimum values by the minimum value. In general, wider ranges apply to jobs that are determined to have larger salary values (e.g., executive jobs), whereas narrower ranges apply to jobs with smaller salary values (e.g., clerical jobs). Midpoint differential is a characteristic of salary structure design that describes the percentage difference between the midpoint values of adjacent salary ranges. In general, if the company's job evaluation approach doesn't discriminate finely between levels, the result will be fewer salary range levels. Another factor to consider in concluding midpoint differentials is the company's policy with regard to the cost of promoting employees into jobs at higher salary range levels. For example, a policy that limits promotional salary increases to 8%, but with a midpoint differential of 15%, may result in salaries for the promoted employees to fall below the new grade minimum salary value. The degree to which ranges overlap each other's salary values is a function of midpoint differentials and range spreads. Analyze range overlap after decisions have been made about midpoint differentials and range spreads to ensure that there is a reasonable progression between the range levels that compose the salary structure; and adjust if necessary.

Traditional Structures

Many salary ranges that have narrow range spreads, small midpoint differentials, and broad overlap between adjacent ranges characterize traditional structures. Traditional structures tend to place greater emphasis on internal equity, as opposed to external equity. Traditional structures focus on job content evaluation to arrange a job worth hierarchy.

With a focus of internal factors to create traditional structures, evaluation of market salary levels is limited to having a secondary influence on the arrangement of the job worth hierarchy. As a consequence, the company is likely to make many more distinctions between company jobs than may actually exist in relevant recruiting markets.

Traditional structures are best suited to companies that recognize and reward employee performance with promotions to jobs assigned to higher salary ranges, as opposed to moving an employee's salary deeper within the range over time.

Broadbanding

Broadbanding is a method of grouping jobs and determining pay that makes compensation administration more flexible and more responsive to the needs of changing organizations. Broadbanding eliminates the present hierarchical grading structure and narrow salary ranges. In broadbanding, jobs with similar responsibilities and skill requirements are grouped in "bands" of job families, and pay is linked to the market. The approach reinforces and values the employees' role within the University and the development of competencies to perform the role successfully.

Broadband Structures

By definition, broadbanding is a salary structure that consolidates the relatively large number of ranges found in a traditional structure into fewer ranges. Because there are fewer ranges, a Broadband salary structure has characteristics that distinguish it from a traditional structure. Fewer salary ranges that have wider range spreads, larger midpoint differentials, and a lesser degree of overlap characterize broadband structures. Broadband structures tend to place greater emphasis on career development opportunities that employees would otherwise seek in the company's recruiting markets.

Broadbanding has been a recognized practice of corporate compensation professionals.Organizations that implemented broadband structures sought to improve the administration of the salary program subsequent to downsizing initiatives that created flatter organizations. In flat hierarchies, greater emphasis tends to be placed on career development as opposed to job promotion. Today, broadbanding still refers to collapsing a company's job worth hierarchy into fewer, wider salary ranges. This is done to manage pay delivery in a manner that recognizes career growth in light of fewer promotional opportunities, and company pay practices that are closely tied to competitive levels.

Broadbanding usually appeals to organizations that want to be more nimble in response to persistent changes in business conditions or recruiting markets. Such organizations would likely implement broadband salary structures in attempt to achieve the following human capital management objectives:

- Broader workforce skills
- Career development among employees
- Improvement in the way of job evaluation, salary structures, and performance rewards are administered and maintained.

Broadbanding is a compensation management's response to changing business conditions. In broadband salary structures, employers reward employees who demonstrate substantial capability improvements with a salary progression that penetrates more deeply into the banded range over time, in lieu of promotions. Whereas the design characteristics of traditional structures emphasize internal equity and focus the employee's attention on the world inside the firm, broadbanding focuses employees on the changing needs of the organization and helps them experience an internal culture that more closely reflects the external business environment and the competitive recruiting market.

Occasionally, employee salaries may fall outside the company's defined salary range for the job. The employee salary will either be above the maximum value or below the minimum value. Salaries that fall above the maximum are referred to as red-circle rates.Red-circle rates may be caused by demotion, an exceptional salary paid to retain a high-potential employee, reorganization or acquisition, or the structure falling behind competitive circumstances. Actions compensation professionals suggest for resolving red-circle rates include freezing the employee's pay until the salary falls back inside the updated range, reducing the employee'spay and paying the excess in the form of a bonus, or reviewing the employee for promotion into a higher salary range.

In contrast to red-circle rates, green-circle rates are where the employee's salary falls below the range minimum. Green-circle rates may be caused by adjustments to the salary structure subsequent to a recent promotion or new hire, reevaluation of the job's value causing reassignment to a lower range in the structure, or reorganization or acquisition.

Compensation professionals recommend that employees not be paid salaries below the company's prescribed minimum value. The employee's salary should be raised to the range of minimum value immediately, or at some scheduled event in the salary administration process, such as annual salary review.

Pay compression can occur when the pay rates of several employees, despite clear differences in capability, are in a cluster. This means highly capable employees are paid similarly to employees with less skill and experience. This eventually creates morale problems, particularly for the more capable employees.

Modern organizations are making very significant changes in their compensation systems in order to better fit the dynamic, highly competitive business environment. Firms increasingly are using things such as skill-based pay, which compensates employees for the number and types of skills they possess instead of the type of job they have. Similarly, there is a strong movement to "at-risk" compensation, where employee pay is tied to performance. Under this system, the employee's bonus does not become part of his or her base pay. Instead, the bonus must be re-earned each year. These changes, and numerous others, are designed to help offset compensation costs by gains in productivity, and to develop more flexible workforces.

The respondents with skill based pay programs indicated that the primary reasons for developing a skill based pay program are as follows:

- encourage skill development
- reward learning
- create fewer titles
- encourage more flexible work assignments.

Table 2.1

Definition	A pay structure is a collection of pay rates or pay ranges.Structure setting and adjustment is the process of developing, adjusting, and maintaining a pay structure.
Purpose	Pay structures are used to help organizations: • maintain pay levels that are competitive with the external labor market, • maintain internal pay relationships among jobs, • recognize and reward differences in the level of responsibility, skill, and performance, and • manage pay expenditures. • Structure setting and adjustment provides a systematic way to manage pay
Elements of a pay structure	A pay structure is defined by several elements, including: • coverage – the occupations, positions, or persons included, • the number of pay ranges or grades, • the differences between pay ranges, and • range width – the difference(s) between the range minimum and maximum structures.

Table 2.2

Types of pay structure	**Common approaches to establishing pay structures include:**	
	Approach	**Common characteristics:**
	Traditional (Grades)	• separate structures for each employee type (e.g., non-exempt, salaried non-exempt, exempt, executive), function, or occupation, • many ranges or grades (often 10 or more), • narrow ranges (15% – 50% for professional positions), and • small to moderate differences between grades
	Broadbanding ("Broad grades")	• separate structures by employee type, · relatively few ranges (4 to 6 bands are common), and • wide ranges (50% to 80% for white-collar non-managerial positions) • Federal broadbanding: • maintains distinctions between developmental and full performance level positions, • may include technical and administrative support occupations, and • typically has more grades and narrower ranges than "pure" broadbanding.
	Career Banding	• one or few structures, • few ranges (4 or less), and • no or extremely wide ranges (150% or more)
	Market Pricing	• separate ranges for each distinct type of job, as defined by the external labour market (jobs and ranges, however, may be grouped for ease of administration.), • the absence of a coherent structure (systematic relationships between different jobs), and • narrow pay ranges, to keep pay levels closely linked to external labour markets

In our experience, flexibility appears to be the more compelling reason because it permits the organization to have a larger pool of well trained workers when and if another person that has a critical skill is absent or otherwise unavailable to perform the necessary work. These reasons track well with the experiences of private sector organizations. In addition to reaping the benefits of a more flexible work force, the organization gets a way to encourage skill advancement and on the job learning. Employees, on the other hand, achieve increased pay.

Skill Based Pay Covers a Wide Variety of Occupational Groups

Skill based pay programs are in use in a wide variety of occupational groups. While the survey did not count the occupations, we found that they are in use among the following job families:

- building inspectors
- police officers
- engineers
- clerical
- fire fighters
- public works jobs
- social workers
- water and waste water treatment plant operators.

The characteristics that these jobs have in common are that the tasks and responsibilities can be broken into smaller, learnable skill blocks and the skills are, for the most part, observable. Management and other "knowledge workers" are noticeably absent from the list. Organizations interested in new pay models for these job families appear to be using broad banding instead of skill-based pay programs because of the subjectivity involved in determining skill block differences and certification.

What is Skill Based Pay

Skill-based pay refers to a pay system in which pay increases are linked to the number or depth of skills an employee acquires and applies and it is a means of developing broader and deeper skills among the workforce. Such increases are in addition to, and not in lieu of, general pay increases employees may receive. The pay increases are usually tied to three types of skills:

- horizontal skills, which involve a broadening of skills in terms of the range of tasks
- vertical skills, which involve acquiring skills of a higher level
- depth skills, which involve a high level of skills in specialised areas relating to the same job.

Skill-based pay differs in the following respects from traditional pay systems which reflect skill differences in a structure consisting of rates of pay for unskilled, semi-skilled and skilled workers:

- Skill-based pay is a person-based and not a job-based system. It rewards a person for what he/she, rather than the job is worth. Job worth is reflected in a basic rate of pay for minimum skills, but pay progression is directly linked to skills acquisition (rather than to general pay increases applicable to all).

- It rewards (and therefore emphasizes) a broad range of skills which makes the employee multi-skilled and therefore flexible.
- It positively encourages skills development.
- A skill-based pay system may not necessarily reflect how well the skill is used, as this falls within the performance component of pay. But there is nothing to prevent injecting performance criteria into the system. In such cases "the system will be more performance-oriented than a structure", which merely recognizes different rates of pay for skills.
- The system needs to be underpinned by opportunities for training which is critical to the success of the system. The traditional structure is not dependent on such opportunities.

Reasons for Skill Based Pay

More than ever before in industrial relations history, a commonality of interests in the skills of employees has developed between employers and employees. Skills provide employees with a measure of protection against unemployment, as well as opportunities for higher earnings. At the same time, skills provide employers with an important means of achieving competitiveness.

Many countries today are seeking to advance to more technology and skill-based industries, while others have become (or are becoming) 'post industrial' societies, in which the application of knowledge determines productivity, performance and competitiveness. Comparative advantage based on, for instance, cheap labour or raw materials, has declined in importance relative to competitive advantage based on the ability to add value to a particular resource or advantage. Such comparative advantage partly (often largely) depends on people - their standards of literacy and education, work attitudes, value systems, skills and motivation. Critical today is the ability to innovate and develop clusters of competitive enterprises in particular industries. For the more industrialized countries, this means 'capturing' some of the key industries of the next century - micro-electronics, biotechnology, new materials, science industries, telecommunications, civil aviation, computers and software, robotics and machine tools and entertainment. An employee with skills is most flexible and productive, when he develops a broad range of skills, he is able to learn the next higher skill, develop analytical skills and is also able to work in a team. Important aspects of today's skills package include multi-skills, cognitive skills, interpersonal and communication skills, positive work attitudes and quality consciousness. Training is no longer only for current competence, but is also to prepare for the next stage of skills. Thus, pay systems which promote current and future skills, needs are increasing in importance among employers.

The impact of rapid technological change, the increasing globalization of product markets, greater customer choice and the emphasis on quality necessitate a frequent updating of skills, and flexibility to respond to rapid changes in the requirements of markets. A flexible workforce, which is one that is multi-skilled, ensures that production is not interrupted due to the narrow skills of workers, and that workers are themselves responsible for the quality of products.

Introducing a Skill-based Pay System

Introducing a skill-based pay system requires several steps to be taken and several issues to be addressed:

- The skills requirements of the enterprise should be analysed.
- The availability of resources for training should be ascertained.

- The jobs to be covered by the scheme should be identified.
- The individual jobs have to be grouped into 'job families' on the basis that in each 'family' the skills needs are similar. The skills within each job family and the tasks needed to perform the job should be analysed.
- The above will lead to an identification of the skill blocks or levels. The skill level is the pay grade relative to the competence to use particular skills, and the skill block is the training input which has to be completed to the satisfaction of the certifying authority in order to gain entitlement to the extra pay. It is not unusual for skill levels to consist of several skill blocks, each to be acquired through training.
- Training modules have to be formulated.
- The way in which certification is obtained that the skill has been acquired should be agreed upon.
- The base rates for 'job families' have to be set, as well as the payments that will be made thereafter when an employee moves upwards through the skills route.
- The criterion for extra payment is not acquisition of the skill, but its application.
- The period during which the skill should be applied before a new one is acquired should normally be decided on, as the skill should benefit the employer who should receive a return on the investment made.
- A difficult question is how obsolete skills should be dealt with e.g. through retraining or redundancy.

Problems in Skill-Based Pay

There are several problems associated with the introduction of skill-based pay which should not be underestimated. They can be extremely costly having regard to:

- the extra payment involved
- training costs
- the fact that some skills may be paid for, but used infrequently
- the possibility that unusable skills may be acquired unless the system is properly administered
- the fact that it is not always easy for an employer to anticipate accurately what skills will be needed in a few years' time.

The administration of the system is complex, both in regard to certification of skills acquisition and payment. Therefore, unless administered properly, the costs can outweigh the productivity and flexibility gains. Further, the employees who reach the maximum of the skill levels can be demotivated when extra payments, as distinct from general pay increases cease. Therefore, the gains from flexibility, improved quality, the elimination of some jobs and so on depend on the employer's ability to administer the system properly, making clear also that it is not the acquisition of any skills, but agreed skills, that fall within the scope of the scheme. Hence, the need to negotiate the system. It is easier to introduce skill-based pay in an entirely new (greenfield) site, than in an already existing one, where there is in existence a pay system based on different criteria.

Factors for Success

Some of the circumstances which contribute to the success of skill-based pay are:

- the employer's commitment to continuous training and development
- the value attached by the employer to personal growth and encouragement of a learning orientation
- dismantling strong bureaucratic hierarchies and narrow job demarcations
- participative management practices, independent and co-operative forms of work.

Skill-based pay systems are most appropriate to enterprises which depend on a high level of skills, and in which labour costs represent a relatively small portion of total costs, unlike in labour intensive industries. Though such pay systems have been commonest in manufacturing organizations, they are applicable to service industries as well, though the objectives may differ. In banks and airlines, for example, skill-based pay can be used to encourage people to work in areas where manpower is most needed at a given point of time due to customer flows. Skill-based pay is particularly consistent with knowledge-based work.

Among the advantages of skill-based pay are the following:

- It contributes to job enlargement and enrichment by breaking down narrow job classifications.
- Flexibility is increased by encouraging the performance of multiple tasks. It enables job rotation, and filling of temporary vacancies due, for instance, to absenteeism. It therefore contributes to a leaner workforce.
- It enhances productivity and quality through better use of human resources.
- It facilitates technological change, which may meet with resistance in a purely job-based system.
- The higher pay levels, continuous training, and job enlargement through the broadening of skills, tend to reduce staff turnover.
- Elimination of unnecessary jobs can result from a workplace having broad, rather than narrow skills. It also reduces the need for supervision.
- Job satisfaction is engendered through employees having greater control over the planning and implementation of their work.
- Broadening of skills leads employees to develop a better perspective of operations as a whole.
- It is an incentive for self-development.
- It provides employment security through skills enhancement.
- It reduces the need to look to promotion to higher levels (which are always limited) as the only way to enhance earnings, and it facilitates the planning of an employee's career development path.
- Since the reward flows from the application of a skill and it does not reduce opportunities for others to similarly increase their skills and earnings, there is likely to be less competition among individuals.

- Since the pay increases on account of skills are linked to a measurable standard, the criticism of subjectivity often associated with performance appraisals and individual-based performance-related pay, is avoided.

COMPETENCY-BASED COMPENSATION PROGRAMME

Performance and skill-based pay systems need to be negotiated and introduced at the enterprise level. Other than for very broad policy issues (e.g. whether such systems should be introduced), performance and skill-based pay cannot be negotiated or designed at the macro, or even at the industry level. It follows therefore that it is not possible to recommend a particular system which could be introduced across several enterprises or even across an industry. This is evident from the following steps that need to be taken before introducing such a scheme:

- A pay expert, or the management, would have to first analyze the existing pay structure.
- The business objectives of the enterprise and its overall human resource management policies should be determined.
- The objectives of the system to be introduced should be clearly identified.
- Whether the scheme to be introduced fits with the overall corporate and human resource management objectives of the enterprise has to be ascertained, as they must all 'fit' together.
- The scheme should be negotiated, and employees consulted to ascertain whether the desired objectives are likely to be achieved.
- Mechanisms to monitor and review the scheme should be agreed upon.

The principles outlined herein could help to guard against possible pitfalls and to identify some of the procedures to be followed, as well as to assist to some extent, in the making of choices between different schemes which may be introduced to achieve the objectives. No blueprint can be provided, however, though the principles can facilitate in identifying the types of schemes suitable to particular types of businesses and tasks.

DIAGNOSIS AND BENCHMARKING

Diagnosis bench-marking: It is defined as a method of defining standard job that is used to anchor the employer's pay scale and around which other jobs are arranged in order of relative worth. The relative worth of bench-mark job is determined with the help of job evaluation. These benchmark jobs are used by the employer's for salary survey.

The main objective of defining the benchmark jobs are to:

- Recruit, reward and retain talented staff.
- Recognize staff's value and their contributions.
- Reward staff for performance.
- Manage pay through a simpler, more flexible and less bureaucratic system.
- Ensure fair and consistent administration.
- Analysis and identification of jobs against consistent criteria and measures them in a uniform and objective manner.

The benchmark or standards of which the plan is to be based should be effective and should satisfy these conditions:

(i) Standards or benchmark jobs are viewed as fair by superiors & subordinates.

(ii) They should be reasonable.

(iii) They should be specific.

(iv) They should be complete and focus on quality rather than quantity.

The compensation surveys are very helpful in providing benchmarks and building databases. Human Resource departments of most mid-sized and large corporations have worked hard to enhance their knowledge and skills in designing appropriate compensation models. Compensation system has started reflecting higher levels of discrimination, and large variation in pay packages which are now accepted by managers in many corporations and professions. Salary or compensation surveys can be formal or informal. Informal telephone or internet surveys are good for checking on a relatively small number of early identified and quickly recognized jobs, such as when a HR director of a bank wants to confirm the salary at which to advertise a newly open cashier's job. Such internet based survey is known as wage access compensation survey, that provides employer with the current and accurate compensation, information needed to attract and retain quality employees. It contains over 500 benchmark positions. Each position includes a detailed job description to ensure a comparable match during the survey data entry process. Survey results are calculated based on the criteria selected and are displayed as mean, weighted mean, median, average low and average high rates of pay.

The degree of match between the survey benchmark jobs and each company's benchmark jobs assessed by various means. The Hay group has installed the same job evaluation plan in many companies that participate in its surveys. Consequently jobs in different organizations can be compared on their job evaluation points and the distribution of points among the compensable factors.

Benchmarking Jobs

Managerial Group	Technical Group	Manufacturing Group	Administrative Group
		Assembler I Inspector I	
Vice Presidents	Head/Chief Scientist	Packer	Administrative Assistant
Division General Managers	Senior Associate Scientist	Material Handler Inspector II	Principal Administrative Secretary
Managers	Associate Scientist	Assembler II	Administrative Secretary
Project Leaders	Scientist	Drill Press Operator Rough Grinder	Word Processor
Supervisions	Technician	Machinist I Coremaker	Clerk/Messenger

Fig. 2.1

Uses of Compensation Surveys

1. To know what the competitors are paying.
2. Development of more integrated pay structures covering all categories of employees.
3. Extent flexible benefit schemes.
4. Align pay strategy more systematically with business strategy.
5. Treat employees as stakeholders who have the right to be consulted on and involved with any reward management developments.
6. Achieve the integration of reward and other HR processes and practices for example, human resource development.
7. Use variable pay rather than consolidated pay increases.
8. Examine more rigorously the cost effective schemes of payment.
9. To analyze pay related problems.

Characteristics of a benchmark job:

1. It's contents are well-known and relatively stable over time.
2. The job is common across a number of different employers. It is not unique to a particular employer.
3. A sizable proportion of the work force is employed in this job.

A representative sample of benchmark jobs will include the entire domain of work being evaluated – office, administration, technical, manufacturing and so on, thus helping to ensure the accuracy of the decisions based on the job evaluation. That means a job evaluation plan is developed using benchmark jobs and then the plan is applied to the remaining non-benchmark jobs to match with jobs at competitors that use a traditional job-based approach, Market data must be converted to fit the skill or competency structure. The simplest approach is to identify the lowest and highest paid benchmark jobs for the relevant skills in the relevant market and to use the wages for these jobs as anchor for the skill based structures; work at various levels within the structure can then be slotted between the anchors.

INFLUENCE OF PAY ON EMPLOYEE ATTITUDES AND BEHAVIOUR

Because compensation practices heavily influence recruitment, turnover, and employee productivity, it is important that applicants and employees view these practices in a favourable light. In the following section, we discuss how people form perceptions about a firm's compensation system and how these perceptions ultimately affect their behaviour.

One would expect that an individual's satisfaction with his or her compensation would simply be a function of the amount of compensation received: the higher the compensation rate, the greater the satisfaction. However, in reality things are not that simple. In fact, the amount of pay is less important than its perceived fairness or equity. To put this finding in perspective, consider the behaviour of many professional athletes when negotiating a new contract. The average NBA salary in 2003 was $4.9 million; the average baseball salary was $2.4 million; the average NFL salary was $1.3 million. Yet, ball players continue to ask for more money. In many instances, these demands stem from neither need nor greed. Rather, the demand for greater salaries often stems from perceptions of inequity. For instance, despite a $15 million salary, a player may feel that his pay is inequitable because a less capable player (or someone he perceives as being less capable) is earning an equal or greater salary.

Regarding the returns they get (e.g., pay) for the work they perform. People judge the equity of their pay by comparing their outcome-to-input ratio (O/I) with another person's ratio. This comparison person is referred to as one's "referent other." People feel equity when the O/I ratios of the individual and his or her referent other are perceived as being equal. A feeling of inequity occurs when the two ratios are perceived as being unequal. For example, inequity occurs if a person feels that he or she contributes the same input as a referent other, but earns a lower salary.

A person's referent other could be any one of several people. People may compare themselves to others:

- Doing the same job within the same organization
- Working in the same organization, but performing different jobs
- Doing the same job in other organizations.

For example, an assistant manager at a Wal-Mart department store might compare her pay to other assistant managers at Wal-Mart, to Wal-Mart employees in other positions (either above or below her in the organizational hierarchy), or to assistant managers at Kmart department stores.

While the mechanism for choosing a referent other is largely unknown, one study found that people do not limit their comparisons to just one person; they have several referent others. Thus, people make several comparisons when they assess the fairness of their pay; perceived fairness is achieved only when all comparisons are viewed as equitable. When employees' O/I ratios are less than that of their referent others, they feel they are being underpaid; when greater, they feel they are being overpaid. According to equity theory, both conditions produce feelings of tension that employees will attempt to reduce in one of the following ways:

1. Decrease inputs by reducing effort or performance.
2. Attempt to increase outcomes by seeking a raise in salary.
3. Distort perceptions of inputs and/or outcomes by convincing themselves that their O/I ratio already is equal to that of their referent other.
4. Attempt to change the inputs and/or outcomes of their referent other(s). For example, they may try to convince their referent other(s) to increase inputs (e.g., work harder for their pay).
5. Choose a new referent other whose O/I ratio already is equal to their own.
6. Escape the situation. This response may be manifested by a variety of behaviours, such as absenteeism, tardiness, excessive work-breaks, or quitting.

While equity theory poses six possible responses to inequity, only two of them typically occurs. Research findings, for example, have linked underpayment to increases in absenteeism and turnover and to decreases in the amount of effort exerted on the job. These linkages are especially strong among individuals earning low salaries.

Contrary to equity theory's predictions, these responses occur only when employees believe they are underpaid. Overpaid individuals do not respond because they feel little, if any tension, and thus have no need to reduce it. (The research findings on the issue of overpayment find overpayment to be either just as satisfying as equity, or somewhat dissatisfying but not nearly as dissatisfying as underpayment.) When feeling underpaid, why do some people choose to decrease their inputs, while others choose to escape the situation? A recent study sheds some light on this issue. The study found that reaction to inequity depends on the source of the comparison; people react differently depending on whether they judge equity on the basis of external (referents outside of the organization) or internal (referents employed by the individual's own organization) comparisons. When perceptions of inequity are based on external comparisons, people are more likely to quit their jobs. For instance, a nurse working for Hospital A may move to Hospital B if the latter pays a higher salary. When based on internal comparisons, people are more likely to remain at work, but reduce their inputs (e.g., become less willing to help others with problems, meet deadlines, and/or take initiatives).

KEY TERMS

Pay grade	Range spread
Pay structure	Broadbanding
Pay compression	Bench-marking

SUMMARY

The present competitive environment requires new strategies toward employee compensation, new management and employee practices, and new methods of educating employees to the shifting competitive environment that has brought about the necessity for these changes. Careful attention must be placed on the development of reward systems that reflect the financial capability of the company as well as reinforce the new directions associated with contemporary organizational strategies. Thus, compensation decisions should be fully integrated into the organization's business and operations strategy, through its compensation philosophy.

Strategic pay. "Pay structure has strategic value that assigns different pay rates offer jobs of different values which differentiate individual employee contributions. A well designed pay structure is one which attract and retain potential employees.

Compensation specialist develop pay structure based on five steps:

(i) Deciding on how many pay structure to construct. (ii) Determining a market pay line.

(iii) Defining pay grades. (iv) Calculating pay ranges for each pay grade. (v) Evaluating the results.

Effective administration of pay structure requires a balance between the pay levels for employees inside the company (internal equity) and they pay level those employees could command in the company's recruiting markets (external equity).

Technical considerations for pay structure design include the number of range levels, width of the ranges from minimum to maximum values (i.e., range spreads), the distance between adjacent range midpoint values (i.e., midpoint differentials), and the degree of overlap between adjacent ranges.

The "range spread" is a characteristic of salary structures that describes the distance between the minimum and the maximum salary range Traditional Structures Many salary ranges that have narrow range spreads, small midpoint differentials, and broad overlap between adjacent ranges characterize traditional structures. Traditional structures tend to place greater emphasis on internal equity, as opposed to external equity. Traditional structures focus on job content evaluation to arrange a job worth hierarchy.

Broadbanding: It is a method of grouping jobs and determining pay that makes compensation administration more flexible and more responsive to the needs of changing organizations. Broadbanding eliminates the present hierarchical grading structure and narrow salary ranges. Pay compression can occur when the pay rates of several employees, despite clear differences in capability, are in a cluster.

Skill-based pay refers to a pay system in which pay increases are linked to the number or depth of skills an employee acquires and applies and it is a means of developing broader and deeper skills among the workforce. The pay increases are usually tied to three types of skills:

- horizontal skills, vertical skills, and depth skills

Diagnosis and bench-marking: It is defined as a method of defining standard job that is used to anchor the employer's pay scale and around which other jobs are arranged in order of relative worth.

REVIEW QUESTIONS

1. Why would an organisation use more than one pay structure? Describe some factors that influence the design of a pay structure.
2. Explain some issues underlying overlap between pay grades?
3. What is a benchmark or a key job? Why are these jobs so critical in various job evaluation methodologies.
4. Justify the high remuneration paid to executives. What steps can be taken to remedy this situation.
5. Bring out the differences between executive remuneration and wages of workers.

References

Adams, J.S., "Injustices in Social Exchange." *In Advances in Experimental Social Psychology.* 2nd ed., Berkowitz. New York: Academic Press, 1965.

Henderson, Richard I., *Compensation Management in a Knowledge-Based World.* 9th ed. Upper Saddle River, NJ: Prentice Hall, 2003.

Kleiman, Lawrence S., *Human Resource Management: A Tool for Competitive Advantage.* Cincinnati, OH: South-Western College Publishing, 2000.

Mathis, Robert L., and John H. Jackson, *Human Resource Management.* 11th ed. Mason, OH: Thomson/ South-Western, 2006.

Milkovich, George T., and Jerry M. Newman. *Compensation. 8th ed. New York:* McGraw-Hill/Irwin, 2005.

Warner, S. and Ward S. G. (2004), Recent compensation research: An eclectic review. *Human Resource Management Review,* 14: pp.201-227.

Balkin, D.B. & Gomez-Mejia, L. R. (1990). Matching Compensation and Organizational Strategies. *Strategic Management Journal,* 11: pp.153-169.

Barkema, H. G. & Gomez-Mejia, L. R., (1998). Managerial Compensation and Firm Performance: a General Research Framework. *Academy of Management Journal,* 41: pp135-145.

Bloom, M., & Milkovich, G.T. (1998), Relationships among risk, incentive pay, and organizational performance. *Academy of Management Journal,* 41(3): pp.283-297.

Carpenter, M.A., Sanders, W.G. & Gregerson, H.B., (2001). Bundling Human Capital with Organizational Context: the Impact of International Assignment Experience on Multinational Firm Performance and CEO Pay. *Academy of Management Journal,* 44 (3): p. 493.

MANAGING COMPENSATION

3

LEARNING OBJECTIVES

After studying this chapter, you will be able to understand —

- ➪ Designing a compensation system
- ➪ Internal and External equity in compensation system
- ➪ Compensation as a retention strategy
- ➪ Competency based programme
- ➪ Framework of compensation policy

DESIGNING A COMPENSATION SYSTEM

Employers receive compensation from a company in return for the work performed. Most people think the pay and compensation to be the same, but the fact is compensation is much more than just the monetary rewards provided by an employer. According to Milkowitch and Newman, "compensation is all forms of financial returns and tangible services and benefits employees receive as a part of an employment relationship". The phrase "financial returns" refers to an individual base salary, as well as short and long term incentives. Tangible services and benefits are such things such as insurance, paid vacations and employer discount.

Any organization's compensation practices and designing have far reaching effects on its competitive advantage. According to Richard Henderson, 'To develop a competitive advantage in a global economy, the compensation program of the organization must support totally the strategic plans and actions of the organization. An organization compensation system can help to reinforce the key corporate values and facilitate the achievement of organizational objectives. It is important to give a lot of consideration to our business compensation structure because it ultimately reflects how employees are valued.

A host of laws such as The Equal Pay Act, Fair Labour Standards Act, and The Employment Retirement Income Security Act, regulate corporate compensation practices. Some pertain to pay issues such as discrimination, minimum wages and overtime pay, others pertain to benefits, such as pensions, unemployment compensation and compensation for work related injures. An organization must understand and fully follow these laws in order to avoid costly lawsuits and design a competency based compensation structure.

The key in designing any compensation is to develop the understating of the forms, vision and direction. As well designed compensation plan becomes one of many tools, a firm can use to help reach its strategic goals. Any failure in compensation design leads to failure to motivate any employee.

A guideline for designing a compensation plan begins at the top by examining the better strategy and ends with a model that is ready to be implemented. There are various steps that help as organization to design a performance based compensation strategy and prepare the organizations disign. Inadequate use of incentive plans and problems with compensation design and strategy often fails to motivate performance of an employee.

Behavioural scientists, employee and management surveys experience show that compensation can be a strong driver of employee behaviour under the right circumstances when properly designed. Also in jobs where significant variability in pay occur in compensation and when it is closely related to key performance factor, then pay can be a big motivator.

The good performers prior to new compensation plan implementation remain good performers and may not improve much because they are already giving close to 100% effort, but the middle and the bottom performers are where there is significant opportunity for change.

(1) Focusing on the strategy objectives

The most important goal in designing an compensation system is supporting the strategic objectives of the organization and ensuring the system that fit in with the organization structure and strategy. There are various questions which should be focused before designing compensation strategy such as:

- What is the rate and mission of the organization?
- Why does it exist?
- What are the strategic goals and objectives for the next five years?
- Whether current employee have the skills to meet these objectives? If so, will they be rewarded for having them? If not, will internal candidates be trained to gain skills or will the organization recruit externally to fill the goals?
- What is the organization's strategy?
- Do employees work individually or in teams?
- Are employees seen as costs or investments?
- What is the cost to replace employees?
- What is the desired turnover rate?
- What should the organization's compensation plan accomplish?
- How would you describe the current total compensation package, including benefits retirement time off etc., at the organization?

- How does it compare with that of other employees in the market. What should the organization pay in relation to the market?
- What is the appropriate balance between external market equity and internal worth.

Once there is an understanding of the answer to these questions, the compensation can be developed, policy guidelines are prepared which reflects thinking, values, strategies and the company is set inconsistency by top management.

(2) Ensuring commitment through communication and participation

An organization must plan for making change to its compensation system.

Before beginning to tackle something, it is important that executive management is absolutely committed to the process, the result and the implementation. All important techniques for participation and communication by the clearly defined, advisory or steering committee. A compensation review committee could help identifying current issues with compensation, job clarification or salary administration. It could contribute ideas and feedback provide valuable advice.

(3) Analyzing job functions

A job analyst develops a current and thorough understanding of the work that is being formed by the employee. It is important to undertake a job analysis before making changes to the compensation plan as job analysis provides a collection of relevant information on the type, scope and responsibility of each job. It is the foundation for job description and how they are in the market. It enables the organization to establish baseline information about a job level of responsibility and qualification, and to compare it to the market place. It also ensures and documents our compliance with legal requirement.

(4) Writing job description

Once the information is collected through the job analysis process, it can be used for preparation of job description. A job description summarizes the important component like the general nature of the work, specific tasks, responsibilities and outcome competence required to perform the job. A written job description should be considered a final document. Before it is finalized, it should be received and accepted by both the employee and the supervisor.

(5) Determining internal pay equity

It determines fairness within the organization. Fair pay is pay that employees generally view as equitable. Internal equity is determined by job evaluation techniques such as whole job ranking method and factor comparison technique.

(6) Determining external pay equity

It is the perceived fairness in pay relative to what other employees are paying for the same type of labour. An externally focused job evaluation method includes the market pricing slotting method. For maximum flexibility, using market pricing is recommended to that of market competitive pay rates. Market competitiveness is more flexible and adaptable than other methods. To gather competitors pay rates, a survey method is developed which includes the following steps:

- Establish a timeline
- Select bench-mark positions to survey

- Target survey participants
- Design questionnaire
- Use other available market data sources
- Follow up and verify answers with participants.

(7) Designing salary structure

Once collection of market data and determination of a hierarchical ordering of position, is done a salary structure can be designed. Salary structure consists of jobs of equal value that are grouped into grades with competitive salary ranges. Pay ranges are the rates from the minimum to maximum of each grade. Positions are assigned to grades and pay ranges based on job content, marketing or external equity and internal equity. Each salary range includes minimum, midpoint and maximum salaries, with the midpoint representing the market or going rate for the job.

Typical compensation design problems includes:

- Failure to tie pay closely to achievement of objective and realistic performance measures.
- Failure to regularly measure and provide feedback on performance.
- Failure to design variances in pay-related to performance that are large enough to be perceived by the employer as worth the effort.
- Over reliance on salary as the only significant method of financial rewards.

Equity in Compensation

Equity means fair pay treatment for employees, which helps to attract, motivate and retain competent employees because equity is such an important concern. Individuals responsible for developing a firm's compensation system need to understand how perception of equity are formed. Equity theory, formulated by J. Stacy Adam attempts to provides such an understanding. The theory states that people form equity beliefs based on two factors:

(i) Inputs

(ii) Outcomes

(i) Inputs refers to the perception that people have concerning what they contribute to the job (e.g., skills or efforts)

(ii) Outcomes refer to the perception that people have regarding the returns they get (e.g., pay) for the work they perform.

People judge the equity of their pay by comparing their O/I (output to input rates with another person ratio. This comparison person is known as 'Referent other'Equity is believed by an individual when his or her O/I ratio is equal to the O/I ratio of the referent.

The referent person can be either–

(i) Doing the same job within the same organization.

(ii) Working in the same organization, but performing different jobs.

(iii) Doing the same job in other organizations.

Any feelings of inequity (underpaid or overpaid) from the referent person produce feelings of tension and frustration that employees will attempt to reduce in one of the following ways:

- Decrease input by reducing effort or performance.
- Attempts to increase outcomes by seeking a raise in salary.
- Distract perceptions of inputs and/or outcomes by convincing themselves that their O/I rates already is equal to that of their referent other.
- Attempt to change the inputs and/or outcomes of their referent others.
- Choose a new referent whose O/I ratio already is equal to their own.
- Escape the situation.

This response may be manifested by a variety of behaviour such as absenteeism, tiredness, excessive work-break or quitting.

These response occurs only when employee believes that they are underpaid or overpaid. Individuals do not respond because they feel little tension and don't want to reduce it.

Thus, it is concluded that employees will feel equity when they perceive that.

(i) Their pay is fair, relative to the pay received by worker in other organization who holds similar position (external equity or external competitiveness).

(ii) Fairly reflects their input to the organization (employee contributions).

Achieving Internal Consistency/Internal Equity

Internal equity refers to the pay relationship among different jobs/skills/competencies within a single organization. To achieve internal consistency, firm's employees must believe that all jobs are paid what they are "worth". In other words, they must be confident that company pay rates reflect the overall importance of each person's job to the success of the organization. For the pay rates to be internally consistent, an organization first must determine the overall importance or worth of each job. It is determined by the process of job evaluation. In general, the evaluation is based on "informed judgments", regarding such things as the amount of skill and effort required to perform the job, the difficulty of the job, and the amount of responsibility assumed by the job-holder. It is used to measure relativities and determine where the job should be placed in a pay structure (the rate for the job). Relative job size assessed in terms of inputs (knowledge and skills), process (behavioural requirement involving the use of competencies) and output (the level of responsibility for result and the impact the job makes on team or organizational performance). Most firms creates a committee of individuals, called job evaluation committee, for the purpose of making the evaluation. The committee members typically include department managers, vice president, plant manager and HR professionals. The committee chair usually is an HR professional or an outside consultant.

Perhaps, the two most serious problems with job evaluation ratings are subjectivity and the rapidity with which jobs fundamentally change, both of which can cause inaccurate and unreliable ratings in order to minimize subjectivity, the rating scales used to evaluate jobs must be clearly defined and evaluators should be thoroughly trained on how to use them. Moreover, the evaluators should be provided with complete, accurate and up-to-date job descriptions.

When job evaluation have been completed, jobs are grouped into pay grades based on the total number of points received (point method). Jobs with the similar or same point values are placed in the same grade. Once the jobs are classified into grades, all jobs within the same grade are treated alike for pay purposes that is, the same range of pay applies to each job in a grade. As companies develop pay grade system, they must decide how many pay grade to establish. Most firms use thirty to fifty pay grades. However, some use as much as one hundred or more, while others use as few as five or six. The practice of limiting number of grades eases the firm's administrative burdens.

Determining External Pay Equity

It is the received fair in pay, relative to what other employees are paying for the same type of labour. An externally focused job evaluation method includes the market pricing setting method. For maximum flexibility using market pricing is recommended to that market competitive pay rate. Market competitiveness is more flexible and adoptable than other methods. To gather competition pay rates, a survey method is developed

A firm achieves external competitiveness when employees perceive that their pay is fair in relation to what their counterparts in other organizations earn. To become externally competitive, organizations must first learn what other employers are paying and then make a decision regarding just how competitive they want to be. They then establish pay rates consistent with this decision. Following is an elaboration of how these steps are carried out:

1. The firm begins by conducting or acquiring a salary survey. This survey provides information on pay rates offered by a firm's competitors for certain bench-mark jobs (i.e., jobs that are performed in a similar manner in all companies and can thus serve as a basis for making meaningful comparisons). Some firms gather this information from existing surveys already conducted by others, such as those produced by the Bureau of Labour Statistics. Trade associations also conduct surveys routinely for their members, or companies may hire consulting firms to gather such information. Salary surveys conducted by others should be used when they contain all the information needed by the company in question. When no such surveys exist, companies generally conduct their own.
2. After the pay practices of other companies have been identified, the organization must determine how competitive it wants to be (or can afford to be). Specifically, it must set a pay policy stipulating how well it will pay its employees relative to the market (i.e., what competitors pay for similar jobs). The determination of a pay policy is a crucial step in the design of a pay system. If pay rates are set too low, the organization is likely to experience recruitment and turnover problems. If set too high, however, the organization is likely to experience budget problems that ultimately may lead to higher prices, pay freezes and layoffs.
3. The majority of firms pay at the market rate, which is the rate offered by most of the competitors for labour. Those paying above market are referred to as "market leaders." These typically are companies with the ability to pay and the desire to attract and retain top-notch employees (e.g., "cream of the crop"). Those paying below market ("market laggards") generally do so because they are unable to pay higher salaries. Such companies often attempt to attract employees by linking pay to productivity or profits, so that the employees can earn more if the company does well.

4. When setting its pay policy, a company must consider its strategic plan. For example, if long-term employee commitment is a strategic goal, then the organization should attempt to develop compensation strategies that will enhance retention, such as establishing a generous retirement plan for long-service employees or adopting a profit-sharing system tied to tenure.
5. Once market rates for jobs are determined and a pay policy is established, an organization must price each of its jobs. Since market rates identified by a salary survey usually are restricted to bench-mark jobs, how do organizations determine these rates for their non-benchmark jobs? Using the data collected on the bench-mark jobs, an organization would determine the statistical relationship (i.e., simple linear regression) between job evaluation points and prevailing market rates. This regression line is referred to as the pay policy line. The appropriate pay rates for non-bench-mark jobs are set based on this line.

Achieving Employees Contribution Equity

Employees contribution equity is achieved when employees believe their pay fairly reflects their level of contribution to the organization. To achieve this aim, an organization must first establish a range of pay for each pay grade; it must then place each employee within that range based on his or her contribution to the organization.

A pay range specifies the minimum and maximum pay rates for all jobs within a grade. When establishing pay ranges, most employers set the market rate at the midpoint of the range. The spread from the midpoint usually varies, becoming larger as one progresses to higher pay grades. Most organizations establish a range spread of 10-25 percent for office and production work, 35-60 percent for professional and lower-level management positions, and 60-120 percent for top-level management positions.

The mechanism for recognizing employee contributions differs for new and existing employees. Contributions made by new employees are recognized by varying the level of starting pay they receive. New employees usually are paid at the minimum rate unless their qualifications exceed the minimum qualifications of the job. Those exceeding minimum qualifications are paid more because they can make a greater contribution, at least initially. Existing employees' contributions usually are recognized in the form of pay raises, typically granted on the basis of seniority and performance.

One may conclude that employees will believe their pay is equitable when they perceive that it:

- Is fair relative to the pay received by co-workers in the same organization (internal consistency).
- Is fair relative to the pay received by workers in other organizations who hold similar positions (external competitiveness).
- Fairly reflects their input to the organization (employee contributions).

COMPENSATION AS A RETENTION STRATEGY

Compensation plays a very important role in retaining potential employees. Implementing compensation and benefits programs that reward the right behaviour and performance will help attract the right people to the organization, and will also help the best people to become more productive. There are various key learning retention strategies that company must incorporate to retain top talent and remain competitive in the current labour market. It is important to search key areas that are important to the organization's employees in terms of compensation and benefits. Mapping this information into the overall plan and budget of the organization ensures that salary and benefits program add value to employees and the organization.

Total compensation includes a total rewards approach because monetary compensation is not always the only factor that employees consider when evaluating a job. Compensation professionals must be very aware of the many elements in addition to money. Our global economy has become more apparent that these different elements, approaches, techniques and tools should be used while designing the compensation plan.

Some of the key learning strategies of retention that defines compensation role are:

- ❖ There should be an effective performance management system that compensation employees fairly in addition to above market pay, employee's seek flexible work schedule, opportunities for advancement, an enhancement in profits and operations of the organization.
- ❖ Managing poor performance is just as important as reorganizing good performance, as non-performers can demotivate good employees.
- ❖ Terms and conditions for designing compensation are not key to a retention strategy as they are perceived as competitive with the market and equitable among employees. The organization should regularly benchmark its salaries and benefits and communicate to employees that their salary and benefits are distributed in a fair and equitable manner.
- ❖ Hiring and promoting the right people ensures company's success and helps in achieving organization's business strategy.
- ❖ Promotion provides employees with a motivating factor to remain in the organization and to be productive.
- ❖ Career development motivates employees and also allows them to build for promotion.

COMPETENCY BASED PROGRAM

"Skill is nothing but a mere hoard of gold, till it is set to work."

Competencies are knowledge, skills and attitude (KSA) and most importantly behaviours that enables one to perform a job that correlates with performance on the job, that can be measured against well accepted standards and that can be improved via training and development. Competencies effectively translate the strategic vision and goal of the organization into behavioral actions. Competency based compensation system focuses on the skills and knowledge required to do a particular job in addition to the attitude and ability to do the job.

Competency-based models help in the organization to:

1. Drive business results.
2. Retain key talent.
3. Raise the bar of individual and organizational performance.
4. Integrate cultures following a merger.
5. Increase in competitive advantage.

Human capital is the most important resource for any organization in the globalized and skill based economies around the world. It is important for any organization to align the employee behaviour to the strategic objectives for sustained success.

Competency based Human resource Management is being increasingly recognized as effective way of talent management over the previously adopted job-description related approach. It involves a transition from the traditional way of managing human resources based on what people have (qualifications) to what people can do (performance).

The advantages of using the competency based framework for Human Resource sub-systems such as selection, promotion, training and developmentper formance management, career and succession planning, compensation, etc. are:

❖ Provide a systems approach to human resources activities and make them more effective.

Competency modelling is based on the fundamental belief that every employee should be given the opportunity to do his or her best. It provides both the structure and discipline to help bring out the best effort in people and ultimately the best performance for the organization. Today's competitive marketplace, constant change, the need for the most cost-effective approaches and potential labour shortages are driving organization to implement new competency based approaches to drive higher performance. As more employers recognize the economic value of multi skilled employees who can work as a team, they are rethinking traditional, job based pay programs that don't fully support skill development or achievement of results. Compensation strategies and programs are changing dramatically and the competency based approach to pay is quickly gaining adherents. It develops the critical behaviour and abilities employees need to achieve specific business results. By linking compensation directly to individual contributions that make a difference to the organization, a company can also maintain company's philosophy related to how equity-based compensation will be distributed within various levels of the company.

❖ The company's philosophy relating to the dilution of existing equity owners. In this, the company uses equity-based tools in its compensation program and articulate how the company will address the issue of dilution.

❖ The parameters by which the company will use severance packages, if at all. The policy should include a definitive statement related to how the company views severance agreements.

Competencies bring out the synergy between different sub-systems by reinforcing each other and minimize the needless overlaps and contradictions if they were treated independently.

❖ Provide a common language to Human resource activities for easy implementation.

❖ The competency based approach to Human Resource Management helps people understand this aspect much better by providing an organization-wide common language to understand different roles and responsibilities and how they can grow to fulfill their aspirations.

❖ Provide management a view of available and required competency level. The competency based form work helps in identifying the interventions needed and in what form to achieve this strategic objective.

Many organizations are using competencies as the means for identifying and developing talent. Unless the competency framework is well planned and defined, organizations will not have the proper foundation for developing and implementing a system of human resource programs and initiatives for renewal and sustained success.

The importance of competency based HRM is increasingly being accepted as an explanation of superior performance. This is based on the fact that the performance of an employee is based on not only skills or knowledge, but is also a function of internal and external environment. From the Indian context, companies are increasingly becoming aware of the importance and an article on "competency profiling" in Business Today (1999 July), reported the steps Indian Organizations are taking with respect to competency based HR practices.

Research in 1999-2000 by three leading performance management companies worldwide, indicate that competency based practices are an integral tool for "talent management", shareholder return and value creation. It is found that companies using competency based HR programs returned between 20-30 percent, more to shareholders than companies using the traditional method (job description, salary grades). Some of the companies using competency based practices are L & T, Smithkline, Pepsico, Escort, P & G, Xerox, Mahindra & Mahindra, etc.

FRAMEWORK OF COMPENSATION POLICY

A compensation framework supports a long term strategic vision for compensation and implements new initiatives, provides the needed direction and innovative concept towards solving special salary problems. The shift from the traditional compensation system to new flexible system increases delegation to managers, focus on long term approach to compensation management, eliminates duplication and increases efficiency.

Objectives of Compensation Policy

- To ensure that compensation is maintained at the desired competitive level by taking into account changing market conditions, and in particular the prevailing market wage rate.
- Attract and retain the desired quality mix of employees so as to achieve the company's objective.
- Motivate employees to perform their duties and responsibilities to the best of their abilities.
- Ensure an equitable compensation system.
- Integrating compensation with other areas of human resource management to emphasize on transparency, monitoring, reporting and accountability.
- Creating and maintaining an organizational structure and culture that facilitates both employee and organizational performance.
- To provide broad guidelines by which company uses alternative form of compensation and the relative weight in relation to overall compensation if "other" forms of compensation will be utilized (Pension's benefits, perks, loans, etc.).

A good rewards and remuneration system ensures that each person receives appropriate financial and non-financial recognition to account for the personal contribution they are making and the overall value of their position to the organization. If the rewards are not fair and equitable, dissatisfaction arises which leads to absenteeism and demotivation. Therefore, there is a need to develop a new structure or framework of compensation which can be tied to a completely new performance management approach, unloading better performance appraisal mechanisms. This includes:

1. Creating and maintaining an organizational structure and organizational performance.
2. Recognizing and rewarding individual and team performance, financially and otherwise, in relation to the overall contribution made.
3. Implementing compensation systems that fairly treat and recognize all employees, regardless of their level within the organization.
4. It involves matching remuneration with the contribution made.
5. A feedback loop between motivation and performance exists, which potentially impact each other.

An integrated system of compensation policy is as follows:

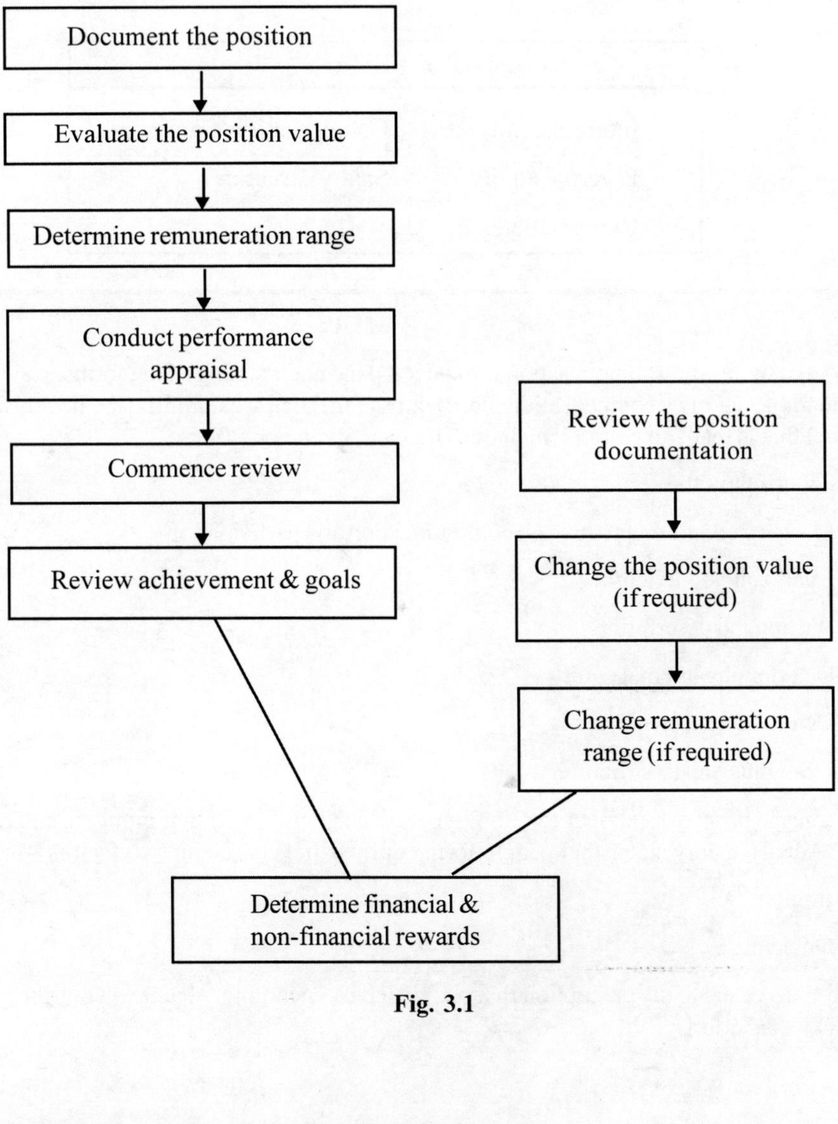

Fig. 3.1

Executive compensation policies should contain, at a minimum, the following components:

1. The bonus and long-term incentive compensation. The policy should clearly articulate how the company ensures optimal alignment of interests with shareowners through the design and implementation of its executive compensation program.
2. The company's intended forms of incentive and bonus compensation including what types of measures will be used to drive incentive compensation.
3. The policy should include the company philosophy related to the major components of incentive compensation, including the strengths and weaknesses of each and how the overall incentive component of the plan provides optimal alignment of interests with shareowners, Performance based plans should be constructed including the specific drivers to construct performance based plan.
4. The company's intended distribution of equity based compensation.

KEY TERMS	
Internal equity	Compensation framework
External equity	Salary structure
Competencies	

SUMMARY

The key in designing any compensation is to develop the understating of the forms, vision and direction. A guideline for designing a compensation plan begins at the top by examining the better strategy and ends with a model that is ready to be implemented. There are various steps–

(1) Focusing on the strategic objectives

(2) Ensuring commitment through communication and participation

(3) Analyzing job function

(4) Writing job description

(5) Determining internal equity

(6) Determining external equity

(7) Designing salary structure.

Equity means fair pay treatment for employees, which helps to attract, motivate and retain competent employee. Adams theory states that people form equity beliefs based on two factors —

(i) Inputs

(ii) Outcomes

(i) Inputs refers to the perception that people have concerning what they contribute to the job (e.g., skill and effort)

(ii) Outcomes refers to the perception that people regarding the returns they get (e.g., pay) for the work they perform).

Internal equity refers to the pay relationship among different jobs/ skills/ competencies within a single organization.

External pay equity is the received fair in pay relative to what other employees are paying for the same type of labour. Employee contributions equity is achieved when employees believe their pay fairly reflects their level of contribution to the organization.

Compensation plays a very important role in retaining potential employee.

Competencies are knowledge, skills and attitude (KSA) and most importantly behaviours that enables one to perform a job that correlates with performance on the job, that can be measured against with accepted standards and that can be improved via training and development.

Competency-based models help in the organization to:

- Drive business results.
- Retain key talent.
- Raise the bar of individual and organizational performance.
- Integrate cultures following a merger.
- Increase in competitive advantage.

A compensation framework supports a long term strategic vision for compensation and implements new initiatives, provides the needed direction and innovative concept towards solving special salary problems.

REVIEW QUESTIONS

1. What is more important for organizational effectiveness – internal equity or external equity?
2. Explain the importance of compensation as a retention strategy.
3. What steps can be a taken to design a competency based compensation program?
4. What are the factors responsible for the failure of a successful compensation program?

References

Adams, J. S., "Injustices in Social Exchange." *In Advances in Experimental Social Psychology.* 2nd ed., Berkowitz. New York: Academic Press, 1965.

Henderson, Richard I., *Compensation Management in a Knowledge-Based World.* 9th ed. Upper Saddle River, NJ: Prentice Hall, 2003.

Kleiman, Lawrence S., *Human Resource Management: A Tool for Competitive Advantage.* Cincinnati, OH: South-Western College Publishing, 2000.

Mathis, Robert L., and John H. Jackson., *Human Resource Management.* 11th ed. Mason, OH: Thomson/ South-Western, 2006.

Milkovich, George T., and Jerry M. Newman, *Compensation.* 8th ed. New York: McGraw-Hill/Irwin, 2005.

HT Careers "Benchmarking Study on Retention Strategies Conducted by Synergy Consultants", (HT Careers 11 Oct. 2001).

PERFORMANCE BASED COMPENSATION

4

LEARNING OBJECTIVES

After studying this chapter, you should be able to understand —

- What is performance appraisal?
- Importance of performance apprasial system.
- Effect of compensation on performance and motivation
- Pay for performance system
- Meeting the challenges of pay for performance system
- Types of pay for performance plan
- Does compensation motivate performance?

WHAT IS PERFORMANCE APPRAISAL?

According to Peter Drucker, "an organization is like a tune, it is not constituted by individual sounds but by their synthesis. The success of an organization will therefore depend on its ability to measure accurately the performance of its members and use its objectivity to optimize them as a vital resource."

Organization are run and steered by people. It is through people that goals are set and objectives are realized. The performance of an organization is thus dependent upon the sum total of the performance of its members. Performance appraisal refers to all those procedure that are used to evaluate the personality, the performance and the potential of its group members.

DEFINITION

Performance appraisal may be defined as a structured formal interaction between a subordinate and supervisor, that usually take the form of periodic interview – annual or semiannual, in which the work performance of the subordinate is examined and discussed, with a view of identifying weaknesses, strengths as well as opportunities for improvement and skills development.

Nikol defined Performance as

The outcome of behaviour: Behaviour is individual activity where outcomes of behaviour are the way in which the behaving individual environment is somehow different as a result of his or her behaviour.

Overview of Performance Appraisal:

- Ideally performance appraisal allows management to specify what employees must do, combines feedback and goal setting.
- Everyone involved needs to recognize that performance appraisal involve human judgment and information processing can never be totally objective or infallible.
- System should aim to be easy to operate, easy to explain, easy to maintain and, easy to administer.
- System should be job related, relevant, sensitive, reliable, acceptable, practical, open, fair and useful.
- Ratee should participate in the development.
- Need to take legal issues into account.

Importance of Performance Appraisal system

- An effective system of performance appraisal. helps the supervisor to evaluate the performance of his employees systematically and periodically. It helps in the placement of the employees on the job for which they are best suited.
- Recent research (Bannister and Balkin, 1990) has reported that appraisee seems to have greater acceptance of the appraisal process and feel more satisfied with it, when the process is directly linked to rewards.
- Performance measures quantitatively tell us something important about our product services and the processes that produce them. They are the tool to help us understand to manage and improve what our organization's do.
- Performance measures are always tied to goal or an objective (the target) and tell us if and where improvements are necessary.
- Performance appraisal can also be used for transfer and promotions of employees.
- It facilitates human resource planning, career planning and succession planning. It is used to analyze the training and development needs and evaluating the effectiveness of existing training program.
- Performance appraisal provides the management an objective basis for discussing salary increases and special increments of the staff.
- The result of performance appraisal may be used by the supervisor in constructively guiding the employees in the efficient performance of their jobs.

EFFECT OF COMPENSATION ON PERFORMANCE AND MOTIVATION

The design and implementation of a performance measurement and compensation system can strongly effect the motivation of employees. There exists a significant positive relationship between the perceived characteristics of the compensation system and extrinsic motivation. Intrinsic motivation is not affected by the design of the monetary compensation system, but is affected by promotion opportunities. The compensation system also significantly affects other indicators of motivation, namely work satisfaction and turnover intent.

A conceptual model, particularly a derivative of a model by Lawler (1986), includes the interrelationships between employee effort, employee performance, the firm's compensation system, and the motivational level of individuals.

The performance measure is used to evaluate the performance of the employee, which forms the basis for determining the amount of variable monetary compensation an employee will receive and for making career decisions. Fixed compensation, as opposed to variable compensation, does not induce effort and its role is limited to retention and selection. In practice, completely fixed compensation that is totally unrelated to performance is extremely rare, for instance, the probability of being fired creates an incentive to perform.

The combination of elements of the compensation system, i.e. performance measurement and evaluation, monetary compensation and career concerns link employee performance to motivation, which in turn affects effort and other indicators for the level of motivation.

The Lawler Porter model gives following guidelines to motivate their employees:

- Place the right person on the right job and match the abilities and trait of individuals to the requirement of the job.
- Carefully explain to employees what their roles are,and make sure that they understand their roles.
- Prescribe in concrete terms the actual performance levels expected of the individuals.
- Make sure that the employees value the reward dispersed.

There are certain conditions, which are necessary for employee motivation.

1. Employees must believe effective performance (or certain specified behaviour) will lead to certain rewards. For example, attaining certain results will lead to a bonus or approval from others.
2. Employees must feel that the rewards offered are attractive. Some employees may desire promotions because they seek power, but others may want a fringe benefit, such as a pension, because they are older and want retirement security.
3. Employees must believe a certain level of individual effort will lead to achieving the corporation's standards of performance.

It is found that motivation to exert effort is triggered by the prospect of desired rewards: money, recognition, promotion, and so forth. If effort leads to performance and performance leads to desired rewards, the employee is satisfied and motivated to perform again.

The ability of a reward system both to motivate and to satisfy depends on who influences and/or controls the system's design and implementation. Even though, considerable evidence suggests that participation in decision making can lead to greater acceptance of decisions, participation in the design and administration of reward systems is rare. Such participation is time-consuming.

Therefore, it can be seen as an important managerial tool, for an increase in the level of motivation is not limited to an increase in effort. A well perceived compensation system also has a beneficial effect for companies on major indicators of motivation: work satisfaction and turnover intent. We can conclude that a compensation system can be of great importance for managers in order to increase both motivation and individual performance.

PAY FOR PERFORMANCE SYSTEM

The term "Pay for Performance" refers to a pay strategy where evaluations of individual and for organizational performance have significant influence on the amount of pay increases or bonuses given to each employee. If employees see that pay is not distributed on the basis of merit, they are more likely to lack commitment to the organization, which decreases their level of satisfaction. Pay for performance system is also known as incentive system where outstanding performers will receive the greatest rewards, to acknowledge their superior contributions and to motivate them to continue high performance. Average performers will receive substantially smaller raises, which may encourage them to work harder to achieve larger raises in the future.

Pay for performance is a pay strategy which emphasises on the performance evaluation processes that produces the most significant gains. It involves initial clarifying of organizational goals and translating them into individual expectations, thus, emphasis on ongoing communication and progress checks, and the careful assessment of individual accomplishments, which are used to justify the variation in rewards in improving organizational performance.

Objectives of Pay for Performance System

- The main aim is to improve the organization's ability to attract and retain high performers.
- It helps in improving individual efforts and consequently, organizational performance.
- It is a fair way of pay since those who contribute more to the organization receives a large salary in return.
- It helps in inducing a performance-oriented culture and contributes to business objective.
- It helps in linking overall compensation strategy with the organization's business strategy.
- It is an effective motivational technique and improves productivity.
- It helps in upgrading skills of team members by increasing a competitive environment.

Though the system of pay for performance is very effective in increasing performance and motivation, yet it is complex processes that demand a large investment from those who seek to use it. The effectiveness of Pay for Performance System can be undermined by flaws in the design, implementation and operational phases. Above all the performance evaluation system must be accurate and supervisors must be well-versed in its use. Checks and balances should be built in to help supervisors accountable for their decisions. It is also associated with conflict and competition and many times discourages co-operation if not properly evaluated. A competency based pay structure requires practices to commit to ongoing staff training and can entail higher costs. Once implemented, pay for performance system creates a psychological contract i.e., a set of expectations based on past experience, and is very resistant to change between the employee and the firm. In many cases, pay for performance leads to job dissatisfaction and stress. Therefore, to avoid these unfavourable consequences, it is important to have a well-designed pay for performance system.

MEETING THE CHALLENGES OF PAY FOR PERFORMANCE SYSTEM

(a) Competency Based Pay Model

It should be developed to motivate staff and to accomplish the objectives. The main focus of this model should be on the person or individual rather than paying for the job. It includes following features:

(i) Thorough job analysis should be done followed by job description. Conducting a job analysis means identifying the critical behaviours, knowledge, skills, abilities and other personal characteristics that will establish a clear link between job's content, a person's qualifications and optimal performance of that job. A systematic job analysis not only is the basis of your pay system, it's the cornerstone of effective staff management because it gives us accurate information on which effective staff selection, training and performance review system is built.

(ii) Based on the job analysis, identify the competencies needed to perform the job.

(iii) Develop assessments to measure staff member's performance of these competencies.

(iv) Price the competencies by analyzing compensation using data. An investigation is done to analyse staff salaries of local or regional data sources.

(v) Establish a salary for each staff member based on the competencies an individual uses to perform his task.

(b) Development of Practice – Effectiveness Pay Model:

It is one of the methods to combine fixed and variable compensation. It involves setting base salaries plus establishing a method that will provide bonus payment based on certain performance criteria. It offers' certain advantages:

(i) This model helps to control operating costs. A portion of each staff members' salary is tied to the practice performance. In addition, the model itself has low overhead, in that, much of the administrative work related to it involves data collection that should already be taking place as a part of sound management practice.

(ii) It rewards the right behaviours that build unity. Staff members are reinforced only for actions that clearly benefit the practice performance, which focus everyone on the most important work and promote a culture of "we are all in this together". It builds an environment of change and adaptability and is compatible with TQM (Total Quality Management) and CQI (Continuous Quality Improvement).

(iii) It encourages self-management and helps in increased understanding of a practice business interest, which improves staff members' motivation to perform. It also encourages employees to co-ordinate their work with others more effectively and to make decisions that reflect the best interests of the practice.

(iv) It encourages innovation and improves operational efficiency producing tangible rewards for staff.

(c) Developing Employee Trust Relationship

A well designed pay for performance system is effective only if there is a relationship of mutual trust and confidence between the employer and employee. This relationship if implemented successfully helps in making major changes in the organization climate. An employer should care about employee's needs and be aware of the work they do. Also they need to keep employees informed and involved while making any changes in the management or compensation plan.

(d) Enhancement of Employees' Participation

An old saying among Compensation Practitioner is, "Acceptability is the ultimate determinant of success in any compensation plan"(Mejia & Cardy p. 365). Employees should be consulted in the formation of plan to increase their motivation. Employee's involvement is also done sometimes in the areas to design the reward strategies, through attitude survey prior to the consideration of a new reward strategy. Employee involvement will result in a greater understanding of the rationale behind the plan and a better matching between individual needs and pay- plan design.

(e) Use of Performance Linked Incentives

It is important for all participating companies to make use of bonus/profit sharing schemes in their compensation system. Also the use of performance bonuses to motivate executive staff whose salaries are close to or at the maximum of their salary range is done. Instead of using the traditional performance appraisal system, which involves a high degree of subjectivity, companies are adopting performance management system. Employees are assessed on their ability to meet "key results" (i.e., quantifiable targets/objectives).

Some Other's are:

(i) An already well functioning performance management system.

(ii) Strong collaboration with unions.

(iii) Involvement of staff in the reform.

(iv) Clear communication of the objectives and functioning of the performance related pay scheme to staff.

(v) Linkage between individual and organizational objectives.

(vi) Measurement of performance against specific goals or with quantitative measures of performance.

(vii) Clear feedback to staff on the allocation of rating and rewards.

The PRP policy needs to be seen as fair and equitable by all employees.

(i) Organization should provide clear guidance's to participants in PRP scheme on the standards, which are to be used to discriminate between levels of awards and its distribution.

(ii) High level and well differentiated reward.

(iii) Possibility of internal and external review.

(iv) Combination of pay with other incentives such as promotions.

Advantages of Performance Related Pay Scheme

(a) The main rationale for establishing performance related pay policies is to improve performance and motivation of managers or employees. This objective is coupled with the need to provide departments and individual managers with greater flexibility to recognize and reward individual or team performance contributions.

(b) The introduction of PRP at the employee level is also a way to forge a closer link between individual job goals and organizational goals.

(c) This scheme especially at the managerial level helps to attract and retain talent of currently employed worker.

(d) PRP can be used to assist or stimulate organizational change. It might help to achieve cultural change by letting employees know the values and expectations of the organization.

(e) PRP mechanism creates alternative paths, where performance is more important than grade and seniority. This has an important impact on strategic human resources management and constitutes strong incentive for improving staff development and training.

(f) The real motivation to use PRP is to be an instrument to obtain political support for more funding or flexibility over pay. It may also be seen as a way to have better control of the pay bill. It can indeed be a way to contain salary costs by reducing the incidence of automatic progression through salary levels.

(g) The individualization of pay may sometimes also be a way to circumvent collective bargaining process, thus reducing the influence of trade unions' and reestablishing managerial control.

(h) With the introduction of PRP in the organization, opportunities for professional growth are possible for staff, which builds acceptance for change. As staff learns to accept change, the practice becomes better able to react to staff turnover, expansions, mergers or changes in the health care environment.

TYPES OF PAY FOR PERFORMANCE PLANS

There are variety of approaches to reward performance in an organization. The pay for performance plans can be designed to reward the performance of the individual, team, business unit or plant or the entire organization.

There are 3 types of Pay-for-performance Plans on the basis of level of aggregation at which performance is defined.

(a) Individual Based Plans.

(b) Team Based Plans.

(c) Organizational Level Plans.

(a) Individual Based Plans:

The key to individual performance based programs is that they focus specifically on the individual. They are the most widely used pay-for-performance plans in the industry. The assumptions underlying these programs are that an individual can control their own behaviour and given some feedback about the behaviour that is good and that which needs improvement, the employee will choose to improve. Typically, individual performance based system involves one individual, usually a supervisor, evaluating the performance of another individual. If there is enough behaviours that meet their approval, the employee is rewarded. Some of the individual performance plans are:

(i) Merit system.

(ii) Piece rate.

(iii) Executive bonus.

(iv) Individual awards.

(i) Merit System

Merit pay consists of an increase in base pay, normally given once a year. Once a merit pay is given to an employee, it remains a part of that employee' base salary for the rest of his or her tenure within the firm. It is a reward for individual performance based on the performance standards established for their job and is designed to differentiate pay based on differences in work performance. This helps in improving accuracy of performance. However, it was found that merit system is expensive and does not achieve the desired goal of improving employees and corporate performance.

(ii) Piece rate

The straight piece work system is where rate wages vary directly as a function of the production level. This system finds difficulty in setting an appropriate standard straight piece rate plan.

Differential Piece Rate

F.W Taylor started this method as a part of the scheme of Scientific Management. The underlying principle of the system is to reward an efficient worker and penalize the inefficient person. The standard time was fixed for completing a task with the help of time and motion study. He set two piece work rates.

- One rate goes into effect when a worker exceeds the published standard for a given time period – this rate is set higher than the regular wage incentive level.
- A second rate is established for production below standard, and this rate is lower than the regular wage. This method offers good incentive to efficient workers but workers' feels insecure, as no minimum wage is guaranteed.

(i) **Executive Bonus. (Lumpsum payments):** It is similar to merit programs but differ in one important respect. Bonuses are given on a one-time basis and do not raise the employees' base pay permanently. It can be larger than merit pay increases because they involve lower risk to the employer as they are not permanent.

- It is increasingly used as a substitute for merit pay.
- It is based on employee or company performance, employee receives an end-of-year bonus that does not increase base pay.
- Since employees must earn this increase each year, it is viewed as less of an entitlement than merit way.
- This approach will cost an employer considerably less over the long run due to lack of compounding.

However, employees typically do not view lumpsum bonuses favourably since base pay does not increase.

(ii) **Individual Awards:** Awards, like bonuses , are one time rewards, but tends to be given in the form of tangible prize, such as a paid vacation, a television set etc.

(iii) **Employees are usually awarded for exceptional performance,** often on special project or for performance that exceeds expectations by a wide margin.

(iv) **According to recent survey,** 74% of companies reported these awards were highly or moderately effective.

Advantages of Individual Incentive Plan

- These plans lead to unexpected and undesired behaviours since employees, being rational, do more of what the incentive system pays for performance that is reward is likely to be repeated or people tend to do those things that are rewarded.
- It helps to make employee's behaviour consistent with the organization goals, which will increase employee's efforts and make their performance goal oriented.
- It helps to reduce job turnover and absenteeism by maintaining equity in the incentive plan. If high performer is not rewarded they may leave the firm or reduce their performance level.

Disadvantages

- The disadvantage of individual based plan is that they focus on a small part of what it takes for a company to be successful.
- It may create competition and destroy co-operation among peers.
- Although all organizations claim to reward individual performance, it is difficult for employees to determine to what extent their companies really do so. They do not believe that pay and performance are linked.
- Individual based plans work against quality programs as individuals rewarded for meeting production goals often sacrifice attention to product quality.
- Supervisors often do not know how to justify particular pay raise recommendations to an employee.

(b) Team Based Plan: (Group incentive Plan):

Team or Group pays Incentive plan: This plan pay incentive to the team based on the team's performance. If a team is to function effectively, firms should provide a reward based on the overall team performance. For this, the work standards are set for each team member and then output of each member is calculated. By doing so, firm's result becomes more effective, efficient and productive. Group members are paid on the basis of these formulas.

- All members receive the pay earned by the highest producer.
- All members receive the pay earned by the lowest producer.
- All members receive pay equal to the average pay earned by the group.

(***Source:*** Dessler Gary p. 336)

Advantages of Team based Incentive Plan

- It is easier to develop performance standards for groups than for individuals.
- All the group members may be more inclined to assist others and work collaboratively, of organization rewards on the basis of team's output.
- An environment of mutual trust and confidence develops among group members.
- Team based plan reinforce team planning, problem solving and creativity.
- Team based approach reduces jealousy conflict and encourages sense of co-operation among group members.
- It also facilitates training, since each member has an interest in getting new members trained as fast as possible.
- Sometimes, intergroup competition leads to decline in overall performance.

Disadvantages

- It generates a feeling of dissatisfaction, if individual employee perceives that they contribute more than other employees in the group and are not properly rewarded.
- The payment of workers may not be proportionate to their efforts which may demotivate hard workers.
- Lack of communication is a familiar factor in failure of team based plan.

Some of the Group or Team Based Plan include:

(i) Gainsharing

(ii) Scanlon Plan

(iii) Rucker Plan

(Explain in detail in Chapter 6)

(c) Organization Wide Incentive Plan:

Many employees have incentive plans in which most employees can participate. Two important ways organization measure their performance are in terms of profit and their stock price. In a competitive market place, profits result when an organization is efficiently providing products that customers want at a price they are willing to pay. Stock is the owner's investment in a corporation. Employer's offer stocks to their employees for several reasons such as attraction, retention and motivation. This organization –level incentive can motivate employees to align their activities with the organization's goals.

Advantages

- These plans offer a possible alternative of incentive plan as compared to others already discussed.
- These plans are generally based on firm's productivity, cost savings or profitability.
- Organization-wide plan motivate employees to align their activities with the organization's goals.
- Increase employee commitment when they are entitled to profitsharing and ESOP's.

Disadvantages

- This plan is involved with high degree of risk and uncertainty, as incentive is linked to organization's profits or stock price.
- There are maximum chances of falling of stock price and profits, as compared to its hike.
- These plans are only effective in organizations that emphasize growth and innovation which tends to need employees who strive in risk-taking environment.
- Organization-wide plan include profit sharing and employee stock ownership plan (ESOP).
- Initially intended to focus attention on costs.
- Formula is tied to group or department performance measures.
- Based upon factors controllable by the group.
- Typically target a specific problem area.
- Direct employee attention to the area or issue.
- Timings are generally monthly or quarterly payouts.
- Reinforces the Performance-reward link.

Types of variable pay plans: Advantages and Disadvantages

Plan Type	What is it?	Advantage	Disadvantages	Why?
Cash profit Sharing	• Award based on organizational profitability • Shares a percentage of profits(typically above a target level of profitability) • Usually annual payout • Can be cash or deferred 401(k)	• Simple, easily understood Low administrative costs	• Profit Influenced by many factors beyond employee control • May be viewed as an entitlement • Limited motivational impact	• To educate employees about business operations • To faster teamwork or "one-for-all" environment
Stock Ownership or Options	• Award of stock shares or options	• Option awards have minimal impact on the financial statements of the company at the time they are granted • If properly communicated, can have powerful impact on employee behaviour • Tax deferral to employee	• Indirect pay/ Performance link • Many factors outside individuals influence affect stock price • Employees may be required to put up money to exercise grants	• To recruit top quality employees when organization has highly uncertain futures (i.e., start -ups, high-tech, or biotech industries) • To address employee retention concerns
Balanced Scorecard	• Awards that combine financial and operating measures for organization, business unit and/or individual performance • Award pool based on achieving performance targets	• Communicates organisational priorities	• Performance criteria may be met, but if financial targets are not met, there may be a reduced payout or no payout at all • Can be complex	• To focus employees on need to increase shareholder value • To focus employees on organization, division, and/or individual goals • To link payouts to a Specific financial and/or operational target
Productivity/ gain sharing	• Multiple performance measures may include 1. Non-financial/Operating quality improvements productivity gains, customer service improvements 2. Financial EPS, ROE, ROA, revenues • Awards that share economic benefits of improved productivity quality, or other measurable results • Focus on group, plant, department, or division results • Designed to capitalize on untapped knowledge of employees	• Clear performance reward links • Productivity and quality improvements • Employees knowledge of business increases • Faster teamwork, co-operation	• Can be administratively complicated • Unintended effects, like drop off in quality • Management must "open the books" • Payouts can occur even if companys financial performance is poor	• To support a major productivity quality initiative (such as TOM or reengineering) • To faster teamwork environment • To reward employees for improvements in activities that they control
Team/group incentives	• Awards determined based on team/group performance goals or objectives • Payout can be more frequent than annual and can also extend beyond the life of the team • Payout may be uniform for team/group members	• Reinforces teamwork and team identify results • Effective in stimulating ideas and problem solving • Minimizes distinctions between team members • May better reflect how work is performed	• May be difficult to isolate impact of team • Not all employees can be placed on a team • Can be administratively complex • May create team competition • Difficult to set equitable targets for all teams	• To demonstrate an organizational commitment to teams • To reinforce the need for employees to work together to achieve results

Source: Kenam S. Abosch,"Variable Pay: Do We Have the Basics in Place?" *Compensation and Benefits Review*, 30(4) 1998, pp. 12-22

Fig. 4.2

DOES COMPENSATION MOTIVATE PERFORMANCE

Psychologist Herzberg says that money only buys temporary compliance, and that as soon as you remove the incentive, the motivation disappears. He said employers' should provide adequate financial rewards and then build other more effective motivators (like opportunities for achievement and psychological success) into jobs.

Motivation and performance are very complex issues affected by many factors.. No one factor can guarantee motivation or performance in the absence of other critical factor. Some people think that money cannot be used to motivate employees and that is true for some employees, but for a large percentage of the workforce it does not have to be that way. The studies shows that, almost everyone is motivated by money to some degree, many to a moderate degree, and most to a great degree when compensation is properly designed. Some psychologist would argue that money does not change behaviour because they do not consider it properly termed a "motivator " but rather they call it a "director" of behaviour. This is a semantic argument. The idea is whether money can be used as a tool to change employee behaviour in a desirable direction. Inadequate use of incentive plans and problems with compensation design and strategy often fails to motivate performance of an employee.

Behavioural scientist, employee and management survey experiences show that compensation can be a strong driver of employee behaviour under the right circumstances when properly designed. Also in jobs where significant variability in pay occurs in compensation and where it is closely related to key performance factor, then pay can be a big motivator.

The good performers prior to new compensation plan implementation remain good performers and may not improve much because they are already giving close to 100% effort, but the middle and the bottom performers are where there is significant opportunity for change. It has been found that failure in poor compensation design leads to failure to motivate. Typical compensation design problems include–

(i) Failure to tie pay closely to achievement of objective and realistic performance measures.

(ii) Failure to regularly measure and provide feedback on performance.

(iii) Failure to design variances in pay related to performance that is large enough to be perceived by the employee as worth the effort.

Thus, it is found that compensation motivates performance but one of the single impediments to the use of compensation as motivator is the managers' inability to measure employee performance accurately and regularly and failure to set goals or standards that are challenging, realistic and have strong relationship to business success.

KEY TERMS	
Pay-for-performance	Organisation-wide plan
Individual based plan	Piece-rate
Team based plan	

SUMMARY

Performance Appraisal may be defined as a structured formal interaction between a subordinate and supervisor, in which the work performance of the subordinate is examined and discussed. The design and implementation of a performance measurement and compensation system can strongly effect the motivation of employees.

The term "Pay-for-Performance" refers to a pay strategy where evaluations of individual and for organizational performance have significant influence on the amount of pay increases or bonuses given to each employee. The main rationale for establishing performance related pay policies is to improve performance and motivation of managers or employees.PRP can be used to assist or stimulate organizational change.

There are 3 types of Pay-for-performance

Individual Based Plans, Team Based Plans and Organizational level Plan.

The key to individual performance based programs is that they focus specifically on the individual. They are the most widely used pay-for-performance plans in the industry. They are Merit system, Piece rate, Executive Bonus. and Individual awards.

Team or Group pays Incentive plan pay incentive to the team based on the team's performance. If a team is to function effectively, firms should provide a reward based on the overall team performance. It is easier to develop performance standards for groups than for individuals. It reduces jealousy, conflict and encourages sense of co-operation among group members.

Some of the Group or Team Based Plan includes, Gainsharing, Scanlon Plan and Rucker Plan.

Organization-wide incentive plan:Many employees have incentive plans in which most employees can participate. These plans offer a possible alternative of incentive plan as compared to others already discussed and are based on firm's productivity, cost savings or profitability.

REVIEW QUESTIONS

1. What is performance appraisal and what are the perquisite conditions that must exist before instituting formal performance appraisal.
2. Is there any relationship between incentives and motivation? Examine the potential advantages and limitations of incentives.
3. What are the major types of individual incentive plan? Point out the prerequisites, advantages and disadvantages of these systems and examine their relevance in India.
4. What are the various types of performance related pay (PRP)? Explain in detail the merits and demerits of each.
5. "Performance appraisal is not merely for appraisal but is for accomplishment and improvement of performance." Discuss.

References

Bolar, M., (1978), *"Performance Appraisal"* New Delhi: Vikas Publications.

Cumming, M. W., (1972), *"Theory and Practice of Personnel Management"*, London: William Heineman. Ltd.

Werther, W. B. and Keith Davis, (1996) *"Human Resources and Personnel Managemnt"*, New York: Mc-Graw Hill.

Kleiman, Lawrence S., *Human Resource Management: A Tool for Competitive Advantage.* Cincinnati, OH: South-Western College Publishing, 2000.

Warner, S. and Ward S. G. (2004) *Recent Compensation Research: An Eclectic Review.* Human Resource Management Review, 14: pp.201-227.

Mathis, Robert L., and John H. Jackson., *Human Resource Management.* 11th ed. Mason, OH: Thomson/ South-Western, 2006.

Dessler Gary, *Human Resource Management,* 9th ed, Prentice Hall of India, New Delhi, 2003.

Hollen beck Noe and Wright Gerhart, *Fundamentals of Human Resource Management.*

Mejia Gomez, and Cardy Robert, *Managing Human Resources,* Pearson Education, New Delhi, 2001.

Bloom, M., & Milkovich, G. T., (1998)., Relationships Among Risk, Incentive Pay, and Organizational Performance. *Academy of Management Journal,* 41(3): pp. 283-297.

WAGES AND SALARY ADMINISTRATION

5

LEARNING OBJECTIVES

After studying this chapter, you will be able to understand —

- Definition and concept of wages
- The wage determination process
- Methods of wage fixation
- Theories of wages
- Types of wages
- Wage differentials
- Wage policy and its importance
- Objectives of national wage policy

DEFINITION AND CONCEPT OF WAGES

A wage or pay is the remuneration paid, for the service of labour in production, periodically to an employee/worker. "Wages" usually refer to the hourly rate paid to such groups as production and maintenance of employees ("Blue Collar Workers"). It is a general term referring to direct monetary compensation.

Wage levels:

The wage levels represent the money an average worker makes in a geographic area or in his organization. It is only an average as specific markets or firms and individual wages can vary widely from the average.

Wage structure:

The term wage structure is used to describe wage/salary relationships within a particular grouping. The grouping can be according to occupation or organization such as wage structure for craftsman (carpenters, mechanics etc.)

Wage and Salary Administration refers to the establishment and implementation of sound policies and practices of employee compensation. They affect levels of employee commitment to the organization. The basic purpose of wage and salary administration is to establish and maintain an equitable wage and salary structure. Its secondary objective is the establishment and maintenance of an equitable labour cost structure.

Wages have at least two connotations from the viewpoint of employers and employees in organizational settings.

The employer perceives wages as a cost of their business efforts and is keen to reduce labour cost per unit of output. Also they realize that it would not be possible for them to attract and maintain an effective work force without compensating it adequately. The employees consider wages as a means for satisfying their needs in terms of an expected standard. They desire to receive at least as much remuneration as other individuals equipped with similar skills get for performing same nature of task.

According to S.P. Robbins: The term wage and salary administration denotes the process of managing a company's compensation program. The goals of compensation administration are to design a cost-effective pay structure that will attract, motivate and retain competent employees.

According to Beach, wage and salary programmes have four major purposes:

(i) To recruit persons for a firm.

(ii) To control payroll costs.

(iii) To satisfy people, to reduce the incidence of quitting, grievances and frictions over pay.

(iv) To motivate people to perform better.

Elements in Wage and Salary Administration

Beach visualizes seven elements or issues in wage and salary administration:

1. **Pay levels:** It relates to the problem as to whether the wage structure is high, average or low and are determined by competitive labour market and industry rates, financial position of the enterprise managerial policies and allied considerations.

2. **Internal pay structure:** It relates to the hierarchy of pay rates, pay grades and job classification and revolves around the job evaluation.

3. **Individual pay system:** It relates to the classification of individuals into job titles and pay grades involving determination of how much compensation, they should be paid. This issue revolves around seniority and merit.

4. **Payment by time:** It relates to remuneration paid in terms of time spent on the job while payment by output involves financial compensation in terms of units of output as indicated by wage incentive plans.

5. **Special issues related to salesman, managers and professional personnel:** It relates to inventive plans, tax saving and fringe benefits, plans and pay plans in terms of qualifications and performance as compared to pay plans based on the intrinsic job content for other personnel in the organization.

6. **Fringe benefit and pay supplements:** It is in the form of insurance, pensions, paid holidays, bonuses, profit sharing and allied factors are significant components in the compensation system involving substantial labour costs to enhance the attractiveness of a job.

7. **Control of wages and salaries:** It is exerted by several measures such as a table of organization, annual review of job classifications, evaluation of incentive plans and careful budgeting of pay increases. Explicitly, the entire problem of wage and salary administration is likely to be solved by carefully considering these elements in organizational settings.

THE WAGE DETERMINATION PROCESS

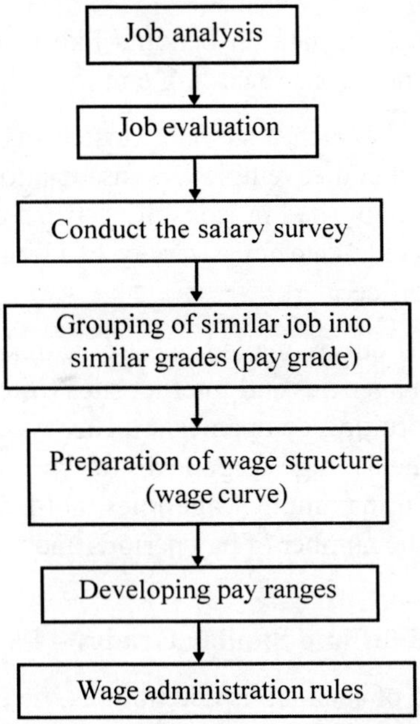

Fig. 5.1

1. Job Analysis

It involves the identification and precisely identifying the required tasks, the knowledge and skills necessary for performing them and the conditions under which they must be performed. It is the basic technical procedure that is used to define the duties, responsibilities and accountabilities of a job. It involves determination of methods and equipments used and the skills and attitude required for successful performance of the job.

2. Job Evaluation

It is the formal process used to assign wage and salary rates to job. A variety of systems and products exist to guide this process, each different from the other in packaging, pricing, philosophy, procedures and utility. It is a systematic technique determining the worth of a job. Once the worth is determined, it becomes easier to fix the wage structure that will be fair and remunerative.

3. Conduct the Salary Survey

Once the process of job evaluation has determined the relative worth of jobs, the actual amounts to be paid must be determined. This is done by making wage or salary surveys in the area concerned. Employers use these surveys in three ways.

(i) They use survey data to price 'benchmark jobs', which are usually known as good indicators on the basis of this, the firm then slots its other jobs, based on their relative worth to the firm.

(ii) The employers typically price 20% or more of their positions directly in the market place based on a formal or informal survey of what comparable firms are paying for comparable jobs.

(iii) The surveys also collect data on benefits like insurance, sick leave and vacations to provide a basis for decisions regarding employee benefits.

There are various ways to make such a survey. Most firms either use the results of 'packaged surveys' available from the research bodies, employers' association, Government Labour Bureaus etc. Also many employers use surveys published by consulting firms or professional associations. Around 200 annual area wage surveys provide data for a variety of clerical and manual occupations ranging from secretary to messengers to office clerk.

These surveys may be carried out by mailed questionnaires, telephone, and personal interviews with other managers and personnel agencies and Internet sites (Site is http:// Stats.bls.gov.) Some of the private consulting or executive recruiting companies are Hay Associates, Hewitt Associates, Heidrick and Struggles etc. In addition to the average wage level for specific job, other information frequently requested includes entry- level and maximum wage rates, shift differentials, overtime pay practices, vacation and holiday allowances, the number of pay periods and the length of the normal work-day and work-week.

4. Grouping of Similar Jobs into Similar Grades – Pay Grades

Once the relative worth of each job is determined, the task of assigning pay rate to each job is done which is possible only by first grouping jobs into pay grades. It comprises of jobs of approximately equal nature or importance, as established by job evaluation. The committee used various techniques for pay grades such as point method (Job falling within a range of points), Ranking method, where the grade consists of all jobs that fall within two or three ranks and the classification method categorises jobs into classes or grades.

5. Preparation of Wage Structure – Wage Curves

The next step is to determine the wage structure. For this, several decisions need to be taken, such as:

(a) Whether wage ranges should provide for merit increases or whether there should be single rates.

(b) Whether the organization pays around above, below or equal to the averages in the community or industry.

(c) The number and width of the 'pay grades" and the extent of overlap.

(d) The jobs placed in each of the pay grade and the actual money value to be assigned to various pay grades.

(e) Differentials between pay plans.

For this purpose, 'wage curve' is used to help assign pay rates to each pay grade (or to each job). It shows the relationship between the value of the job and the average wage paid for this job. It is a two-dimensional graph on which job evaluation points for key jobs are plotted against actual amounts paid or against desired level. It shows pay rates on the vertical axis, and pay grades (in terms of points) along the horizontal axis, The purpose of the wage curve is to show the relationship between:

(i) The value of the job.

(ii) The current average pay rates for your grades.

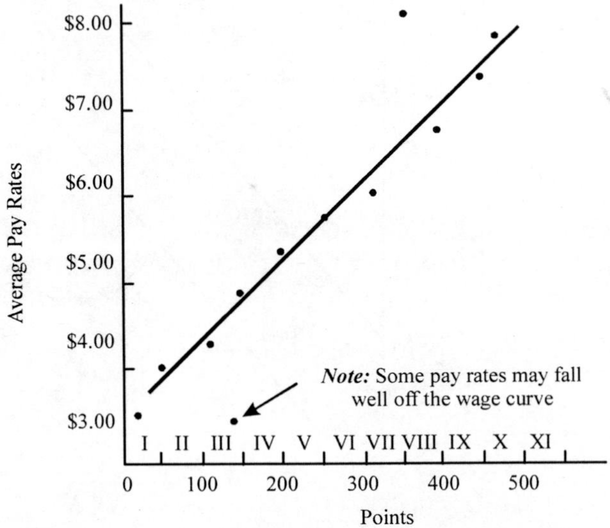

Fig. 5.2

There are various steps involved in drawing a wage curve:

(i) Find the average pay for each pay grades, since each pay grade may have several jobs.

(ii) Plotting the wage rate for each pay grade.

(iii) Drawing 'wage lines' through the points plotted. This can be done freehand or by using a statistical method.

(iv) Finally, price the jobs. Wages along the 'Wage line' are target wages or salary rates for the jobs in each pay grade. It is possible that some of the plotted points may fall off the wage line i.e., average for that grade is too high or too low. If the current rates being paid for any of your jobs or grades fall above the wage line that indicates rates are high and the overpaid employees are often called "red circle", "flagged" or "overrates. If the plot falls below the line, raises for jobs in this pay grade may be required. Such under-valued jobs carry a "green circle" rate and attempts should be made to make raises either immediately or in one or two steps.

6. Developing Pay Ranges: (Wage Structure):

It is only a short step from plotting a wage curve to developing the organization wage structure. Jobs that are similar in terms of classes, grades or points are grouped together. Most employers do not pay just one rate for all jobs in a particular pay grade. Instead, they develop vertical pay range (rate range) for each horizontal pay grade. These pay range makes it easier to attract experienced employees from other organization and allow the management to provide for performance differences between employees. These pay ranges may appear as vertical boxes within each grade, showing minimum, maximum and mid point pay rates for that grade.

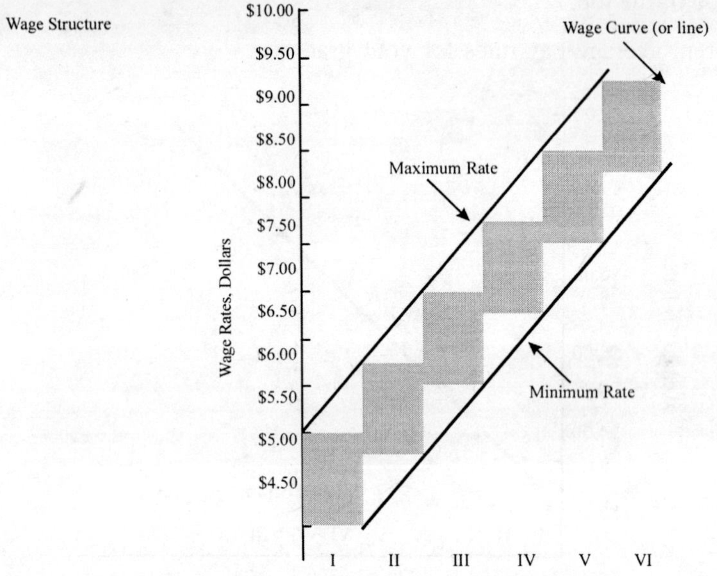

Fig. 5.3

'Rate ranges' can be developed in various ways. A maximum and minimum range for each grade, such as 15% above and below the wage line, may be arbitrarily decided. The maximum and minimum lines may then be drawn on the curve. The 'range'may be allowed to become wider for the higher pay grades, reflecting the greater demands and performance variability inherent in more complex jobs.

While deterring pay ranges it is important to keep in mind that there is an adequate difference between superiors and subordinates and regional differences should be maintained. The existing pay structure should be regularly reviewed and revised to make the process more acceptable to employees.

7. Wage Administration Rules

Once the pay ranges have been determined, the development of rules of wage administration has to be done. The rules developed should determine —

- Whether degree of advancement of service be based on seniority or merit.
- How control over wage and salary costs can be maintained.
- Frequency of pay increase.

The employees are to be informed of the details of wage and salary program. Finally, the employee is appraised and the wage fixed for the grade he is found fit.

METHODS OF WAGE FIXATION

There are several methods employed in fixing the workers' wages. Different bodies such as the Pay Commissions, Wage Boards, Industrial Tribunals and Labour Courts' as well as the High Court and the Supreme Court can fix the wages. Wages are also fixed through Collective Bargaining and Job Evaluation.

Some of the popular methods are:

- Legislation.
- Wage Boards.
- Pay Commissions.
- Job Evaluation.
- Collective Bargaining.
- Arbitration and Adjudication.

1. Legislation

The major wage laws include the Payment of Wages Act, 1936 and its subsequent amendments, the Minimum Wages Act, 1948 and the Equal Remuneration Act, 1976. (Discussed in detail in chapter 10).

The terms, which have acquired currency in discussing wage problems since 1948 are:

(i) statutory minimum wage;

(ii) bare or basic minimum wage;

(iii) fair wage;

(iv) living wage; and

(v) need based minimum wage.

The first term owes its origin to the provisions of the Minimum Wages Act, 1948. The second is used in awards and judicial pronouncements. The other three terms are introduced in the report of the Committee on Fair Wages (CFW) and the last named one in the resolution of the 15th session of the Indian Labour Conference in July 1957. There is need for amplification, rationalization and consolidation of the laws relating to the wages. The wages fixed under the Minimum Wages Act were also to be revised every 3 years. Also there is a need of constant adjustments, taking into account changes in the value of money and workers' productivity. There is a proposal by the Association to make a provision in the law for the establishment of a wage guarantee fund to ensure the payment of wages and other statutory dues of the employees in case if employer fails to pay the same due to closure or insolvency. On further consideration, it has been decided to incorporate such provisions in social security legislation.

2. Wage boards

This is another method of fixing wages. The history of wage boards in India dates back to the 1930s'. The Royal Commission on Labour recommended the setting up of wage boards for the determination of wages. Wage Boards are also known as Trade boards, wage councils, wage committee, wage commission etc. The first wage boards were set up in 1957 for the cotton textile industry.

Composition of Wage Boards: A wage board is tri-partite in character, and is a non-statutory body. It consists of representative of employers and workers and is headed by an independent Chairman. The labour and management representatives are nominated in equal numbers by the government, after consultation with the major central organizations. Usually, the Chairman is a Judge serving or retired and is nominated by the Government as well as an economist and a consumers' representative, both being independent also. The consumer representative is a Member of Parliament, who is expected to safeguard Consumers' interests. The total number of members of wage boards constituted so far has varied from 7 to 9.

Objectives of Wage Boards: The objective of Wage Board include more durable results, improved climate for industrial relations, promotion of interests of consumers and community, safeguard the interests of the community, derived standardized wage structure for the concerned industry, suggest a system of payment by results, work out the principles that should govern bonus to workers in industries and support to social and economic policies of the Government.

Functioning of wage Board: The procedure adopted by a wage board to make recommendations is as follows:

(i) To prepare a comprehensive questionnaire designed to collect information on the prevailing wage rates and skilled differentials and related issues and is sent out to labour unions, employers' association, interested individuals, academic organization and Government agencies.

(ii) Making an assessment of the views of the parties.

(iii) It involves recommendations regarding wage structure and convenes secret sessions at which members of the board make proposals and counter-proposals, regarding the related issues. Finally, the decision of the board is written down and submitted to the Government, which can be modified if found necessary. The wage structure recommended by a wage board is in operation for 5 years. The wage structure recommended may not always be implemented by the management.

3. Pay Commission

Wage boards were set up to deal with the pay structure in different industries outside the Government whereas the pay structure of Government employees is based on the recommendations of pay commissions. It covers a wide range of employees in the public sector as compared to wage board, which is concerned, with limited range of employees. The Central Government has so far set up five pay commissions, which reported in 1947, 1959, 1973, 1984 and 1995, respectively. They are set up at regular intervals and function non-statutorily. They make recommendations to the Government after inquiring problem in their own way. Though, these recommendations are given much weightage, the ultimate responsibility lies with the Government whether to accept, reject, or modify the plan.

The First Central Pay Commission (1947) asserts that the "living wage' should form the basis for determining the minimum wage which should not be too low to cause under nourishment.

The Second Central Pay Commission (1957) also referred to the belief that "minimum wages or salary should not be determined merely an economic considerations, but should satisfy also a social test- both because of its intrinsic validity and because of its bearing on efficiency. The lowest rate of remuneration should not be lower than a 'living wage' and the highest salaries also should be kept down, consistent with the essential requirements of recruitment and efficiency. The commission further states "If the Governments were to function as a model employer, in the sense that they paid higher wages and salaries than other good employers for comparable work, the community would be required to pay a price which the efficiency of the public service did not demand and which should not in fairness be asked of the community. The Government cannot, therefore, in our opinion be a model employer in this sense".

The Third Central Pay Commission (1973) viewed that the minimum wage fixed should be realistic and should match the conditions prevailing in the economy, if paid considerable attention to fair comparison under the principle of 'equal pay for equal work'. A sound pay system should be inclusive and comprehensible providing the true picture of the total remuneration system. The commission denied the role of the model employer to the Government. It observes " we should be labouring under a delusion if we were to suggest that the Central Government should now take upon itself the responsibility of being a pace-setter, and of bettering the wages paid by reputable concerns in the private sector". The commission concluded "the adoption of the minimum remuneration based on the 15th ILC norms at this stage would be tantamount to a misdirection of resources.

The Fourth Central Pay Commission observed that the capacity of the employer to pay the employees is a factor to be given due consideration. The report of the commission relates to structure of emoluments, conditions of services of Central Government employees and also deals with the pension structure of pensioners. The commission said that the fairness of the payments has to satisfy a double test, in the sense that it has to be fair from the point of view of the employees as well as the people they serve. According to this commission, a model employer need not necessarily pay higher wages than other good employers. A model is above the ordinary or higher than what others are content with or what is good enough to serve their purpose.

The Fifth Pay Commission underlined the need to have competent, professional, productive and motivated employees in the Government sector. There is recommendation for increasing the pay of lower level employees by 20 to 40 percent and that of senior level rates by almost 130 percent. There is also a proposal to reduce hiring, abolish currently vacant posts and restructure government department. The commission also made suggestions for creating a modern non-feudal style of administration.

4. Job Evaluation

It is the systematic method of appraising the value of each job in relation to other jobs in the organization. It helps to identify with precision the key tasks, especially in measurable, output oriented jobs.

The first requirement of job evaluation is to gather relevant data about the jobs in the organization, to be obtained from job descriptions. For this, the compensable factors are classified as skills, efforts, responsibilities and working conditions. Each organization will have to decide the weightage it desires to give each of these factors and then to translate this data into a pay structure with grades and pay rates. The committee of job evaluation performs this task which comprises of representatives of the personal department, industrial engineers and the union representatives. Before the committee fixes salaries, a number of issues have to be decided.

(i) Should the wage structure be formulated after determining the highest and lowest rates?

(ii) Should it be determined after an industry-cum-regional community survey?

(iii) Whether there should be single rates for job or should be 'wage spreads' within each job grade.

5. Collective Bargaining

It is a process of negotiation and other related pressure tactics adopted by the employers and the organized workers represented by their union in order to determine the terms and conditions of employment. The main objective is of reaching an agreement by specifying the rules pertaining to employment relationship. It is, moreover, a technique by which an attempt is made to reconcile the needs and objectives of workers and employers and is, therefore, an integral part of an industrial society.

The agreement in collective bargaining brings both labour and management together to determine the conditions of employment and lays down fair rates of wages and norms of working condition. It is a procedure, which determines the quantum of compensation which employees should receive and which influences the distribution of economic ills.

6. Arbitration and Adjudication

These methods are not generally successful in India. For some time wage fixation through arbitration used to take place in the cement industry when the President of the Indian National Trade Union Congress and the President of the Indian Cement Manufactures' Association together used to arbitrate over wage revision. However, this does not continue because of the existence of multiple unions in the industry. Also wage issues are best settled through collective bargaining rather than through adjudication.

THEORIES OF WAGES

Wage theories ascertain the levels and sources of wages. How much and on which basis wages should be paid to the worker for services rendered by them has been a subject matter of great concern among economic thinkers. Attempts have been made by them to interpret prices and price systems from the standpoint of demand and supply and macro and micro approach. Some important wage theories are:

(i) Wage Fund Theory

Adam Smith (1723-1790), developed this theory. His basic assumption was that wages are paid out of a predetermined fund of wealth to the workers. This fund is created as a result of savings and could be utilized for employing labourers for work. The demand for labour and rate of wages depend on the size of the wage fund. If the fund was large, wages would be high; if it was small, wages would be reduced to the subsistence level. It was held that the lumpsum had been distributed equally among the workers obtained in the labour market.

(ii) The Subsistence Theory

David Ricardo (1772 – 1823), developed this theory. Also known as "Iron Law of Wages" was of the opinion that "labourers are paid to enable them to subsist and perpetuate the race without increase or diminution". If the workers are paid wages more than subsistence level, workers' number will increase and, as a result, wages will come down to the subsistence level. If the wages fall below the subsistence level, the number of workers would decrease – as many would die of hunger, malnutrition, disease, cold etc., the wage rate would go up to the subsistence level. The subsistence wages refers to minimum wages.

(iii) The Surplus Value Theory of Wages/The Labour Theory of Value

This theory was developed by Karl Marx (1849-1883). It is based on the assumption that the value of a particular commodity is equivalent to the magnitude of labour involved in it. The labour was an article of commerce, which could be purchased on payment of 'subsistence price' i.e., wages. The price of any product was determined by the labour time needed for producing it. The labourer was not paid in proportion to the time spent on work, but much less. The surplus, thus created, was utilized for paying other expenses.

(iv) Residual Claimant Theory

This theory was developed by Francis A.Walker (1840-1897). According to him, there were four factors of production/business activity *viz.* land, labour, capital and entrepreneurship. He views that once all other three factors are rewarded what remains left is paid as wages to workers. Thus, labour is the residual claimant.

(v) Marginal Productivity Theory

Phillips Henry Wicksteed developed this theory. According to this theory, wages depend upon the demand for and supply of labour and price economy. Wages are based upon an entrepreneurs' estimate of the value that will probably be produced by the last or marginal worker. Wage that is paid to an employee should be equal to the extra value of productivity that the employees add to total production. The revenue the employer can realize from the workers' productivity determines the value of the workers' production. As the employer hires additional workers, a point eventually is reached at which the last worker hired just produces enough products to pay his or her own wages. The latest worker hired is called the "marginal employee", and the increased production attributed to the worker is called "marginal productivity". The result is that the employer has a larger share in profit as he has not pay the non-marginal workers.

(vi) The Bargaining Theory of Wages

John Davidson propounded this theory. This theory assumes that wages are determined by interaction of management and labour in a collective bargaining process. When a trade union is involved, monetary benefits, incentives, fringe benefits and individual differences tend to be determined by the relative strength of bargaining agents. If workers are strong in bargaining process, then wages trends to be high and if employers' bargaining power is high, then wages tends to be low.

(vii) The Investment Theory

H.M.Gitelman developed this theory. He recognized that labour markets vary in the scope of "worker investment" required for their particular industry. The individuals are paid in terms of their investment in the form of training, education and experience. Thus, according to this theory, individual workers' compensation is determined by the rate of return on that workers' investment i.e., what the individual,s "bring to" a job.

(viii) The Contingency Theory

It has been found that there is no single 'best way' to evolve payment system. The effectiveness of a particular scheme is a function of a match between it and the specific organizational factors depending on the motivation. According to Lupton and Bowey. "Essentially, a contingency approach is one in which it is argued that in some industries and in some environments one kind of managerial practice will contribute to some desired objectives. But in other industries and circumstances entirely different result may occur. Accordingly, as they further suggest, while designing payment system, managers are required to take into consideration the following issues:

(i) Objectives towards which the payment system is geared.

(ii) Available payment system.

(iii) Payment system most likely to contribute towards the desired objectives in the context of situational factors prevailing in the company.

(ix) Expectancy Theory

Vrooms' expectancy theory focuses on the link between rewards and behaviour. According to this theory, motivation is the product of valence, instrumentality and expectancy. Remunerating system is based on the impact on these motivational components.

(x) Equity Theory

Adams' equity theory assumes that an employee who perceives inequity in his or her rewards seeks to restore equity. There should be equity in pay structure of employees' remuneration. There should be a feeling of 'a fair day's work for fair day's pay' among the employees which denotes a sense of equity. Any feeling of inequity leads to job dissatisfaction, high employee turnover, absenteeism and lower productivity.

(xi) Agency Theory

The agency theory focuses on the divergent interests and goal of the organization stakeholders and the way employee remuneration can be used to align these interests and goals. It provides the most relevant implication for the design of a compensation system for the organization. The fundamental compensation problem is how to develop either an explicit or an implicit incentive-reward contract that aligns the interests of management with those of the stockholders. Employers and employees are the two stakeholders of a business unit, the former assuming the role of principals and the later the role of agents. The wages paid to the employees are the agency costs. The agency theory says that the principal must choose a contracting scheme that helps align the interest of the agents with the principal's own interests. These contracts can be classified as either behaviour oriented (merit pay) or outcome oriented (stock option scheme, profit sharing and commissions). As profits go up, rewards also increase and remuneration falls when profits go down.

TYPES OF WAGES

Wages are broadly based on the needs of the workers, organizational capacity to pay and general economic conditions prevailing in a country. Since 1948, several terms have been propounded in the wage concepts such as statutory minimum wage, the basic minimum wage, the minimum wage, the fair wage, the living wage and the need based minimum wage.

(a) Statutory Minimum Wage: It is the wage determined according to the procedure prescribed by the relevant provisions of the Minimum Wages Act, 1948. Once the rates of such wages are fixed, it is the obligation of the employer to pay them.

(b) Base or Basic Minimum Wage: It is the wage to be fixed in accordance with the awards and judicial pronouncements of Industrial Tribunals and National Tribunals.

(c) Minimum Wages: A Minimum wage is a compensation to be paid by an employer to his employees, irrespective of his ability to pay. According to Committee on Minimum Wage "the wage which must provide not only for the bare sustenance of life, but for the preservation of the efficiency of the worker. For this purpose, the minimum wage must provide for some measures of education, medical requirements and amenities. The content of the Minimum Wage is dynamic and vary from time to time and place to place. It may be fixed by an agreement between the management and the workers but is usually determined through legislation. This is more in the unorganized sector where labour is unionized.

The International Labour Organization (ILO) lists three criteria for fixing the minimum wage. These are:

(i) The needs of workers

(ii) The capacity to pay and

(iii) Wages paid for comparable work elsewhere in the economy or more generally, the standard of living of other social groups.

Living Wage: According to the Committee on Fair Wages, the living wage is the highest and is ultimate goal in a wage policy. It is defined as "one which should enable the earner to provide for himself and his family not only the bare essentials of food, clothing and shelter but a measure of frugal comfort, including education for his children, protection against ill health, requirement of essential social needs and a measure of insurance against the more important misfortunes, including old age". A living wage must be fixed considering the general economic conditions of the country. There are three possible ways of obtaining some indication as to what constitutes a living wage. (i) It should be sufficient to purchase the minimum theoretical needs of a typical family, calculated in accordance with some more or less scientific formula. (ii) It should be sufficient to pay for a satisfactory basic budget, as revealed by a survey of actual family expenditures. (iii) It should be comparable with a living wage already established in similar circumstances.

Fair Wage: Fair wage, according to the committee on fair wage, is the wage, which is above the minimum wage but below the living wage. The lower limit of the fair wage is the minimum wage, the upper limit is set by the capacity of the industry to pay. It is understood in two ways. In a narrow sense, wage is fair if it is equal to the rate prevailing in the same trade and in the neighbourhood for similar work. In a wider sense, it will be fair if it is equal to the predominant rate for similar work throughout the country and for the trades in general. According to the Committee on Fair Wages, 1948, fair wages should be determined taking the following factors into account:

(i) The productivity of labour.

(ii) The prevailing rates of wages in the same or similar occupation in the same or neighbouring localities.

(iii) The level of national income and its distribution.

(iv) The place of the industry in the economy of the country.

The committee observed that it was not possible to assign any definite weight to the above factors in the actual calculation of the fair wage.

Need Based Minimum Wage: The Indian Labour Conference in its 15th session held in July, 1957, suggested that Minimum Wage should be need based and should ensure the minimum human needs of the industrial worker, irrespective of any other consideration.

The conference accepted the following norms for calculation of the minimum wage:

- The standard working class family should be taken to consist of 3 consumption units for the earner, the earnings of women, children and adolescents should be disregarded;
- The minimum food requirements should be calculated on the basis of the net intake of 2,700 calories, as recommended by Dr. Akroyd, for an average Indian adult of moderate activity.
- The clothing requirements should be estimated at a per capita consumption of 18 yards per annum, which would mean, for an average worker's family of four, a total of 72 yards.
- In respect of housing, the norms should be the minimum rent charged by the Government in any area for houses provided under the subsidized housing scheme for low-income groups, and
- Fuel, lighting and other miscellaneous items of expenditure should constitute 20 percent of the total minimum wage.

WAGE DIFFERENTIALS

When wages differ in different industries, firm's, jobs, area, skill or geographical region it is known as wage differential, on the basis of which, there are regional, inter industry, intra industry, geographical, skills and gender differentials. Wage differentials perform important economic functions like labour productivity, attracting the potential candidates to different jobs, maximizing productivity, development of skills, utilization of human resources and labour mobility among different regions. It may occur due to following reasons:

(1) Occupational Differentials

This indicates that wage differential arises because of varying occupational proficiencies. Occupation in an organization is widely differed from one another in terms of skill requirement and degree of responsibility. It induce the person to undertake "more demanding" and more challenging jobs; encourage workers to develop their skills, to perform social functions and motivate employees for training and development program. This differential plays an important role in manpower development and employment programs, for they considerably help in bringing about an adequate supply of labour with skills corresponding to the requirement of product plans.

(2) Inter-firm Differentials

It reflects the relative wage levels of workers in the same area and occupation. There are varied reasons for inter firm differential such as differences in the quality of labour employed by different firms, imperfection in the labour market, differences in the efficiency of equipment, supervision, firm size, technical advancement, financial capabilities and other non-labor factors.

(3) Inter-area or Regional Differentials

This differential arises when workers are in different geographical area, but in the same industry or occupation, paid different wages. These differences are the result of working conditions prevalent in different regions of the country, disparities in the cost of living and availability of manpower. Regional differential is merely a part of inter industry differentials in a particular region. It affects the supply of manpower for various plants. In some cases, these differentials are used to encourage planned mobility of labour.

(4) Inter-industry Differentials

These differentials arise when workers in the same occupation and same areas but in different industries are paid different wages. These differences are the result of varying skill requirements, level of unionization, nature of product market, ability to pay, labour-capital ratio and the stage of development of an industry.

(5) Interpersonal Wages Differentials: These differential arises between workers in the same occupation and plant but with different skills, age and other personal characteristics. Though the principle of 'Equal pay for equal work' is recommended, but it is not pragmatic. There are cases where female employee is paid less as compared to male for the same nature of job.

Importance of Wage Differentials

Wage differentials have a great economic and social significance. Its importance arises because–

1. It enables full employment of the resources of the economy to be attained.
2. It provides an important incentive for labour mobility as it brings about a re-allocation of the labour force under changing circumstances, so as to maximize the national product.
3. It facilitates desirable rate of economic progress. It is found that wage differentials giving the wide differences in demand and supply of jobs along with wide variations in job requirement like skill, ability, knowledge and experiences so on, ensures full exploitation of the national resources and thus is justified.

WAGE POLICY

The importance are of wage policy is obvious as it forms a highly sensitive and complex dimension of labour policy and influences employee's level of motivation, morale, productivity and standard of living. Its importance has been recognized by the Constitution of India. The provisions in the Indian constitution and the policy statements in successive five-year plan documents provide useful insights into the Government's approach towards wage policy. The second National Commission on labour recommended the appointment of a high-level committee with technically Competent people including economists, trade unionists, entrepreneurs and consumers to formulate a national wage policy.

OBJECTIVES OF NATIONAL WAGE POLICY

Despite several theoretical guidelines for the formulation of a wage policy, there are various concrete facts that must be taken into account in designing a wage policy. Accordingly, in view of the realities of the situation, there are several hurdles in the formulation of a wage policy in a developing economy like India's which adheres in a democratic system. Ideally, wage revision should be higher than the rate of growth in gross domestic product (GDP) and lower then the rate of inflation. This ensures that real wages are maintained.

The term "Wage Policy" refers to the legislation or Government action undertaken to regulate the level or structure of wages or both, for the purpose of achieving specific objectives of social and economic policy. According to ILO, the wage policy means "legislation or government action calculated to affect the level or structure of wages, or both for the purpose of attaining specific objectives of social and economic policy".

Objectives of National Wage Policy

The objectives of a wage policy in the developing countries as enumerated by ILO are as under:

1. To abolish malpractices and abuses in wage payment.
2. To set minimum wages for workers having weak bargaining power because either they are unorganized or inefficiently organized, accompanied by separate measures to promote the growth of trade unions and collective bargaining:
3. To obtain for the workers a just share in the fruits of economic development.
4. To bring about a more efficient allocation and utilization of manpower through wage differentials and where appropriate systems of payment by results cost.

KEY TERMS	
Pay levels	Arbitration and adjudication
Wage curve	Pay commission
Wage differential	Wage board

SUMMARY

A wage or pay is the remuneration paid, for the service of labour in production, periodically to an employee/worker.

The wage levels represent the money an average worker makes in a geographic area or in his organization.

The term wage structure is used to describe wage/salary relationships within a particular grouping.

The elements in wage and salary administration are:

Pay levels, internal pay structure, individual pay system., payment by time, special issues related to salesman, managers and professional personnel , fringe benefit and pay supplements and control of wages and salaries:

Wage determination process involves job analysis,job evaluation, Conduct the salary survey, grouping of similar jobs into similar grades – pay grades:

Preparation of wage structure – Wage curves and developing pay ranges: (wage structure) and wage administration rules:

Methods of Wage Fixation: There are several methods employed in fixing the workers' wages. Some of the popular methods are:

- Legislation.
- Wage Boards.
- Pay Commissions.
- Job Evaluation.
- Collective Bargaining.
- Arbitration and Adjudication.

Wage theories ascertain the levels and sources of wages. Some important wage theories are: Wage Fund Theory, The Subsistence Theory, The Surplus Value Theory of Wages/The labour Theory of Value, Residual Claimant Theory, Marginal Productivity Theory,The Bargaining Theory of Wages: The Investment Theory, The contingency Theory: Expectancy Theory: Equity Theory and Agency theory.

Types of wages: Statutory Minimum Wage Base or Basic Minimum Wage,: Minimum Wages, Living Wage and Fair Wage

Wage Differentials is when wages differ in different industries, firm job, area skill or geographical region it is known as wage differential, on the basis of which, there are regional, inter industry, intra industry, geographical skills and gender differentials, resources and labour mobility among different regions. The term wage policy refers to the legislation or government action undertaken to regulate the structure or level of wages.

REVIEW QUESTIONS

1. What do you understand by wage and salary administration? State its objectives and basic principals that any wage plan must follow.
2. What do you understand by minimum wages? What is the difference between minimum wages and statutory minimum wages?
3. Fair wage is a sandwich of minimum wage and living wage. Do you agree? Illustrate.
4. What is the machinery for fixing minimum wages?
5. Discuss the institutional machinery for wage determination? Examine their pros and cons.
6. What should be the basis for wage differential?
7. Should there be a national wage?
8. Statutory wage fixation remains true in principle only but is never transferred into real action why?

References

Henderson, Richard I., *Compensation Management in a Knowledge-Based World.* 9th ed. Upper Saddle River, NJ: Prentice Hall, 2003.

Kleiman, Lawrence S., *Human Resource Management: A Tool for Competitive Advantage.* Cincinnati, OH: South-Western College Publishing, 2000.

Mathis, Robert L., and John H. Jackson., *Human Resource Management.* 11th ed. Mason, OH: Thomson/ South-Western, 2006.

Milkovich, George T., and Jerry M. Newman., *Compensation.* 8th ed. New York: McGraw-Hill/Irwin, 2005.

Beach D. S., *Human Resource Management/Personnel Management,* New york: Tata McGraw-Hill.

Dessler Gary, *Human Resource Management,* 9th ed, Prentice Hall of India, New Delhi, 2003.

Dunn J. D., and Frank Rachel, *"Wages and Salary Administration",* 1972.

Dwidedi R. S., *Managing Human Resource,* Galgotia Publishing Company, New Delhi, 1999.

Decanzo A. David and Robbins P. Stephen, *Personnel/HRM,* Prentice Hall of India, 3rd Ed. New Delhi, 1989.

K. Asahwathappa, *Human Resource Management,* 4th ed., Tata McGraw-Hill, New Delhi, 2005.

Milton L. Rock, *Handbook of Wages and Salary Administration.*

Mejia Gomez, and Cardy Robert, *Managing Human Resources,* Pearson Education, New Delhi, 2001.

Milkovich, G. T, and Newman J. M, *Compensation,* (4th ed.). Homewood, ILL:Irwin

Subramaniam K. N., *"Wages in India",* Tata McGraw-Hill, New Delhi.

INCENTIVE PLANS AND FRINGE BENEFITS

6

LEARNING OBJECTIVES

After studying this chapter, you will be able to understand—

- Basic concept of incentives
- Benefits of incentive plan
- Types of wage incentive plan
- Merits and demerits of individual and group incentive system
- Limitations of incentive plan
- Suggestive measures to make incentive system effective
- Definition of fringe benefits, nature and its needs
- Types and objectives of fringe benefits
- Fringe benefits in India and its significance

INCENTIVE PLAN

Basic Concept: Wage Incentive also called 'Payment by results', is anything that attracts the worker and motivates him to work. It determines their standard of living and their attitude towards the company. Incentive schemes provide payment based on either individual output or group output. The use of incentive assumes that people's actions are related to their skills and ability to achieve important goals.

According to the National Commission on Labour, "Wage incentives are extra financial motivation. They are designed to stimulate human effort by rewarding the person, over and above the time rated remuneration for improvements in the present or targeted results."

Psychologists have also defined incentive as a spurring force introduced as a means of accomplishing a goal or an outward stimulus, which activates a need or brings the motive to work.

According to Dale Yoder, "Incentive wages relate earnings to productivity and may use premiums, bonuses or a variety of rates to compensate for superior performance".

Characteristics of Incentive Plan

- Incentives have direct linking to performance.
- Incentives induce the employee to move from existing level of performance to optimum achievable performance.
- It helps to improve level of technology and thus increases productivity.
- Incentives are measurable in monetary terms.
- The timing, accuracy and frequency of incentives or the very basis of successful incentive plans.
- Incentive plan encourages attendance and reduces absenteeism.
- Incentives vary from person to person, depending on their performance.
- Minimum wages are guaranteed to all workers.

Benefits of Incentive Plans

- Incentives are beneficial to both employer and employees. They help to attract and retain employees in the organization and improve employer-employee relations.
- It helps to reduce employee absenteeism and turnover.
- The amount paid in incentive scheme is linked with output i.e., Payment by results (PBR) which helps in rewarding employees for higher performance.
- Incentive motivates people to work more and thus creates culture of efficient and motivated workforce.
- Incentives are also desired from the standpoint of equity theory. Explicitly, individual working better receives greater rewards.
- This system provides a desirable outcome (pay), which tends to reinforce appropriate behaviour positively.
- Wage incentive is concerned with an effective utilization of manpower, which is the cheapest, quickest and surest means of increasing productivity.
- A spirit of mutual co-operation and teamwork is created among workers and therfore, morale of the employees are increased.

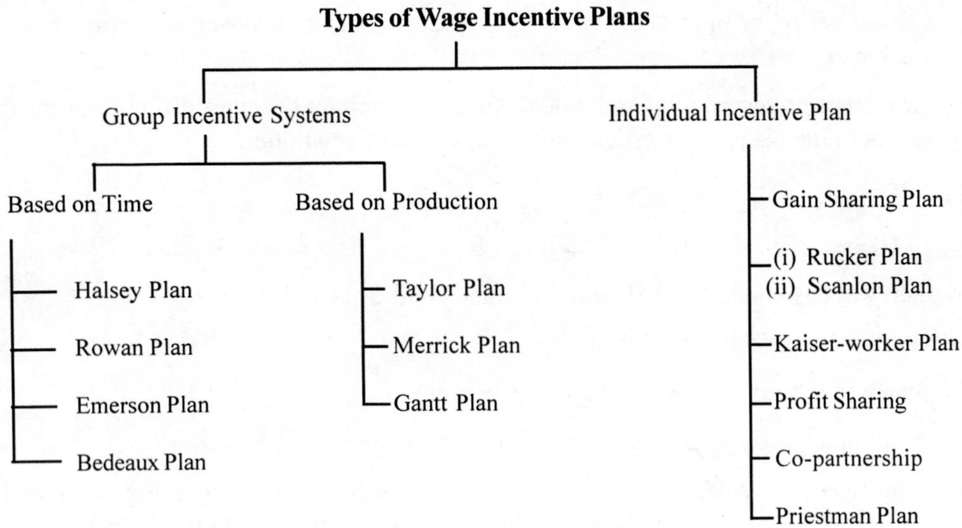

Fig. 6.1

Individual Incentive System

Individual incentive plans reward employees for meeting work-related performance standards such as quality, productivity, customer satisfaction, safety or attendance. It is based on either time, where workers are paid according to the work done during a certain period of time at the rate of per hour, per day, per week, per month or any other fixed period of time. The essential part is that the production of a worker is not taken into consideration in fixing the wages; he is paid at the settled rate as soon as the time contracted for is spent.

Merits of Time Based Plan

- It is simple, for the amount earned by a worker can be easily calculated.
- As there is no time limit for the execution of a job, workmen are not in a hurry to finish it and this improves quality of work.
- As all the workmen employed for doing a particular kind of work receive the same wages, it reduces jealousy among them.
- Due to slow and steady pace of the worker, rough handling of machineries are avoided.
- This system requires less administrative attention then others because the very basis of the time wage contract is good faith and mutual confidence between the parties.

Demerits

The main drawbacks of this system are:

(i) It does not take into account the fact that competent workers' will be paid more. This will therefore, reduce motivation and morale of employees.

(ii) The labour charges for a particular job do not remain constant. This creates difficulty for the top management in terms of doing payment.

(iii) As there is no specific demand on the worker that a piece of work needs to be completed in a given period of time, there is always the possibility of a systematic evasion of work by workmen.

(iv) As there is no record of an individual workers' output, it becomes difficult for the employer to determine his relative efficiency for purposes of promotion.

Based on Time

(1) Halsey Plan

This plan was designed by F.A Halesy and Rand Deill Co. Canada

The main features of this plan are:

(i) Standard time is fixed for each job or operation.

(ii) A minimum time wage is guaranteed to every worker.

(iii) Time rate is guaranteed and the workers receive the guaranteed wages, irrespective of whether he completes the work in the time allotted or takes more time to do the same.

(iv) The payment for time saved varies from 33-1/3% to 66-2/3%, but generally wages are paid at one half of time saved.

Total Earnings = Time taken × Hourly rate + Bonus.

$$= T \times R + \frac{(S-T)}{2} \times R$$

(Bonus = 50% of time saved).

Merits of Halsey Plan

- It is simple to operate and easy to understand.
- It guarantees minimum wages to all workers, whether efficient or inefficient.
- It provides incentive to efficient and competent employees.
- Both the employer and employee gets the benefit of time saved.
- There is no need to detroit quality as incentive is based on time saved rather than production.

Demerits

(i) The system lacks fixing of standard time for fixing a job.

(ii) It depends on past performance instead of making new standards.

(iii) It does not provide sufficient incentive to highly competent employees as it involves sharing of the benefit with employers.

(iv) Difficulty in maintaining record of time saved of each worker.

(2) Rowan Plan

This plan differs from Halsey Plan only in regard to the determination of the bonus. A worker is guaranteed minimum wages for time spent on the job and also gets bonus for completing the job in less than the standard time. Efficiency is measured as:

$$\text{Bonus} = \frac{\text{Time saved} \times \text{Time taken} \times \text{Hourly rate}}{\text{Standard time or time allowed}}$$

Total earnings = Time taken × Hourly rate + Bonus.

Merits of Rowan Plan

- It assures minimum guaranteed wage and is more liberal than the Halsey Plan, as it provides incentive to work and earn extra remuneration.
- It gives more bonus than the Halsey Plan as a worker gets his maximum bonus, when he completes the task in half the standard time allowed.
- Both the employer and employee are benefited by the plan.
- The increase in production will reduce overhead cost per unit.

Demerits

- It is associated with complex method of premium calculation for ordinary workers.
- This method is not fair to potential workers, as bonus is paid at decreasing rate.
- Labour cost is generally higher in this method.

(3) Emerson Plan

Under this system, a standard time is established for a standard task. There is no sudden rise in wages on achieving the standard of performance. Efficiency is determined by the ratio between the standard time fixed for a performance and the time actually taken by a worker. A worker reaching unto $66\frac{2}{3}\%$ of efficiency is paid only minimum wages and bonus is paid when a worker cross this limits. This bonus goes on increasing till, when he achieves 100 per cent efficiency, the bonus comes to 20 percent of the guaranteed wage. Efficiency of workers is well acknowledged in this system.

Merits of Emerson Plan

- This method is simple and easily understood by workers.
- It gives minimum guaranteed wage to all workers.
- It is a good source of motivation, as the rate of bonus is directly related to efficiency in a rational manner.
- It helps to reduce job turnover and dissatisfaction and helps to increase the efficiency of workers.

Demerits

- It is not a good source of encouragement for very efficient workers as, benefit is nominal above the standard level of output.
- It is difficult to maintain a separate record of workers of different categories.

(4) Bedeaux Plan

This plan was devised by Charles E. Bedeaux in 1911. Under this plan, every operation or job is expressed in terms of so many standard minutes, which are called 'Bedeaux points' or "B's". Such B representing one minute through time and motion study. If a particular job is rated at 60 Bs or (1 B hour), the worker is allowed one hour for its completion and receives a bonus of 75 percent for the number of Bs i.e., time saved. This means bonus is paid when actual performance exceeds standard performance in terms of B's.

Merits

- It is applicable to any kind of job.
- It ensures minimum wages to workers.
- It is suitable for plants where workers are assigned diverse kinds of jobs.
- The method is simple and easily understood.
- Since ¼ of wages for time saved go to the supervisor, they feel motivated to get higher productivity from the workers.

Demerits

(1) The process is complicated in terms of calculation.

(2) Workers' avoid sharing their efforts with supervisors.

(3) The speedy job of the workers to save time may affect, quality of product.

Based on Production

Under this system, workers are paid according to the amount of work done or the number of units completed, the rate of each unit being settled in advance, irrespective of the time taken to do the task. This does not mean that a worker can take any time to complete a job because if his performance far exceeds the time, which his employer expects he would take, the overhead charge for each unit of article will increase.

The worker working in a given situation and with given machinery is paid exactly in proportion to his physical output. He is paid in direct promotion to his output, the actual amount of pay per unit of service being approximately equal to the marginal value of his service in assisting to produce that output. This system is adopted generally in jobs of a repetitive nature, where tasks can be readily measured, inspected and counted. It is of great appeal to efficient and skilled workers who can increase their earnings by working to their full capacity.

Merits

- It pays the workman according to his efficiency as reflected in the amount of work turned out by him. It is a good source of motivation for efficient employees.
- Supervision charges are not so heavy, for workers are not likely to waste their time since they know that their wages are dependant upon the amount of work turned out by them.
- The method of production is improved along with output and wages.
- The workers take greater care to maintain machinery's and equipment for continuity in the job.
- The total unit cost of production comes down with a larger output because the fixed overhead burden can be distributed over a greater number of units.

Demerits

- The system is not favoured by most of the employees, as the fixation of piece rate by the employer is not done on a scientific basis.
- As the worker's wish to perform their work at breakneck speed, they generally consume more power, overwork the machines, and do not try to avoid wastage of materials. This results in a high cost of production and lower profits.
- There is a greater chance of distribution in the quality of work owing to over zealousness on the part of workers to increase production, which may result in loss of efficiency and health.
- Excessive speeding of work may result in frequent wear and tear of plant and machinery and frequent replacement.

(1) Taylor Plan

F.W. Taylor, father of scientific management initiated this scheme under which an efficient employee is rewarded and one who is inefficient is penalized. He suggested differential piece rate plan where standard workload for every worker is calculated on the basis of time and motion study. If a worker completes the task in the standard time, he is paid at higher rate and lower rate is paid if more than the standard time is taken. No minimum wages are guaranteed. The system is designed to encourage the efficient workforce by providing higher rate of payment and induce them to produce up to their full capacity.

Merits

- There is a clear demarcation of efficient and inefficient employees.
- Easy to understand and calculate.
- It helps to motivate efficient employees and induce them to utilize their maximum potential.
- It helps to remove inefficient workers from the organization.

Demerits

- No minimum wage is guaranteed.
- The feeling of jealously and conflict generate among slow workers.

- It adversely affects the health of workers because of over-exertion for achieving the standard output.
- It causes severe punishment to low or inefficient workers.

(2) Merrick Plan

This system is similar to Taylor's Plan, except that three rates are established.

(i) High for production exceeding 100% of standard.

(ii) Medium for production between 83 and 100% of standard.

(iii) Low for production less than 83% of standard.

Thus, this system is an improvement over the Taylor's plan as it reduces the severity of the Taylor's plan. Such a scheme is usually introduced in an organization where the performance level is already high and management is aiming at 100% efficiency.

Merits

- It is liberal for the efficient workers.
- It reduces the severity of Taylor's plan and is an improvement over Taylor's plan.

Demerits

- No minimum wage is guaranteed for the workers.
- A feeling of insecurity develops among low performers due to wide gap in slabs.

(3) The Gantt Task and Bonus Plan

This plan has been devised by H.L. Gantt and unlike Taylor's and Merrick's plan, minimum time wage is guaranteed to every worker, taking standard time or more. This is the only plan that pays a bonus percentage multiplied by the value of standard time. If a worker achieves standard performance, he gets extra wages varying between 25% to 50 % of the hourly rate for the time allowed for the task. But if he fails to complete the task within the standard time, he receives only the wages for actual time spent at the specified rate.

E.g., a standard time of 8 hours is allowed to complete a task at hourly rate of Rs.2. A person completing the task in standard time (8 hrs.) will get Rs.16 and if the same task is completed in 6 hrs. then wages will be Rs. 18 i.e., Rs.12 will be for time spent and Rs.6 for bonus (50% as the rate of bonus).

Merits

- Minimum wage is assured to every worker.
- The worker's with lower efficiency are not punished as in Taylor's plan.
- This plan is a motivating factor for employees to increase their efficiency as it is directly related to incentive.
- This system is most profitable for workers where efficiency is very high as the bonus is paid on the increased wage.

Demerits

- Since minimum wage is guaranteed to every worker, they are reluctant to achieve the target and increase their efficiency.
- There is a wide gap between wages of efficient and inefficient workers, which increases feeling of jealously, and conflict among them.
- It increases labour cost for low production.
- Adequate attention is paid in fixing the guaranteed time rate and determination of standard output, as any error creates disturbances among workers.

GROUP INCENTIVE SYSTEM

Group incentive plans focus on an established standard against which team performance is compared to determine the magnitude of incentive pay. Historically, financial measures have been the most widely used performance indicator for group incentives. The total earnings of a group are first determined in accordance with the incentive method, which is followed, and the earnings are then distributed among the group members on some equitable basis. If the group consists of members with same competencies and skills, the earnings are equally divided among them. If the members are of unequal competencies then earnings are divided in proportion to specified percentage.

Merits

- Effective teamwork is recorded among group members.
- Innovation and creativity
- Better co-operation among employee's management and the union to accomplish broader objectives.
- Strengthening of employee loyalty to the company.
- Decreased rate of job turnover and absenteeism.
- Minimum time wage is generally guaranteed to each member of the group.

Demerits

- There are certain team members who do not carry their share of the workload, yet share equally in the distribution of rewards.
- Rivalry among the members of the group defeats the purpose of teamwork and co-operation.
- There is always a problem of rewarding team at various levels e.g., if teams are defined at a broad level (entire organization) the motivational impact of incentives can be lost, since a single employee is unlikely to believe his/her efforts effecting the overall organizations performance.
- Sometimes an efficient worker may be penalized for the inefficiency of the other members in the group.
- There are some plans, which are too complex for employees to understand and execute.
- Lack of control and communication among team members often exist which reduces the outcome.

(1) Gain Sharing Plan

It is an incentive plan that engages many or all employees in a common objective. These plans focus on cost components associated with an organizations income and identify savings over which employees have impact i.e., reduced scrap, lower labour costs, reduced utility costs, etc.

KEY-ISSUE IN DESIGNING GAIN SHARING PLAN

- Strength of reinforcement– What role should base pay assume relative to incentive pay.
- Productivity standards– What standard will be used to calculate whether employees will receive an incentive payment?
- Sharing the gains (split between management and workers)– Plan must address relative cuts between management and workers of any profits or savings generated.
- Scope of formula– These were based on inclusions for both labour inputs and productivity outcomes.
- Perceived fairness of the formula– One way to ensure the plan is perceived as fair is to let employee's vote on whether implementation should proceed.
- Ease of administration– Sophisticated ,complex plans require more effective communication and higher levels of trust.
- Production variability– Establishing standards that are "controllable" by employees is a key issue.
- Developing involvement system– Most commonly used systems include steering committees, suggestion systems, co-ordinators, problem solving teams, department committees, inside letter, etc.

There are various types of Gain-sharing plans, differentiated by their focus on either cost savings or some measure of revenue. Some are:

(a) Scanlon Plan

(b) Rucker plan

(a) Scanlon Plan

The plan was devised by Joseph N. Scanlon to accomplish widespread employee participation, industrial harmony and increased productivity. It involves a wage formula where incentives are derived as a function of the ratio between labour costs and sales value of production (SVOP) it includes sales revenue and value of goods in inventory.

The plan has two basic features:

(i) Both employees and managers can participate in the plan by submitting their suggestions for cost cutting methods.

(ii) Financial incentives aimed at cutting cost and thereby increasing efficiency are installed. This plan is essentially a suggestion scheme where both quality and quantity of decision are higher as compared to the usual suggestion system.

If a suggestion is implemented and successful, all employees usually share in 75% of the savings and develop a sense of partnership among employees and increases motivation level.

Merits

- It encourages a sense of partnership and sharing among workers.
- This plan enhances productivity and profits, improves union management relations, and increases inter-group and superior subordinate co-operation.
- It increases sense of motivation among employees.
- It demands a high level of competence from employees at all levels.
- Good supervision and healthy labour relations seems essential.
- The Scanlon Plan helps in reducing costs and fosters a sense of sharing and co-operation among the employees.
- It encourages involvement at departmental level and the executive level. The suggestions for improvement are transmitted from the departmental level to the executive level committee, to implement the suggestion.
- There is an assurance of fair and balanced return to customers, owners and employees.

Demerits

- The biggest criticism is that incentive benefits being similar to all group members, the best performer may lose incentive.
- The plan is a failure where market condition is too difficult to sell increased output and thus, enhanced productivity cause unemployment to numerous individuals.

(b) Rucker Plan

It involves a more complex formula than a Scanlon plan for determining incentive bonus. It ties incentives to a wide variety of savings. The ratio is calculated that expresses the value of production required for each dollar of the total wage bill. More attention is focused on organization behaviour variables.

Features of Gain sharing plan:

(a) Employees earn bonuses based upon a predetermined Gain sharing formula.

(b) Initially intended to focus attention on costs.

(c) Formula is tied to group or departmental performance measures.

(d) It is based upon factors controllable by the group.

(e) It typically targets specific target area and directs employee interest to the area or issue.

(f) It reinforces the performance-reward link.

(2) Kaiser Plan

This plan was devised in 1863 by a committee consisting of union and public representatives .The main aim was to overcome the threats of strikes by equally distributing the company's financial gains among the employees, stockholders and the public. This plan is characterized by guaranteed employment to workers against technological employment, sharing of the gains resulting from cost reduction in view of enhanced efficiency between the company and the employees, increase in wage rate and fringe benefits. This plan has achieved mixed success like Scanlon plan.

(3) Profit Sharing Plan

This plan is popular because the focus is on a predetermined index of profitability. It is an agreement by which an employee receives a share fixed in advance of profits. It usually involves the determination of an organization's profit at the end of the fiscal year and distributes the profit percentage to workers who are qualified to share in the earnings. It is basically a method of remuneration under which an employer undertakes to pay his employees a share in the net profits of an enterprise, in addition to regular wages. The very purpose of this plan is to strengthen the loyalty of employees to the organization.

Features of Profit Sharing

- The profit to the worker is on the basis of certain percentages of ones' monthly wage.
- The payment is based on seniority for wages of the workers.
- It enhances employee security and provides a group incentive to the participants.
- Both the employer and employee mutually accept the agreement of Profit Sharing Plan.
- The amount to be distributed among the participants is computed on the basis of some agreed formula, which is to be applied in all conditions.

Type of Profit Sharing

- Current: Under this form, profit is paid to the employees in cash or by cheque or in the form of stock option immediately after the determination of profit.
- Deferred: Profits are credited to employee's accounts to be paid at the time of retirement or in circumstances like death, disability, etc.
- Combination: In this, a part of the profit is paid in cash and a part is deferred and placed in the employee's account in a trust fund.

Merits

- It strengthens the unity of interest and encourages the spirit of co-operation among employees.
- It enhances employee security.
- Attract and retain competent resources.
- It develops a sense of partnership and commonality of interests.
- It increases employees' interest in the company.
- It induces motivation in the workers' for better work, which increases the profit of the firm and in twin share of worker therein.
- It reduces labour turnover and maintain cordial relationship between the employer and employees.

Demerits

- There is always an uncertainty of profit due to number of factors which in turn effects employees' share.
- These schemes are not supported by Trade Unions.
- It demotivates efficient employees as all the workers without considering their contribution shares profits in a specific ratio.
- Profit sharing being a long term scheme does not work as incentive due to the absence of immediate feedback about the efforts and rewards.

(4) Co-partnership

It is an improvement over profit sharing as employees also participate in the equity capital of a company. The employees are offered shares of the enterprise at reduced rates and they share profits of the concern as its members. It also offers recognition of the claim of the dignity of labour as the worker is viewed as partner in the business. This creates sense of belongingness among workers and stimulates them to contribute their best for the success of the organization. The system tries to eliminate friction between capital and labour.

(5) Priestman Plan

According to this plan a standard production is fixed for the whole factory. If productivity exceeds the standard then bonus is paid in accordance with the increase and in case production does not reach the standard, then worker gets minimum wage only. There is sense of team work and cooperation as their collective efforts increases production and sufficient incentive. There is no other provision for the individual worker.

Limitation of Incentive Plans

- Performance pay cannot replace good management.
- Psychologist says that people put their efforts to achieve reward but it detroit's quality of product when produced in excess.
- Workers may disregard safety measures in order to produce more.
- This scheme also increases the feeling of jealousy and conflict among the employees, if pay for performance is strictly followed.
- Workers may also lead to unethical and illegal behaviour for task completion.
- Incentive schemes are sometimes too complex to be understood and to implement.

Prerequisites for Effective Incentive Plan

- There must be a commitment on the part of the top management to the incentive program.
- The incentive plan should reward employees in direct proportion to increased productivity or quality.
- The standards of performance and criteria for measurement should be fair, clear and aligned with firm's strategy and objectives.

- There should be active participation of workers and union while installing incentive plan.
- A good incentive plan should be simple, clear and easy to operate. An average worker should know the linkage of pay for performance.
- There should be proper communication of details of the scheme to all the concerned persons.
- There should be a supportive environment from the employees for the scheme as any restriction can undermine the plan.
- The incentive plan should be in consistent with the corporate' culture.
- An incentive wage plan must be fair and equitable to both employers and the employees. It should be motivating to employees and economical to the management.
- The time gap between actual performance and reward should be as small as possible.
- There should be an atmosphere of mutual trust and understanding between employer and employee.
- A minimum wage rate should be guaranteed to every worker irrespective of his performance. It increases sense of security among workers.

Fringe Benefits

The term fringe benefits refer to various extra benefits provided to the employees, in addition to the compensation paid in the form of wage or salary. These benefits can be defined as any wage cost not directly connected with the employee's productive effort, performance, service or sacrifice. It is also defined as those benefits which are provided by an employer or for the benefit of an employee and which are not in the form of wages, salaries and time-related payments."

Definition of Fringe Benefit

According to Cockman "Employee benefits are those benefits which are supplied by an employer for the benefits of an employee and which are not in the form of wages, salaries and time related payments."

Different terms are used to denote fringe benefits. They are welfare measures, social charges, social security measures, supplements, sub-wages, employee's benefits etc. The ILO described fringe benefits as "Wages are often augmented by special cash benefits, by the provision of medical and other services or by payments in kind, that forms part of the wage or expenditure on the goods and services". In addition, workers commonly receive such benefits as holiday with pay, low cost meals, low-rent housing etc. Such additions to the wage proper are sometimes referred to as fringe benefits.

Benefits that have no relation to employment or wages should not be regarded as fringe benefits, even though they may constitute a significant part of the workers' total income.

These fringe benefits are those monetary and non-monetary benefits given to the employees during the post employment period which are connected with employment but not to the employee's contributions to the organization.

Features of Fringe Benefit

- Fringe benefit is indirect compensation as they are not directly related to performance but extended as the conditions of employment.
- They are paid to the employees based on their membership in the organization.
- They are helpful in raising the standard of living of employees.
- Benefits and services are provided to the employees on the basis of genuine interest in the protection and promotion of their well-being.
- They are supplementary forms of compensation.
- Fringe benefits must satisfy a real need of an employee. If benefit is not liked by him he will resist to it.
- Employees are educated to make use of fringe benefits.
- They may be voluntary or statutory (provident fund is voluntary and transport is statutory benefit).

Examples of Fringes

Table 6.1

1.	**Legally required payments:**
(i)	Old age, survivors, disability and health insurance (commonly known as social security)
(ii)	Worker's compensation
(iii)	Unemployment compensation
2.	**Contingent and deferred benefits:**
(i)	Pension Plans
(ii)	Group Life Insurance
(iii)	Group health insurance
(a)	Medical expenses (hospitalization and surgical)
(b)	Disability income (short-term and long-term)
(iv)	Guaranteed annual wage
(v)	Prepaid legal plans
(vi)	Military leave and pay
(vii)	Jury duty and bereavement paid leave
(viii)	Maternity leave
(ix)	Child care leave
(x)	Sick leave
(xi)	Dental benefits
(xii)	Tuition aid benefits
(xiii)	Suggestion awards
(xiv)	Service awards

(xv)	Severance pay
3.	**Payments for time not worked:**
(i)	Vacations
(ii)	Holidays
(iii)	Voting pay allowances
4.	**Other benefits:**
(i)	Travel allowances
(ii)	Company car and subsidies
(iii)	Moving expenses
(iv)	Uniform and tool expenses
(v)	Employee meal allowances
(vi)	Discounts on employer's goods and services
(vii)	Child care facilities.

Source: Terry L. Leap and Michael D.Crino, Personnel/HRM, MaCmillan 1990,p.-438.

Need for Fringe Benefits

During the World War II, certain non-monetary benefits were extended to employees as means of neutralizing the effect of inflationary conditions. These benefits, which include housing, health, education, recreation, credit, canteen etc., have been increased from time to time as a result of the demands and pressures from trade union. It has been recognized that these benefits help employees in meeting some of their life's contingencies and to meet the social obligation of employers.

Most of the organizations have been extending the fringe benefits to their employees, year after year, due to the following reasons:

- **Employee demands**

  Employee demands more and varied types of fringe benefits rather than pay hike because of reduction in tax burden on the part of employees and in view of the galloping price index and cost of living.

- **Trade Union demands**

  Trade unions compete with each other for getting more a new variety of fringe benefits to their members such as life insurance etc.

- **Employers' preference**

  As fringe benefits motivate the employees for better contribution to the organization, it is more in demand as compared to pay hike. It is a good tool for employees to improve employee's moral and job satisfaction.

- **As social security**

  It is a type of safety that society furnishes through appropriate organization against certain risks to which its members are exposed. Employees have to provide certain benefits like safety measures, compensation in case of any contingencies of life such as accident, sudden death, occupational disease etc.

- **To improve human relations**

  Human relations are maintained when employees are satisfied economically, socially and psychologically. Therefore, fringe benefits are helpful in maintaining cordial human relations as they satisfy all the three form of needs. It includes credit facilitation, recreational and retirement benefits.

OBJECTIVES OF FRINGES BENEFITS

- To motivate employees and in turn reduces job turnover and absenteeism.
- To attract and retain potential employee.
- To enhance employee's competencies and skills e.g., accelerated promotion provided to an employee.
- To improve industrial relations and work environment.
- To develop a sense of belongingness and loyalty among workers.
- To ensure health, safety and welfare of employees.
- To meet voluntary and statutory requirements.

Fringe benefits have been classified in several ways. From the standpoint of Accounts, these items can be classified in three categories, such as:

(a) Payment for time on the job; overtime payment.

(b) Payment for time not on the job involving paid holidays, vacations, sick leave.

(c) Payment for varied benefits such as insurance, pension, meals, bonuses etc.

According to Chamber of Commerce, U.S.A., Fringe benefits have been classified into 5 categories including:

(a) Legally required benefits such as group insurance, wage, pension plan etc.

(b) Payment for pension and allied agreed upon payments.

(c) Paid rest period or lunch period.

(d) Payment for time not worked.

(e) Other benefits such as profit sharing, general use of companies' cars, discount on property or services, Membership in Country Club or other social clubs, reallocation expenses etc.

Fringe benefits are also categorized as statutory or legal and voluntary benefits. The statutory benefits include social security and medical care, unemployment compensation and workmen's compensation. Voluntary fringe benefits include pension plan premiums, payment for holidays not worked, paid sick leave, recreational bonus, profit sharing payments, death benefits, free meals, employee education refund, discount on property or services, etc.

FRINGE BENEFITS IN INDIA

- Employee security
- Workmen's compensation
- Voluntary arrangements
- Safety and health
- Old age benefit
- Medical benefit
- Welfare and recreational facilities
- Payment for time not worked.

(a) Employee Security

Employees security is in terms of wages security or income security which is assured by Minimum Wage Act, 1948, The Payment of Wages Act, 1936 and Payment of Bonus Act, 1965. Also, the Industrial Dispute Act, 1947, providing the payment at the time of lay off and retrenchment. It also provides Payment of compensation at the rate of 50 percent of wages to workers in factories, mines and plantation. The retrenchment and closure compensations are lumpsum, payments means to give some staying power to the affected workmen who have lost their jobs.

(b) Workmen's Compensation

The Workmen's Compensation Act, 1923 provides for payment by certain classes of employers to their workmen of compensations for injury by accident. This Act is intended to meet the contingency of death, injuries or any disability arising out in the course of employment. The law applies to certain specified categories of workers other than that employed on casual basis for purpose not connected with the employer's trade or business.

(c) Voluntary Arrangement

These are arrangements such as setting up hospital, dispensaries, canteen, free meal and accommodation etc. by the employer.

(d) Safety and Health Benefits

Employees safety and health should be taken care of in order to protect the employees against accidents, exploitation, worker's productive capacity, etc. For this, Fatal Accident Act, 1985 was introduced which was the first law enacted in India providing social security type of protection to the workers. The Act provides for payment of compensation to families for loss occasioned by the death of person caused by wrongful act, negligence or on the part of another person. The Factories Act, 1948, stipulated certain conditions and requirements regarding working conditions with a view to provide safe working environment.

(e) Old Age Benefit

There are the benefits provided to the employees, after retirement and during old age, with a view to create a feeling of security about the old age. These include:

(i) ***Provident Fund Act*** –

This Act provides for the establishment of a compulsory Provident fund for certain industries and other classes of establishments specified therein. There are three schemes under this Act, namely, the employee's Provident Fund Scheme, the Employee's Family Pension Scheme and the Employee's Deposit-linked Insurance Scheme.

At the time of death of a member of the Provident Fund scheme while in service, the members of his family are paid pension and insurance benefit under the Family Pension Scheme and the Deposit-linked Insurance Scheme.

Similar schemes have been introduced under certain other laws e.g., Coal Mines Workers Provident Fund, 1948, Assam Tea Plantations Provident Fund Scheme Act, 1955 and Seamen's Provident Fund Act, 1966.

(ii) ***The Payment of Gratuity Act, 1972*** –

This Act provides for payment of gratuity to employees engaged in factories, mines, oilseeds, plantations, shops and establishments on termination of employment after completion of a minimum period of five years of service. Payment of gratuity is subject to a maximum.

(f) Medical Benefit

The employees are entitled to medical attendance and treatment either under the contributory Health Service Scheme or under the Medical Attendance and treatment rules, which provide for reimbursement of the expenditure incurred on medical attendance and treatment of employees and their family members.

(i) ***The Maternity Benefit Act, 1961*** –

This Act seeks to regulate employment of women in certain classes of establishments during certain periods before and after childbirth and provide for payment of a benefit called the maternity benefit.

(ii) ***Employee's State Insurance Act, 1948*** –

It deals comprehensively about the health benefits to be provided. It is a contributory scheme for which the employees as well as the employers make contributions. Benefits include are sickness benefit, maternity benefit, employment injury benefit, and dependant's benefit.

(g) Welfare and Recreational Facility

Welfare and recreational benefits include:

(a) Canteens, *(b)* Consumer Societies, *(c)* Credit Societies, *(d)* Housing, *(e)* Legal aid, *(f)* Employee counseling, *(g)* Welfare Organizations, *(h)* Holiday Homes, *(i)* Educational facilities, *(j)* Transportation, *(k)* Parties and Picnic, and *(l)* Miscellaneous.

It includes other benefits like organizing games, sports with awards, setting up of clubs, community service activities, Christmas or Diwali gifts, leave travel concession, productivity / Performance awards, etc.

(h) Payment for Time not Worked:

This category includes

(i) Hours of work

(ii) Paid holidays

(iii) Shift premium

(iv) Holiday pay and

(v) Paid vacation.

(i) Hours of Work: According to Factories Act, 1948, no adult worker shall be required to work in a factory for more than 48 hours in any week. Even in some organizations, the number of working hours is less than the legal requirements.

(ii) Paid Holidays:An adult worker shall have weekly paid holidays, preferably Sunday, according to the Factories Act, 1948. Some workers are even allowed to have holidays in a week. If a worker works for the whole week including Sunday, then he is eligible for compensatory holiday of the same number in the same month.

(iii) Companies operating second and third shifts pay a premium to the workers who are required to work during the odd hour's shift.

(iv) Holiday Pay: Generally, organizations offer double the normal rate of the salary to the workers, who work during holidays.

(v) Paid Vacation: Workers in manufacturing, mining and plantation who worked for 240 days during a calendar year are eligible for paid vacation at the rate of one day for every 20 days worked in case of adult workers and the rate of one day for every 15 days worked in case of child workers.

SIGNIFICANCE OF FRINGE BENEFITS IN INDIA

Fringe Benefits are an integral part of the reward system in the public sector undertakings and related to management motivation similar to basic compensation. The employers provide it to their employees under the statutory provisions or on a voluntary basis. The social services provided under the Factories Act, 1948, in the manufacturing industries include canteen, rest shelter, crèche, storage or locker, sitting arrangement, overtime payment, appointment of welfare officers, etc. Other benefits provided to the workers include festival, year-end profit sharing, attendance and production bonuses, free supply of uniforms and other allied items supplied on concessional rates. Social security system provides benefits such as provident fund, employee's state insurance (ESI) scheme, retrenchment, compensation, maternity benefits, gratuity, pension, dependant allowance and pension claims. Also there are arrangements for adult literacy, vocational training and for education of worker's children.

There are Fringe Benefits provided in large establishments in different industries compared favourably with those provided in many advanced countries. The management is becoming extremely concerned with fringe benefits and requires constant research, analysis and control of this system to balance the cost with the returns in the form of improved job satisfaction and productivity.

KEY TERMS

Incentive plan	Co-partnership
Profit sharing	Fringe benefits
Scanlon plan	The Gantt plan

SUMMARY

Wage incentives are extra financial motivation. They are designed to stimulate human effort by rewarding the person, over and above the time rated remuneration for improvements in the present or targeted results. Incentives have direct linking to performance. They induce the employee to move from existing level of performance to optimum achievable performance and helps to improve level of technology and thus increases productivity.

There are basically two types of wage incentive plans

(a) Individual incentive system and (ii) Group incentive system

Individual is further classified on the basis of time and production, They are Halsey plan, Rowan plan, Emerson plan, and Bedeaux plan on the basis of time. On the basis of Production, it is classified into Taylor Plan, Merrick Plan and Gantt plan.

Group incentive plan includes Gain sharing plan, which is of two types.

Scanlon plan and Rucker plan. It also includes Kaiser-worker plan, Profit sharing, Co- partnership, and Priestman plan.

Fringe Benefits**:** The term Fringe benefits refer to various extra benefits provided to the employees, in addition to the compensation paid in the form of wage or salary.

Most of the organizations have been extending the fringe benefits to their employees, year after year, due to the following reasons:

Employee demands, Trade Union demands: Employers' preference as Social security: and to improve human relations.

Fringe benefits has been classified into 5 categories including:-

(i) Legally required benefits such as group insurance, wage, pension plan etc.

(ii) Payment for pension and allied agreed upon payments, (iii) Paid rest period lunch period, (iv) Payment for time not worked and (v) Other benefits such as profit sharing, general use of companies' cars, discount on property or services, membership in Country Club or other social clubs, reallocation expenses etc.

Fringe Benefits are also categorized as statutory or legal and voluntary benefits. The statutory benefits include social security and medical care unemployment compensation, workmen's compensation. Voluntary fringe benefits include pension plan premiums, payment for holidays not worked, paid sick leave, recreational bonus, profit sharing payments, death benefits, free meals, employee education refund, discount on property or services, etc.

Fringe Benefits in India are classified as Employee Security, Workmen's Compensation, Voluntary Arrangement, Safety and Health, Old Age benefit, Medical Benefit, Welfare and Recreational Facilities, and Payment for time not worked.

The management is becoming extremely concerned with fringe benefits and requires constant research, analysis and control of this system to balance the cost with the returns in the form of improved job satisfaction and productivity.

REVIEW QUESTIONS

1. What do you understand by wage incentive plan? Describe the prerequisites of sound wage incentive plan?
2. Explain in detail various types of wage incentive plan.
3. Compare and contrast various incentive plans and suggest measures to use team or group incentive plan rather than individual incentive plan.
4. What is Scanlon plan? Explain its basic features.
5. How do group incentive system differ from individual incentive system? Briefly describe various types of group incentive system.
6. What is meant by Profit sharing? What are their objectives and prerequisites?
7. Given the increase in the cost of 'fringe benefits', are no longer as fringe. How do you explain the statement?
8. What do you mean by 'Fringe Benefits'? Explain its need and various types offered in India.
9. Suggest some measures to make incentive and benefits program more successful.

References

Beach D. S., *Human Resource Management/personnel Management,* New york: Tata McGraw-Hill.

Dessler Gary, *Human Resource Management,* 9th ed, Prentice Hall of India, New Delhi, 2003.

Dunn J. D and Frank Rachel, *"Wages and Salary Administration",* 1972.

Dwidedi R. S., *Managing Human Resource,* Galgotia Publishing Company, New Delhi, 1999.

Decanzo A. David and Robbins P. Stephen, *Personnel/HRM,* Prentice Hall of India, 3rd Ed. New Delhi, 1989.

K. Ashwathappa, *Human Resource Management,* 4th ed., Tata McGraw-Hill, New Delhi, 2005.

Milton L. Rock, *Handbook of Wages and Salary Administration.*

Mejia Gomez, and Cardy Robert, *Managing Human Resources,* Pearson Education, New Delhi, 2001.

Milkovich, G. T, and Newman J. M., *Compensation,* (4th ed.). Homewood, ILL: Irwin.

Subramaniam K. N., *"Wages in India",* Tata McGraw-Hill., New Delhi.

Werther W.B and Davis Keith, *Human Resource Management/Personnel Management.* New york: Tata McGraw-Hill.

Wallace M. J, and Fay C. H., *Compensation Theory and Practice,* 1st ed. Tata McGraw-Hill.

JOB ANALYSIS

7

LEARNING OBJECTIVES

After studying this chapter, you will be able to understand —

- ⇨ Understand the nature and significance job analysis
- ⇨ Discuss the need for job analysis
- ⇨ Outline the process involved in job analysis
- ⇨ Discuss the method for data collection for job analysis
- ⇨ Explain the techniques for analysis of job data
- ⇨ Define job description and job specification
- ⇨ Discuss job design and its approaches
- ⇨ Differentiate between job enrichment and job enlargement
- ⇨ Defining the concept of job simplification and job rotation

JOB ANALYSIS

Job analysis is a formal and detailed study of Jobs. It is a systematic process of gathering information about work, jobs and relationship between jobs. Understanding and being able to perform good job analysis is an essential human resource function, forming the basis of selection, promotion, training etc. It is the best way to establish what exists, what is good, and what should be changed.

Definitions

According to Edwin Flippo — "*Job analysis is the process of studying and collecting information relating to the operations and responsibilities of a specific job.*"

According to Richard Henderson — *Job analysis involves the identification and precisely identifying the required tasks, the knowledge and skills necessary for performing them and the conditions under which they must be performed.*"

According to S.P. Robbins and D.A. Decanzo – "*Job Analysis is the systematic exploration of activities within a job. It is a basic technical procedure. One that is used to define responsibilities and accountabilities of a job.*"

It is the process of "determining by observation and studies the tasks, which comprises the job, the methods and equipment used and the skills and attitudes required for successful performance of the job." It provides the following information about a job:

- Identification of job in terms of its title and code number.
- Duties involved in the job along with the frequency of occurrence of each duty.
- Operations involved in doing the job.
- Materials and equipment required for doing the job.
- Relationship of the job with other jobs in the organization.
- Personal qualities required to do the job.

SIGNIFICANCE OF JOB ANALYSIS

- It helps in mapping of potential employees by placing right person at the right place.
- It helps in improving the design of jobs by making comprehensive study of the job elements. It helps in analyzing work processes and work simplification and serves as the basis for time and motion study.
- It can be used in training or needs assessment to identify or develop training content, assessment tests to measure effectiveness of training and methods of training program.
- It facilitates job evaluation and performance appraisal which are necessary for wage determination, for appraising the working conditions and promotions and transfer.
- It helps in proper allocation of authority and responsibility by describing the duties of each job and the interrelationships among jobs.
- It helps in efficient manpower planning by determining the demands of the job in terms of responsibilities and duties and then translates these demands in terms of skills, qualities and other human attributes.
- Job analysis will be helpful in improving labour management relations and to resolve disputes related to workload and work procedures.

PROCESS OF JOB ANALYSIS

The steps involved in job analysis process are as under:

(1) Organizational Analysis

In this, the overall picture of various jobs in the organization has to be obtained. It mainly includes makeup of a job, its relation to other jobs and its contribution. This required background information for this purpose is obtained through organization chart and workflow charts.

(2) Selection of representative positions to be analyzed

It is difficult to analyze all the jobs, being costly and time consuming. Therefore, a representative sample of jobs is to be analyzed for the purpose of detailed analysis.

(3) Collection of job analysis data

In this step, collection of data is done on the job characteristics, required behaviour and personal qualification needed to carry out the job effectively. Data can be collected even through questionnaire, observation or interviews, care should be taken to use only reliable and acceptable techniques in a given situation.

(4) Preparation of job description:

The job information collected in the above ways is now used to prepare a job description which is a written statement describing the contents of the job in terms of task, duties, responsibilities, required to perform the job effectively and efficiently.

(5) Preparing job specification:

The last step involved is to prepare job specification or employer's specification on the basis of collected information. It is also a written statement, which specifies the personal attribute in terms of education, experience, qualities, traits, aptitude, etc., required for effective job performance.

Job Analysis Process

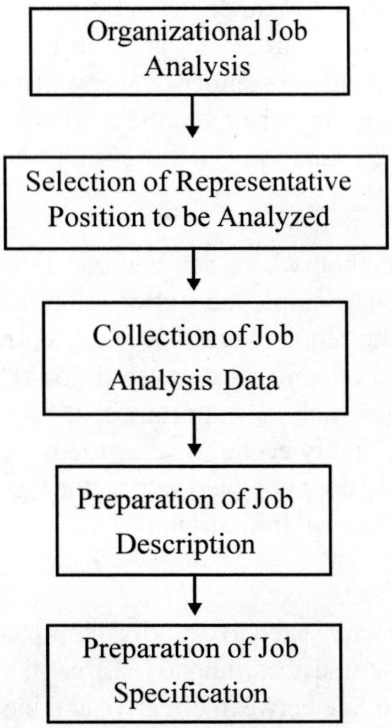

Fig. 7.1

Collection and Describing Data

There are following information sources of gathering information for job analysis.

(1) Interview

In this method, the job analyst directly interviews the job holder and asks questions regarding the various jobs performed by them for collection of data. This method is found suitable particularly for jobs wherein direct observation is not feasible. The interview should be structured and the interviewer must be trained in proper interviewing techniques. It is used as a technique for comparing the data collected by the analyst through observation or questionnaire. The following guidelines, as outlined by Carrol L. Shartle, Otis and Lenhert, may help the interviewer to make his/her interview more effective.

- Introduce yourself to make the worker know who you are and why you are there.
- Allay the worker's fear whatsoever by showing keen interest in both him/her and his/her job.
- Do not advice the worker how to do the job.
- Try to talk to the worker in his/her language, to the extent possible.
- Do not create confusion between work and the worker.
- Make a full-fledged job study within the objectives of the program and
- Verify the job information whatsoever obtained.

(2) Observation

The analyst observes the worker doing the job. This is the most reliable technique of getting information regarding job. It helps to gather information of repetitive nature and analyze the tasks performed, the pace which activities are done, and the working condition during a complete work cycle. The jobs of draftsman, mechanic spinner or weaver are the examples of such job. Observation coupled with discussions with the supervisor and the workers constitute the preferred approach in most of the cases to get the required information. Training is also helpful to make the job analyst skillful.

(3) Questionnaire

This is the widely used method where detailed questionnaire is prepared by the job analyst and distributed among the workers. The employee's after filling structured questionnaire return back to the supervisor, who after making the required and necessary corrections in the information submit to the job analyst. The structured questionnaire must cover all job related tasks and behaviour, each of which is described in terms of factors such as importance, difficulty, frequency, relationships to overall performance. This technique is highly economical as it covers a large number of job-holders at a time but time consuming and generally does not yield satisfactory results, as many employees do not complete the questionnaire because of their own limitation.

(4) Critical Incident

In this method, job-holders are asked to describe their past experiences related to job. The incident so collected is analyzed and classified according to job areas they describe. The job requirement becomes clear, once the analyst draws the line between effective and ineffective behaviour of workers on the job. This method is also time consuming and job analyst requires high degree of skills to analyze the content of description given by the worker.

(5) Checklist

The checklist method of job data collection differs from the questionnaire method in the sense that it contains a few subjective questions in the form of yes or no. The job-holder is asked to tick the questions that are related to his job. It is prepared on the basis of job information obtained from various sources such as supervisors, industrial engineers and other people who are familiar with the job. Once the checklist is prepared, it is then sent to the job holder and the information is tabulated to obtain the job- related data. The method is costly and therefore, is not suitable for small organizations.

(6) Record

Personal department maintains the record of the facts and figures related to the job-holder. The analyst collects the information from the record maintained by the Personal department.

Analysis of Job Data

There is no one best way to conduct job analysis. Experts agree that the choice of job analysis method depends upon the purposes to be served by the data. Wherever possible, multiple methods of job analysis must be followed. Some of the techniques are:

1. Position Analysis Questionnaire

It is a very structured job analysis questionnaire developed at Purdue University to quantitatively sample work-oriented, job element. It permits management to scientifically and quantitatively group interrelated job elements into job dimensions. It is filled in by a job analyst, a person who should already be acquainted with the particular job to be analyzed. The PAQ contains 194 items, each of which represents a basic element that may or may not play an important role in the job. They are divided into 6 sections.

Table 7.1

Employees Activities in PAQ

(a)	Information Input: Where and how do workers get information to do their jobs?	35 elements
(b)	Mental Processes: Decision-making, reasoning planning and information processing activities involved in job performance.	15 elements
(c)	Work Output: What physical activities do the employees perform and what tools or devices he uses.	49 elements
(d)	Relationships: The type of relationships and contact a person is having with others, both inside and outside in performing the job.	36 elements
(e)	Job context: The physical and social context in which the job is performed.	19 elements
(f)	Other Job characteristics: What activities, condition or characteristics not covered by the other categories are relevant?	40 elements

The advantages of PAQ are that it provides a quantitative score or profile of any job in terms of how that job rates on the basic activities.

(2) Management Position Description Questionnaire (MPDQ): MPDQ is a standardized instrument designed specifically for uses in analyzing managerial jobs. The 274-item questionnaire contains 15 sections, which takes 2 ½ hour to complete it. In most cases, respondents are asked to state how important each item is to the position.

W.W. Tomov and P.R. Pinto (Journal of Applied Psychology 61, 1976) have developed the following MPDQ factors. They are:

(a) Product, marketing and financial Strategy Planning

(b) Co-ordination of other organizational units and personnel

(c) Internal business control

(d) Products and services responsibility

(e) Public and customer relations

(f) Advanced consulting

(g) Autonomy of actions

(h) Approval of financial commitments

(i) Staff service

(j) Supervision

(k) Complexity and stress

(l) Advanced financial responsibility

(m) Broad personnel responsibility

(3) Functional Job Analysis (FJA)– It is a technique used in the Public sector, which attempts to describe the whole person on the job. It tries to examine the fundamental components of "data, people and things." The technique collects information on the following aspects of the job:

- The methods and techniques of the job, incumbent use to perform the job.
- The verbal and language facility required performing the task.
- The machines, tools and equipment used by the job incumbent.
- The material, projects, or services produced by the job incumbent.

FJA then identifies performance standards and training requirements. It provides a quantitative score of each job as a function of its complexity in relationship with people, data and things. These results are helpful in fixing wage rates and in developing employee succession plan.

(4) Critical Incident Technique: It is used to develop behavioral descriptions of a job. The CIT technique involves following steps (1) generate dimensions (2) generate incidents (3) retranslate and (4) assign effectiveness values.

A quantitative approach like Position Analysis Questionnaire (PAQ) should be supported by a qualitative approach like critical incident technique (CIT) are used for job analysis.

JOB DESCRIPTION

A job description is a written statement of what the job holder does, how it is done, under what conditions it is done and why it is done. It is a written document that identifies and describes a job in terms of its duties, responsibilities, working conditions and specifications.

A few important definitions of job description are as follows:

According to Edwin B. Flippo, "Tthe first and immediate product of job analysis is job description. As the title indicates, the document is basically descriptive in nature and constitutes a record of existing and pertinent job facts.

According to Pigors and Myres, "Job description is a pertinent picture (in writing) of the organizational relationships, responsibilities and specific duties that constitute a given job or position. It defines a scope of responsibility and continuing work assignment that are sufficiently different from that of other jobs to warrant a specific title.

According to Ernest Dale, the following guidelines are important while writing the job description.

- The job description should indicate the nature and scope of the job, including all important relationships.
- It should be brief, factual and precise; use active verb such as collect mail; sort out mail, etc., avoid statements of opinion. Give a clear picture of the job; explaining all the duties and responsibilities of the job in a greater detail.
- More specific words be chosen to show (i) the kind of work (ii) the degree of complexity (iii) the degree of skill required (iv) the extent to which problems are standardized and (v) the degree and type of accountability.
- The extent of supervision available should also be clearly stated.
- The reporting relationship must also be clearly indicated (e.g., who reports to whom, frequency etc.)

Contents of Job Description

(1) Job title: Tells about the job title, code number and the department where it is done.

(2) Job summary: A short statement that summarizes the job's duties, responsibilities and place in the organization structure.

(3) Duties and responsibilities: It explains what is done on the job, how it is done and why it is done.

(4) Working conditions: The working environment in terms of heat, noise, light, fumes and any other hazards.

(5) Relationship with other jobs: It includes size of work group and interpersonal interaction required to do the job.

JOB SPECIFICATION

It comprises of the entire worker's characteristics required for efficient job completion. It describes the key qualification to perform the job that spells out the important characteristics of an employee in terms of education, experience, skills, knowledge and abilities (KSA).

According to Edwin B.Flippo – "A job specification is a statement of minimum acceptable human qualities necessary to perform a job properly."

A job specification can be developed by talking with the current job-holder's about the attributes required to do the job satisfactorily. There is also a checking of job needs of other organizations with similar jobs. A job specification should include:

(1) Physical characteristics: It includes height, weight, health, etc.

(2) Psychological & Social characteristics: It includes mental ability, decision making skills, initiative, emotional stability, etc.

(3) Personal characteristics: It includes gender, education, family background, job experience, etc.

All the attributes are classified into 3 categories:

- Essential attributes: which a person must possess.
- Desirable attributes: which a person ought to possess.
- Contra indicators: which will become a handicap to do successful job performance.

A well written job specification statement offers a clear picture to new recruiters of what they will be doing in the organization.

Preparation of Job Specification

Job Specification of a Compensation Manager

Education	MBA with specialization in HRM/ MA in social work/ PG Diploma.
Experience	A degree Diploma in Labour Law is desirable.At least 2 years experience in a similar position in a large manufacturing company.
Skills, Knowledge, Ability	Knowledge of Compensation practices in competing industries of job analysis procedures, of compensation survey technique, of performance appraisal system.Skill in writing job description in conducting job analysis interview.Ability to contact meetings, to plan and prioritise work.
Work Orientation Factors	The positions may require up to 15% travel.
Age	Preferably below 30 years

Fig. 7.2

Source: Adapted from Bernardin/bid p.113

Job specification statement is typically developed with the co-operation of the Personnel department and various supervisors throughout the organization. The personnel department co-ordinates the writing of the job specification and description and secures agreement on the desired qualification. The Personnel Manager should confirm that all the specifications are realistic, fair and designed to assist the organization in attaining its goals.

JOB DESIGN

It is the process of organizing work into the tasks required to perform a specific job. The Human Resource Management has realized the importance of designing a job in terms of productivity and job specification. It reduces monotony, boredom, increased job turnover, absenteeism and job dissatisfaction

There are 4 approaches to job design:

(A) Job Enrichment

It is an approach to job design that is based on the assumption that in order to motivate personnel, the job itself must provide opportunities for achievement, recognition, responsibility, advancement and growth. It gives employees more opportunities for autonomy and feedback. It also gives them more responsibilities that require decision making, such as scheduling work, determining quality, etc.

According to Herzberg, an enriched job has eight characteristics. These features are:

(a) Direct feedback: The evaluation of performance system or immediate feedback to the employees.

(b) New learning: A feeling of growing intellectual among employees.

(c) Client relationship: An employee who serves a client or customer directly has an enriched job.

(d) Scheduling own work: Employees who perform creative work are given the opportunity to schedule their own work.

(e) Unique experience: An enriched job provides unique experience or quality.

(f) Control over resources: This approach for employee leads to enrichment.

(g) Direct communication authority: An enriched job allows the worker to communicate directly with people.

(h) Personal accountability: A feeling of personal accountability enhances job enrichment.

(B) Job Enlargement

It involves adding more tasks to a job or assignment of varied tasks or duties of the jobs of employees at the same level. According to Herzberg, "Job enlargement is simply adding a zero to zero. Zero meaning that one set of boring tasks is simply added to another set of boring tasks. A recent study found that by expanding the scope of job, workers found benefits such as mere satisfaction, reduce boredom, monotony and increased motivation.

Enlargement is done only on the horizontal level i.e. the jobs remains the same, but of larger scale than before. According to George Strauss and L.R.Sayles, "Job enlargement implies that instead of assigning one man to each job, a group of men can be assigned to a group of jobs and then allowed to decide for themselves how to organize the work. Such change, permit mere social contact and greater control over the work process.

Difference between Job Enlargement and Job Enrichment

Job Enlargement	Job Enrichment
It involves horizontal or lateral expansion of job in addition of tasks of same nature and at the same level.	It involves vertical expansion of functions and responsibility of the job-holder.
It may not call for acquisition of higher level skills for job-holders.	It calls for development and utilization of higher skills, innovation and creativity for job holder.
The main purpose is to reduce boredom and monotonous nature of job.	The main purpose is to make the job more lively, challenging and motivating.
This method of job design satisfies extrinsic need of the job-holder or Maslow's Lower level need.	This method satisfies intrinsic need or higher level need such as ego, self actualization, self esteem, sense of achievement, etc.
Employees in job enlargement's need more supervision to perform the job.	Employees need less supervision and are more motivated by self direction and self control.

(C) Job Simplification or Work Simplification

Under this method, the complete job is simplified by breaking down into small sub-parts. Then, each part of the job is assigned to a worker who does the same task over and over again. This is done so that employees who gain proficiency in doing the repetitive task require less training. This will lower down training costs and in turn increases productivity and profit. Time and motion study are generally used for job simplification. However, company may not always be benefited from this technique, as it increases absenteeism and boredom due to repetitive nature of job.

(D) Job Rotation

This is one of the methods to reduce boredom which implies moving of employees from one job to another within a working group so that there is some variety and relief from boredom of monotonous jobs. Herzberg characterized this approach as merely substituting "one zero for another zero". It is horizontal or lateral transfer, where employees are shifted to another activity to meet the needs of work scheduling. It not only reduces boredom and monotony of job but also increases employee's skills and knowledge. This method improves the self image and personal worth of the employee. However, employees who look for more challenging job become frustrated.

KEY TERMS

Job description	Critical incident
Job specification	Position analysis
Job design	Questionnaire (PAQ)
Management Position Description	Functional Job Analysis
	Questionnaire (MPDQ)

SUMMARY

Job analysis is a formal and detailed study of jobs. It is a systematic process of gathering information about work, jobs and relationship between jobs. It involves the identification and precisely identifying the required tasks, the knowledge and skills necessary for performing them. It helps in mapping of potential employee by placing right person at the right place and improving the design of jobs by making comprehensive study of the job elements.

It facilitates job evaluation and performance appraisal, which are necessary for wage determination, for appraising the working conditions and promotions and transfer.

The steps involved in job analysis process are as under: (1) Organizational Analysis: (2) Selection of representative positions to be analyzed. (3) Collection of job analysis data: (4) Preparation of Job description and, (5) Preparing job specification.

There are various information sources of gathering information for job analysis such as:
Interview, Observation, Questionnaire, Critical Incident, Checklist Method and Records of Personal Department.

Experts agree that the choice of job analysis method depends upon the purposes to be served by the data. Wherever possible, multiple methods of job analysis must be followed. Some of the techniques arePosition Analysis Questionnaire, Management Position Description Questionnaire (MPDQ), Functional Job Analysis (FJA), and Critical Incident Technique.Quantitative Approach like Position Analysis Questionnaire (PAQ) should be supported by a qualitative approach like Critical Incident (Technique (CIT) are used for job analysis.

A job description is a written document that identifies and describes a job in terms of its duties, responsibilities, working conditions and specifications.

Job specification comprises of the entire worker's characteristics required for efficient job completion and describes the key qualification to perform the job in terms of education, experience, skills, knowledge and abilities (KSA).

Job design is the process of organizing work into the tasks required to perform a specific job. There are 4 approaches to job design: Job Enrichment, Job Enlargement, Job Simplification and Job Design.

REVIEW QUESTIONS

1. What is Job Analysis? Discuss its needs and significance.
2. Distinguish between Job Analysis, Job description, Job specification and Role analysis.
3. What is Job Description? Discuss its features. With the help of an example, prepare the sample of Job Description.
4. "Job analysis is the most basic personnel activity". Discuss Briefly describe common methods of analyzing job.
5. Compare and contrast various methods of data collection and the pros and cons of each method.
6. Explain the following term:

   (a) Position Analysis Questionnaire

(b) Management Position Description Questionnaire

(c) Functional Job Analysis

(d) Critical Incident Technique.

7. Discuss various approaches of Job design.

8. Distinguish between:

(a) Job Description and Job Specification

(b) Job Enlargement and Job Enrichment

(c) Job Analysis and Job Design.

References

Armstrong, M. and H. Murlis (1991), *Reward Management,* 2nd ed., Kogan Page/IPM, London.

Decanzo A. David and Robbins P. Stephen, *Personnel/HRM,* Prentice Hall of India, 3rd Ed. New Delhi, 1989.

Dessler Gary, *Human Resource Management,* 9th ed, Prentice Hall of India, New Delhi, 2003.

Grant. C. Phillips, *What use is a Job Description*? Personnel Journal,Feb. 1988, pp. 44-45.

Henderson Richard, *Compensation Management,* Prentice Hall, N. J.,1994.

Hollenbeck Noe and Wright Gerhart, *Fundamentals of Human Resource Management,*

J. L. Gray, and F. A.Starke, *'Organization Behaviour,* Charles E. Merrill Co., Ohio, 1977.

K. Asahwathappa, *Human Resource Management,* 4th ed., Tata McGraw-Hill, New Delhi, 2005.

Mathis L. Robert and Jackson J. H., *Personnel/HRM,* Tata McGraw-Hill,1990.

Mejia Gomez, and Cardy Robert, *Managing Human Resources,* Pearson Education, New Delhi, 2001.

Paul W.J and Robertson K. B., *Job Enrichment and Employee Motivation,* Gower Press, London, 1970 .

JOB EVALUATION

8

LEARNING OBJECTIVES

After studying this chapter, you will be able to understand —

- What is job evaluation
- Objectives of job evaluation
- Limitations of job evaluation
- Process of job evaluation
- Prerequisite for successful job evaluation program
- Techniques of job evaluation
- Pay structure and its determination.

JOB EVALUATION

Job evaluation is the formal process used to assign wage and salary rates to a job. A variety of systems and products exists to guide this process, each different from the other in packaging, pricing, philosophy, procedures and utility. The degree to which an organization uses a formal job evaluation process is related to the number of jobs in the organization.

Job evaluation is a systematic technique determining the worth of a job and not the man. It considers the demands of the job in terms of efforts and abilities but does not take into account individual abilities and efforts. Once the worth of the job is determined, it becomes easier to fix the wage structure that will be fair and remunerative.

Definition of Job Evaluation

Edwin Flippo — *"Job evaluation is a systematic and orderly process of determining the worth of a job in relation to other jobs".*

Dale Yoder — *"Job evaluation is a practice which seeks to provide a degree of objectivity in measuring the organization value of jobs within the organization and among similar organizations".*

International Labour Organization

Job evaluation may be defined simply as an attempt to determine and compare the demands which the normal performance of particular job makes on normal workers taking into account the individual abilities or performance of the worker's concerned.

Maurice B. Cuming

Job evaluation is a technique of assessing the worth of each job in comparison with all others throughout an organization.

OBJECTIVES OF JOB EVALUATION

- To determine the hierarchy and place the worth of each job of the organization.
- To ensure fair and equitable wage structure on the basis of relative worth or value of jobs.
- To determine upon a standard for performance appraisal for determining relative worth of each job in a plant.
- To form a basis for fixing incentive and different bonus plans.
- To provide information for work organization, employee's selection, placement training, career development, etc.
- To provide a framework for periodic review of wages.
- To ensure the competitiveness of the organization in the labour market.
- To justify the existing pay structure to employees.
- To identify a ladder of progression for employees by providing benchmark for career planning.
- To strengthen compliance with equal pay legislation and regulations that encourage basic pay on difference in job contents.
- To produce pay structure that reconciles the conflicting demands of internal and external equity.
- To provide a sound basis for merit or pay-for-performance systems.
- To undergo organizational development in times of change.

LIMITATIONS OF JOB EVALUATION

- Job evaluation is not concerned with the performance, potential or personal qualities of individual employees.
- It is impersonal, concentrating on measuring work input rather than work output.
- It is a time consuming process requiring specialized technical personnel to undertake it and thus too costly.
- It promotes increase in number of grievances concerning wages.

- It always creates doubt in minds of workers and trade unions because of the difficulty in understanding its techniques.
- It is susceptible because of human error and subjective judgment.
- This technique is not accurate because of lack of scientific basis about efficacy of methods of job evaluation.
- Job evaluation leads to frequent and substantial changes in wage and salary structure, which in turn creates financial budget on the organization.
- Job evaluation results may not exactly coincide with social evaluations, which in turn, result in employee dissatisfaction.

Process of Job Evaluation

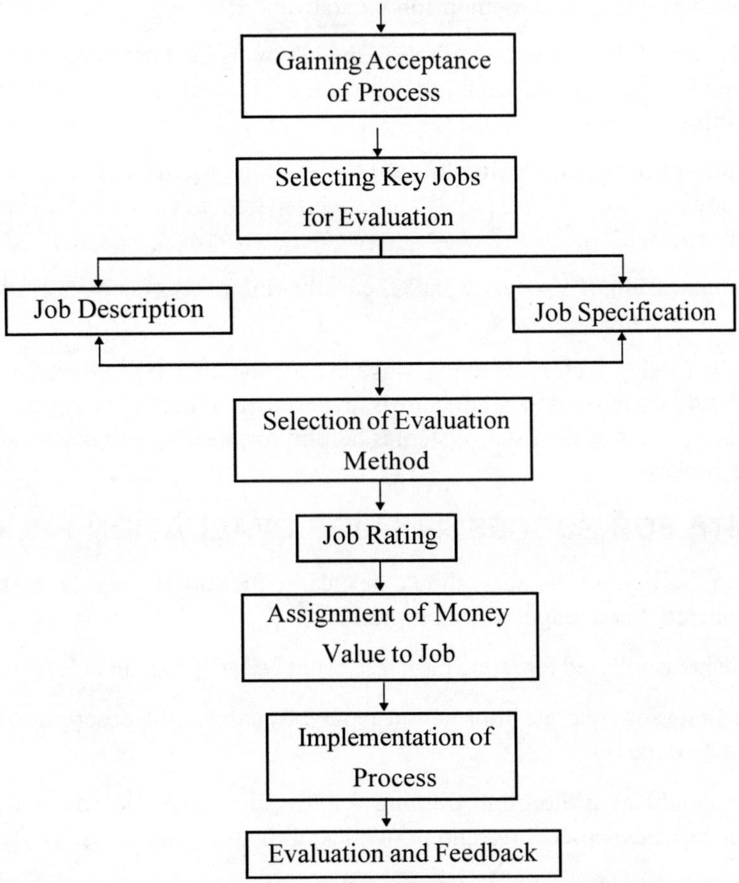

Fig. 8.1

1. **Gaining Acceptance of Process:** The process of job evaluation is explained to the employees and unions before undertaking it. The purpose and importance of job evaluation is made available to everyone with the help of conferences, letters & circulars.

2. **Selecting Key Jobs for Evaluation:** The key jobs are those which are critical in nature and represent the type of work performed. The other jobs are compared with the key jobs or critical success jobs and the process continues.

3. **Job Description:** It is a written statement of what job-holder does, how it is done, under what conditions it is done and why it is done. It is a document identifying responsibilities involved and condition of employment for each job which is essential for job evaluation.

4. **Job Specification:** It comprises of all the characteristics of a worker required for efficient task competition. It describes the key qualification in the form of employee's education, experience skills, knowledge and abilities.

5. **Selecting job Evaluation Method:** There are several technique of job evaluation, but the one, which is most appropriate to the job, and organization is selected. It may also be possible to select more than one method for accuracy.

6. **Job Rating:** It is the method of rating the job by using a predetermined system or plan and studying job description. Each job is assigned with certain value or score depending upon its worth.

7. **Assignment of Money Value to Job:** Once all the scores and values are added, the worth of job is determined. These points are converted into monetary values according to a definite system or scale.

8. **Implementation of Process:** Once the evaluation process is over, management explains it to employees and put into action.

9. **Periodic Review:** This is the final stage in a job evaluation program. In this stage, procedure developed to maintain salary structure is reviewed in the light of changes in their responsibilities and market rates. A feedback system is helpful for the employees who are dissatisfied by the above process.

PREREQUISITE FOR SUCCESSFUL JOB EVALUATION PROGRAMME

- The process of job evaluation should be clear to the supervisors. They should have complete and concrete knowledge of the program.
- The elements selected for rating purpose should be easily explainable to avoid any overlapping.
- An accurate and concrete information about job analysis, job description and job specification should be done.
- There should be a thorough training for the supervisors in advance to enable others to explain policies, procedures and principles of the program.
- All the relevant internal and external factors have been taken into account in arriving at the final form of the scheme.
- The program should have the full approval and support of the top management.
- The details of the administration plan should be made simple to avoid employee's doubts and fears about the plan.

- Before launching a job evaluation program, certain issues to be decided before hand, such as category of employees to be covered, job evaluator and the atmosphere for launching of job evaluation process.
- The scheme should be introduced on a plant-to-plant basis, then applied to a whole industry. This is because it is difficult to standardize job's throughout an industry, unless the plants in it are so familiar that they can be treated as being virtually a single firm.
- There should be an atmosphere of open communication and participation of employees to discuss job ratings to enhance co-operation.
- Changes, if any, in the evaluation method should be carried out before the program is installed.
- The better the state of industrial relations, the easier it is to introduce a job evaluation scheme.

TECHNIQUES OF JOB EVALUATION

There are four basic systems of job evaluation, which are grouped into 2 categories.

1. **Non-quantitative methods/Non-analytical system.**
   (a) Ranking or job comparison.
   (b) Grading or job classification.
2. **Quantitative methods/Analytical system.**
   (a) Point rating.
   (b) Factor comparison.

The basic difference between non-quantitative and quantitative method is that:

- In non-quantitative method, job as a whole is considered.
- Judging and comparing jobs with each other.
- In quantitative method 'compensable factor' are considered i.e., Key factors or critical factors.
- There is an assignment of numerical scores on a rating scale and then key factors are measured.

1. The Ranking System

The ranking method is the simplest method of job evaluation, where each job as a whole is compared with, other i.e., "the whole job" is compared rather than compensable factors. All jobs are ranked in the order of their importance from highest to lowest, or in the reverse order, each successive job being higher or lower than the previous one in the sequence.

The ranking of jobs in university

Ranking Method of University Jobs

Table 8.1

Ranking Order	Pay Scale
Professor/Registrar	Rs. 16,400-450-20,900
Reader/Dy. Registrar	Rs.12,000-420-18,300
Lecturer/Asst. Registrar	Rs. 8,000 – 275 - 13,800

This method involves the following steps:

- Preparation of job description, which is studied, analyzed and ranked.
- Selection of rater or committee of rater is done.
- Identification of key jobs or benchmark is done and rated on the basis of its importance.
- Ranking of all jobs in the organization around the benchmark jobs, until all jobs are placed in their rank order importance.
- Finally, job classification is done based on the rating where the total ranked job is classified into appropriate group by considering the common features of jobs. All the jobs within a single group or classification receive the same range of wages.

Merits

- This method is simple, easily understood, easily explainable and flexible.
- It is suitable for small organizations with clearly defined jobs.
- It is less time consuming.
- It is economical and requires little effort for maintenance.

Demerits

- There is no standard of judgment of one job with another job and hence associated with errors.
- Improper analysis of competencies from rater's point of view.
- This method fails to indicate the degree to which one job is better than the other. It only produces a job order and tells us that one job is higher or lower than the other.
- It is a failure when large number of jobs are to be analyzed.

2. Job Classification or Grading Method

Under this method, a number of predetermined grades or classifications are first established by a committee and then the various jobs are assigned within each grade or class. A job grade is defined as a group of different jobs of similar features, requiring similar skills to perform them. Grade descriptions are the result of the information derived from a job analysis, which includes responsibilities, skills, knowledge, experience, etc. Once the grades are established, each job is placed in its appropriate grade or class depending upon its similarities. Finally, wage/salary rate is fixed for each grade, because of difference in duties, skills and knowledge.

This method involves the following steps:

(i) Preparation of job description.

(ii) Preparation of grade description.

(iii) Selection of grades for key jobs.

(iv) Grading the key jobs.

(v) Classification of all jobs.

Merits

(i) This method is simple, easy to understand and less time consuming.

(ii) It takes into account the entire factor that a job comprises.

(iii) The grouping of jobs into classification makes pay determination problems administratively easier to handle.

Demerits

- It is difficult to write a grade description especially where large number of jobs are involved.
- The system is a failure in large organizations.
- The judgment may produce an incorrect classification because of lack of detailed analysis of job.

3. Point System

This method is widely used, where jobs are expressed in terms of Key of factors or compensable factors and points are assigned to each factor on the basis of priority. The sum of these points gives us an index of the relative significance of the jobs that are rated.

The steps involved are:

- Select key jobs and cluster the jobs on the basis of similar skills, efforts, responsibility etc.
- Divide each major factor into a number of sub-factors. Each sub-factor is defined and expressed in the order of preference along a scale.
- Each factor is assigning a point value which is summed up to find the maximum number of points assigned to each job. This helps to find the relative worth of a job.
- Once the worth of a job in terms of total points is expressed, the money value is assigned to points.

Conversion of Job Grade Points into Money Value

Table 8.2

Point Range	Job Grade	Pay Scale
100-150	1	900-1800
150-200	2	1400-2200
200-250	3	1700-2700
250-300	4	2400-4200
300-350	5	3200-5200

Merits

- It is the most widely used method of job evaluation.
- Job can be easily placed in distinct categories.
- For various factors of job are rated by points which make it possible for one to be accurate in assigning money value to total job points.
- This method is associated with minimum rating error's because rater using similar criteria would get more or less similar answers.
- It is more systematic, reliable and objective than other methods of job evaluation.

Demerits

- This method is very costly complex and time consuming.
- It is difficult to determine the factor levels within factors and assign values to them. Preparing of manual is a difficult process.

Compensable Factors Used in the Point-Factor Method of Job Evaluation

Table 8.3

COMPENSABLE FACTOR	RATING CRITERIA
Skill/know-how	Education Experience Knowledge
Effort	Physical effort Mental effort Judgement/decision-Making Internal business contacts Consequence of error Degree of influence
Responsibility	Supervisory responsibilities Responsibility for independent action

	Responsibility for machinery/equipment Fiscal responsibility Responsibility for confidential information Risks Comfort
Working conditions	Physical demands Personal demands

4. The Factor Comparison Method

The factor method is based on the analysis of jobs in terms of separately defined factors, component that are compensable to the organization. The steps involved are:

(a) Determine the appropriate factors to measure. Factors could include education, training, experience, customer relation, responsibilities and decision making authority.

(b) Weight the factors, when designing the system, each of these factors would be assigned a different weight based on the relative importance of each factor.

(c) Calculate the whole score for each job. Once the factor in weights are established, the whole score is calculated for each job. The total points assigned to a job factor determine the job's relative value and location in the pay structure.

Merits

- This method is more defensible and objection measure of job, worth due to numerical valuation.
- It is easy to communicate and be understood.
- The value of the job is expressed in monetary terms which make the method effective.
- It can be applied to a wide range of jobs.

Demerits

- It is time consuming process due to consistent detail required.
- The method is more expensive to maintain and update.

Table 8.4

METHOD	ADVANTAGES	DISADVANTAGES
Ranking • Jobs are compared to each other based on the overall worth of the job to the organis-ation. The 'worth' of a job is usually based on judgements of skill, effort (physical and mental),	Simple. Very effective when there are relatively few jobs to be evaluated (less than 30).	Difficult to administer as the number of jobs increase. Rank judgements are subjective. Since there is no standard used for comparison, new jobs would have to be compared with the

responsibility (supervisory and fiscal), and working conditions.		existing jobs to determine its appropriate rank. In essence, the ranking process would have to be repeated each time a new job is added to the organisation.
Classification • Jobs are classified into a grade/ category structure or hierarchy. Each level in the grade/category structure has a description and associated job titles. Each job is assigned to the grade/category providing the closest match to the job. The classification of a position is decided by comparing the whole job with the appropriate job-grading standard. To ensure equity in job grading and wage rates, a common set of job grading standards and instructions are used. Because of differences in duties, skills and knowledge, and other aspects of trades and labour jobs, job-grading standards have been developed mainly along occupational lines.	Simple. The grade/category structure exists independent of the jobs. Therefore, new jobs can be classified more easily than the Ranking Method.	Classification judgements are subjective. The standard used for comparison (the grade/ category structure) may have build in biases that would affect certain groups of employees (females or minorities). Some jobs may appear to fit within more than one grade/category.
Factor Comparison A set of compensable factors are identified as determining the worth of jobs. Typically, the number of compensable factors is small (4 or 5). Examples of compensable factors are: 1. Skill 2. Responsibilities 3. Effort 4. Working Conditions • Next, benchmark jobs are identified. Benchmark jobs	The value of the job is expressed in monetary terms. Can be applied to a wide range of jobs. Can be applied to newly created jobs.	The pay for each factor is based on judgements that are subjective. The standard used for determining the pay for each factor may have built in biases that would affect certain groups of employees (females or minorities).

should be selected as having certain characteristics. 1. equitable pay (not overpaid or underpaid). 2. range of the compensable factors (for each factor, some jobs would be at the low end of the factor, while others would be at the high end of the factor). • The jobs are then priced and the total pay for each job is divided into pay for each factor. • This process establishes the rate of pay for each factor for each benchmark job. Slight adjustments may need to be made to the matrix to ensure equitable dollar weighting of the factors. The other jobs in the organisation are then compared with the benchmark jobs and rates of pay for each factor are summed to determine the rates of pay for each of the other jobs.		

METHOD	ADVANTAGES	DISADVANTAGES
Point Method (The point method is an extension of the Factor comparison method. • A set of compensable factors are identified as determining the worth of jobs. Typically, the compensable factors include the major categories of: 1. Skill 2. Responsibilities 3. Effort 4. Working Conditions	The value of the job is expressed in monetary terms. Can be applied to a wide range of jobs. Can be applied to newly created jobs.	The pay for each factor is based on judgements that are subjective. The standard used for determining the pay for each factor may have build in biases that would affect certain groups of employees (females or minorities).

• These factors can then be further defined. **1. Skill** a. Experience b. Education c. Ability **2. Responsibilities** a. Fiscal b. Supervisory **3. Effort** a. Mental b. Physical **4. Working Conditions** a. Location b. Hazards c. Extremes in Environment • The point method is an extension of the factor comparison method. • Each factor is then divided into levels or degrees which are then assigned points. Each job is rated using the job evaluation instrument. The points for each factor are summed to form a total point score for the job. • Jobs are then grouped by total point scores and assigned to wage/salary grades, so that similarly rated jobs would be placed in the same wage/salary grade.	

The quest to compensate employees fairly is an ongoing process. If an organization pays employees too little, it may lose valuable employees. If they pay too much, it loses company resources. Therefore, pay structure play an important role in an organization.

PAY STRUCTURE

Pay structure represents pay rates differences for jobs of unequal worth and the framework for recognizing differences in employee contribution. It defines the boundaries for recognizing employees contribution and therefore helps to retain potential employees.

The purpose of pay structure is to organize and demonstrate organization's compensation philosophy and to reflect and support the advancement of company's culture. An effective pay structure allows attracting and retaining the people who can help active their business goals. An organization's pay structure is a visible demonstration of companies' philosophy and strategy.

There are three challenges in developing a pay structure. We should determine —

(i) The appropriate data for establishing the relative value of a particular job in the organization.

(ii) The appropriate pay range for a job with the stated value to the organization.

(iii) The value of each job position within the allotted pay range.

There are following types of data used to determine pay structures.

(1) Ranking data: Traditionally, organization and pay structures were developed with an internal focus on creating equitable pay ranges dependent on job evaluations. This is known as the internal equity method. A different and currently favoured ranking method for job evaluation is the point factor method. In the point-factor method, certain aspects of job, such as skills required, work environment or level of authority are assigned points. The assigned points determine the ranking of a job in the organization's job hierarchy. Higher ranking jobs are more highly compensated.

The drawback to job evaluation ranking system's is that they depend largely on subjective decision-making and can be time consuming.

(2) Market pay-data: In the past decade, pay structure development has been more extremely focused and driven by market considerations. This is known as market pricing method. This method relies on market pay data usually obtained through commercial or professional association salary survey when certain job position, such as software developer position are highly valued in the market, the use of market data is critical to retain and attract talented candidates. However, jobs with less value in the market place are often overvalued when compared with data from market pay studies.

(3) Compensation approach:

Recently, organization's pay structures have been developed by combining both types of methods.

Compensation Specialists develop pay structure based on the following steps:

- Deciding on the number of pay structures. In this, companies often establish more than one pay structure, depending on market rates and the company's job structure. Companies pay structure includes pay structure based on job families based on geography.
- Group jobs with those that have a similar value to the organization; assess these groupings to determine the number of pay ranges needed to group the jobs by their value to the organization.
- Determine the pay for each job grouping by establishing a salary range that has minimum point, mid-point and maximum point for amounts allotted within the range. Many pay range in percentiles; pay is allotted at 25th percentile, the 50th percentile and the 75th percentile.

- Salary ranges are also determined by company policy. Each organization should consider that, what percentage of increase the organization will extend to an employee for a promotion.

The pay range for executive-level positions is normally the largest; the pay range for lower-level position is normally the narrowest.

Once the pay structure is determined, next assignment of monetary value is done to each employee's job.

- Mid-Point salaries in the range are often assigned to effective, but not outstanding performers.
- Maximum point salaries, or salaries above the 75th percentile, are assigned to the best performers whose job valuation best affects company business results.
- Minimum point salaries in the range are generally given to inexperienced employees.

An organization's compensation philosophy and pay strategy determines the approach one should take to allocate pay across the job ranges. Other factors that include are:

- Number of years of experience.
- Number of reporting staff members.
- Performance evaluation results.
- Hazardous working conditions.
- Education and professional certifications.
- Management opinions.

Developed effectively, the pay structure recognizes career development in addition to promotion. It clearly defines the value of each job and communicates the relationship of jobs to one another.

KEY TERMS	
Job evaluation	Grading method
Job grade	Point rating
Job specifications	Factor comparison
Job description	Pay structure
Ranking method	

SUMMARY

Job evaluation is the formal process used to assign wage and salary rates to a job or "it is a systematic and orderly process of determining the worth of a job in relation to other jobs."

The objectives of job evaluation includes:

(i) Determining the hierarchy and place the worth of each job of the organization,

(ii) To ensure fair and equitable wage structure on the basis of relative worth or value of jobs, to provide a framework for periodic review of wages.

(iii) To strengthen compliance with equal pay legislation and regulations that encourage basic pay on difference in job contents and

(iv) To produce pay structure that reconciles the conflicting demands of internal and external equity.

The process of job evaluation comprises of following steps:

Gaining acceptance of process, selecting key jobs for evaluation, Job description –

Job specification, Selecting job evaluation method, job rating, Assignment of money value to job, Implementation of process and periodic review.

There are four basic systems of job evaluation, which are grouped into 2 categories.

Non-quantitative methods/Non-analytical system.

(a) Ranking or job comparison.

(b) Grading or job classification.

Quantitative Methods/Analytical system

(a) Point rating.

(b) Factor comparison.

Pay structure represents pay rate differences for jobs of unequal worth and the framework for recognizing differences in employees contribution. The purpose of pay structure is to organize and demonstrate organization's compensation philosophy and to reflect and support the advancement of company's culture.

These are following types of data used to determine pay structures.

Ranking data, Market Pay-Data and Compensation Approach:

Other factors that include are:

Number of years of experience, Number of reporting staff members, Performance evaluation results, Hazardous working conditions, Education and professional certifications and Management opinions.

REVIEW QUESTIONS

1. What is Job evaluation? Explain its objectives and prepare the ground for evaluating jobs?
2. "Job evaluation does not usually price jobs." Discuss.
3. Explain different techniques of Job Evaluation. What are the advantages and disadvantages of each technique?
4. Should the job evaluation depend on an appraisal of the job-holder's performance? Why? Why not?
5. Compare and contrast the following methods of Job evaluation:

   Ranking Method

   Point Method

   Factor Comparison Method

   Grading Method.
6. Discuss the procedures involved in the evaluation of jobs.
7. What makes a Job Evaluation Program successful?

References

Armstrong, M. and H. Murlis, (1991) *Reward Management,* 2nd ed., Kogan Page/IPM, London.

Beach D. S., *Human Resource Management/personnel Management,* Newyork: Tata McGraw-Hill.

Dessler Gary, *Human Resource Management,* 9th ed, Prentice Hall of India, New Delhi, 2003.

Dunn J. D. and Frank Rachel, *"Wages and Salary Administration",* 1972.

Dwidedi R. S., *Managing Human Resource,* Galgotia Publishing Company, New Delhi, 1999.

Decanzo A. David and Robbins P. Stephen, *Personnel/HRM,* Prentice Hall of India, 3rd Ed. New Delhi, 1989.

Hollenbeck Noe and Wright Gerhart, *Fundamentals of Human Resource Management,* J.L Gray, and F.A. Starke,'Organization Behavior, Charles E. Merrill Co., Ohio, 1977.

K. Asahwathappa, *Human Resource Management,* 4th ed., Tata McGraw-Hill, New Delhi, 2005.

Mathis L. Robert and Jackson J.H., *Personnel/HRM,* Tata McGraw-Hill,1990.

Milton L. Rock, *Handbook of Wages and Salary Administration.*

Mejia Gomez, and Cardy Robert, *Managing Human Resources,* Pearson Education, New Delhi, 2001.

Milkovich, G. T., and Newman J. M., *Compensation,* (4th ed.). Homewood, Ill: Irwin.

Subramaniam K. N., *"Wages in India",* Tata McGrawHill., New Delhi.

Werther W. B. and Davis Keith, *Human Resource Management/Personnel Management.*

Newyork: Tata McGraw-Hill.

Wallace M.J. and Fay C.H., *Compensation Theory and Practice,* 1st ed. Tata McGraw-Hill.

BENEFITS & ADMINISTRATION

9

LEARNING OBJECTIVES

After studying this chapter, you will be able to understand —

- ⇨ Benefits determination Process
- ⇨ Employee benefits and Services
- ⇨ Legally required benefits – DA
- ⇨ Types of Retirement Plans
- ⇨ Employee Stock Option Plan (ESOP)
- ⇨ Flexible Compensation/Cafeteria plan

BENEFITS DETERMINATION PROCESS

Concept of Benefits: Benefits are considered to be the major factor in attracting and retaining employees. The provision of 'benefits and services' can be and important in maintaining the employees and reducing absenteeism and job turnover. This is called by various names, such as fringe benefits wage supplements, supplementary compensation, non-wage benefits, indirect benefits, hidden payment, etc. Benefits are group membership rewards that provide security for employees and their family members. These include all financial rewards that employees generally receive indirectly. They provide coverage for sickness, injury, unemployment, old age and death, health and life insurance, pensions and child care facilities.

Definition: Belcher defined benefits as *"any wage cost not directly connected with employees' productive, effort, performance, service or sacrifice"*.Cockman describes employee's benefits as *"those benefits which are supplied by an employer to or for the benefits of an employee, and which are not in the form of wages, salaries, and time rated payments"*.

EMPLOYEE BENEFITS AND SERVICES?

Employee benefits protect employees from risks that could jeopardize their health and financial security. They represent increased earnings to employees. The variety of possible benefits helps employers to tailor their compensation to the kinds of employees they need. It would also be simpler to pay all compensation in cash and let employees buy their own insurance and contribute to their own savings plans. Most of the benefits are not taxed and hence are advantageous to employees. The rationale behind providing benefits are:

1. Benefits and services attract and retain efficient and contented employees.
2. It helps to reduce employee dissatisfaction, absenteeism and turnover.
3. Managers that offer enticing benefits can use this advantage to recruit high-quality applicants.
4. There are certain benefits such as vacations, family and medical leave and sick days that helps the managers to be aware of these benefits to effectively manage work schedules.
5. Benefits seeks to enhance employee morale remain cost effective and introduce changes without much resistance.
6. It helps to improve and furnish the organizational image, thus improving its morale position.
7. It helps to maintain economic security, social security and unemployment insurance.

Types of Benefits

Various benefits provided to the employees may be classified on different basis.

U.S. Chamber of Commerce has classified employee benefits into four categories as follows:

(1) Legally required payments:

(i) Old age pension
(ii) Disability pension.
(iii) Unemployment insurance.
(iv) Worker's compensation.

(2) Contingent and deferred benefits:

(i) Pension plans.
(ii) Group life insurance.
(iii) Maternity leave.

(3) Payment for time not worked:

(i) Vacation.
(ii) Holidays.
(iii) Voting pay allowance.

(4) Paid rest periods:

(i) Waste-up time.
(ii) Lunch periods.
(iii) Christmas bonus.

(i) Legally-required Payments or Mandated Benefits

The federal and State Governments require various forms of legally required benefits to protect workers from the financial hardships of being out of work. They include Dearness Allowance, Social Security, Unemployment, Insurance, Worker's Compensation and Family and Medical Leave. These benefits are so designed to give the workforce a basic level of security. The cost of legally required benefits to employers is quite high. They pay a tax on employee's earnings for each of these required benefits.

Dearness Allowance

According to Pension rule 50A, the pensioners and the family pensioners are granted Dearness Allowance against the price rise. During the reemployment under Central or State Government or Government undertaking or Autonomous body or Local Body, they are not eligible to draw D.A., in case D.A. is allowed in addition to fixed pay or time scale. In other cases of reemployment D.A. is allowed subject to the limit of emoluments last drawn. D.A. is not allowed while the pensioner stays abroad and also in case of employees absorbed in public undertaking or bodies. If the pensioner stayed abroad without reemployment, he shall be eligible to draw D.A. on pension.

The Rates of Dearness Allowance

- Prior to 1972 there was no element of D.A. on Pension. From 01.04.1972 there was a flat rate of D.A. to all the pensioners 01.04.1972 @ Rs.5 ; 01.04.1973 @ Rs.10 ; 01.10.1973 @ Rs.15 ; 01.04.1974 @ Rs.20 ; 01.02.1975 @ Rs.28 ; 01.02.1976 @ RS.32 ; 01.04.1977 10 % subject to maximum of Rs.15 till15.09.1977. Rs.10 for those retired prior to 01.06.1961and Rs.5 after 01.06.1961 ; 01.04.1978 5% increase - minimum Rs.10, maximum Rs.25. From 01.04.1979 to 30.09.1984 there were 28 installments of D.A. paid to the pensioners at certain fixed rates for 13 slabs of pension amounts. From 01.10.1984 to date, the pensioners are paid D.A. at certain percentage of basic pension.
- Dearness Allowance is calculated on the original pension without commutation.
- Dearness Allowance is granted at certain percentage of basic pension and it is revised every 6 months from 01.07.1986 onwards based on cost of living index.

Social Security

The measures of social security have introduced an element of stability and protection and reduce stresses and strains of an individual. The ILO defines social security as "the protection which society provides for its members through a series of public measures, against the economic and social distress that otherwise would be caused by the stoppage or substantial reduction of earnings resulting from sickness, maternity, employment injury, unemployment, invalidity, old age and death, the provision of medical care and the provision of subsidies for families with children".

The concept of social security is essentially related to the high ideals of human dignity and social justice. The formation of ILO in 1919 to promote social justice through *(i)* international standards *(ii)* technical assistance and guidance and *(iii)* co-operation with other international organizations, provided the impetus and direction needed by most countries.

To be eligible for full social security benefits, a person must have worked 40 quarter year periods which equals 10 years of total employment. In India, over the years a number of legislative measures have been adopted to ensure benefits to employees of industrial undertaking under the scheme of social security.

The Social Security Act of 1935 created a system of retirement benefits. It also includes income for disabled, survivors of deceased workers and health care for the aged through the Medicare Program. Employers are required to share equally with employees the cost of old age and disability insurance. They pay the full cost of unemployment schemes. Social Security Program are increasingly being accepted as useful and necessary instruments for the protection and stability of the company. Defined benefits plans may be either funded or unfunded. In a funded plan, contribution from the employer and sometimes also from plan members are invested in a fund towards meeting the benefits. The future returns on the investments and the future benefits to be paid are not known in advance, so there is no guarantee that a given level of contributions will be enough to meet the benefits. Typically, the contributions to be paid are regularly reviewed in a valuation of the plans' assets and liabilities, carried out actually. In many countries such as USA, UK and Australia, most private benefit plans are funded, because Governments there provides tax incentives to funded plans.

In an unfunded plan, no funds are set aside. The benefits to be paid are met immediately by contributions to the plan. In some countries, such as Germany, Austria and Sweden, company run retirement plans are often unfunded.

Unemployment Assistant Schemes

The Social Security Act of 1935, established unemployment insurance to provide temporary income for people during periods of involuntary unemployment. In some states, the Governments have undertaken to provide work to the unemployed persons so that they may earn their living and in such cases, financial assistance is given if the Government is unable to provide employment. These are known as employment guarantee schemes. The Central Government has also introduced a variety of schemes to provide employment to the unemployed youths so as to relieve them of the hardships due to unemployment. These include National Rural Employment Programme, Rural Labour Employment Guarantee Program and the Jawahar Rozgar Yojna.

Worker's Compensation

The Principal of worker's compensation makes the employer liable to pay compensation for personal injury caused by accident in course of employment. It is the first social security measure which ensures relief for workmen and their dependants in case of accident in course of employment and resulting in death or disablement of workmen.

The Commissioner of Workmen's Compensation must be notified of the accident resulting in the death of an employee within 7 days of the date of accident. The amount of compensation is equal to 40% of the monthly wages of the deceased workman, multiplied by the relevant factor; or an amount of Rs.20,000/, whichever is more, where death results from injury. If the employer does not pay the compensation within one month from the date it falls due, the Commissioner may order recovery of not only the amount of arrears but also a simple interest at the rate of six percent per annum on the amount due. If there is no justification for the delay in the opinion of the Commissioner, an additional sum not exceeding 50 percent of such amount may be recovered from the employer by way of penalty.

Family and Medical Leave

The employees are entitled to medical attendance and treatment either under the contributory Health services scheme or under the Medical Attendance and Treatment rules which provide for reimbursement of the expenditure incurred on medical attendance and Treatment of the employees themselves as well as the members of their families. The employees are entitled to earned leave on full pay for 30 days and half pay leave for 20 days per year. Earned leave can be accumulated upto 240 days. Half day leave can be commuted into full pay leave on medical grounds up to a maximum of 240 days during one's service.

Voluntary Benefit

Retirement benefits, rest periods, vacations, medical care, compensation for injuries and disablement, subsidized food and housing, educational and cultural facilities, payment on life insurance, cafeterias (flexible compensation), maintenance of canteens, assistance to co-operative societies are some of the benefits voluntarily offered by employers.

1. **Retirement Benefits:** These benefits are provided by good employers, even before compulsion through legislation. There benefits generally consist of providing schemes for pension fund, provident fund and gratuity. (Explained in detail in Chapter 10.)

2. **Rest Period:** It is the time which allows workers some physical and mental diversion from their work. It is particularly popular among office job having heavy exertion or high repetition. These rest periods are however not free to the employer. The absolute cost to US employers for 20 minute rest period permitted to every employee in a day would exceed $ 62 billion a year. In case of adult workers in a factory, the period of work must be so fixed each day that no period shall exceed 5 hours, with an interval for rest of at least half an hour.

3. **Vacations:** Paid vacations vary from 15 days to 30 days in a year. These are given to the employee to provide a break to refresh him. The number of paid employee vacation days varies from employer to employer. The common trend is to relate the length of vacation to the length of tenure and job classification in the organization. For example, after six months' service with the organization, an employee may be eligible for one weeks' vacation, after a year, two weeks, after five years, three weeks, after 10 or more years, four weeks. If the individual is an executive, the vacation time is usually doubled. In contrast to normal paid vacation, the extended vacation is made available to employees every five to seven years, depending on the terms of the negotiation. It was found that vacations develop employee loyalty.

Sick Leave

It provides an employee pay when he is out of work due to illness. It is allocated on the basis of so many days a year, accrued on a cumulative basis, or expanded years of service with the organization.

Sick leave pay causes difficulty for many employees. The problem is that while many employees use their sick days only when they are legitimately sick, others use sick leave as extensions to vacations, whether they are sick or not. Employer has tried several tactics to overcome the problem. They used to repurchase unused sick leave at the end of the year by paying their employees equivalent sum of amount. Some organizations provide their employees with accident insurance to cover loss of income brought about by a long-term illness or disability. The range of payment is normally between 40-60 percent of an individual's weekly wage or salary. In case of permanent disability, coverage may include benefits up to the normal retirement age when pension benefits will be available to provide financial security.

Holidays

There are certain days in the year stipulated as paid holidays. Most organizations define these days to include Christmas, New Years, Labour Day, Thanksgiving day, on which the employees are paid and they do not have to work. These holidays are usually nine to eleven in number regardless of the employees' length of service. In India, Independence Day, Republic Day, Gandhi Jayanti, Deepawali, Dushera, Holi, Id, Christmas, Gurunank Jayanti, Mahaveer Jayanti are gazetted holidays.

Leave of Absence

This cover leave of absence for which pay is provided. This category includes absence for education leave, jury duty or military service Educational leaves are the usual province of managers or management trainees. There are some organizations like IBM and Xerox which permits employees to take a paid six-month or one-year leave in order to engage in community service i.e., Sabbatical leave. Also those employees who are active in their union are frequently given periods of time off each week, with pay, engaged in union administrative activities.

Housing Services

These services includes company-owned housing projects and subsidized housing with the high cost of housing or high risk in ownership, some organizations are building homes and rental units for a selected group of their employees. This service is mainly provided to attract and retain potential employees. Top executives in some organizations are provided free housing as they are required to do considerable entertaining and recreation activities.

Cultural Activities

There are certain activities provided to employees for their overall growth and to broaden the organizations' interest. They are free tickets to plays or operas, use of company library, club membership, organize athlete's events, arrange football and hockey tournaments, and provide picnics for their workers and employees. The cost of such benefits is usually minimal, yet they provide an opportunity for the employee's to grow and develop. It not only increases employee loyalty and interest but also strengthens employer employee relationships.

Disability Income

For people who become disabled, a monthly income comparable to retirement benefits is provided by social security. An individual must meet the requirements of disability insurance status to obtain disability benefits.

Retirement Plans

Many retirement plans have some form of disability retirement benefits. These plans often have some service and age requirement. It is an arrangement to provide people with an income or pension during retirement, when they are no longer earning a steady income from employment. Retirement plans may be set up by employers, insurance companies, the Government or other institutions such as employer associations or trade unions. Retirement plans may be contributory plans, meaning they are funded by contributions from the employer and employee or noncontributory plans, meaning all the contribution come from the employer. Retirement benefits include:

(a) Provident Fund

(b) Pension

(c) Deposit-linked insurance

(d) Gratuity

(e) Medical benefit.

Types of Qualified Retirement Plans

What Is a Qualified Retirement Plan?

It is a Retirement Plan maintained by an Employer that provides retirement income to employees and/or results in the deferral of income by employees for periods extending generally to the end of employment.

The employer is afforded favourable tax treatment (i.e., a deduction) for contributions made to the Plan assuming they fall within the prescribed IRS limits and the Plan meets all of the "qualification requirements" under the Internal Revenue Code.

Why Should a Company Adopt a Qualified Retirement Plan?

A Qualified Retirement Plan is one of the best tax shelters available. The company is allowed current tax deductions for it's contributions to the plan and the employee pays no tax on monies contributed to the Plan until a distribution is made. Also, earnings from investments made with the Plan funds accumulate tax free. Thus, long term employees (i.e., usually key employees) can accumulate large sums of money through the tax free build up of capital.

There are also non-tax reasons for adopting a qualified Plan. They attract good employees, reduce employee turnover; increase employee incentive and accumulate funds for retirement.

What are the Basic Types of Qualified Retirement Plans?

Qualified Retirement Plan Fall into Two Categories: *Defined Contribution Plans* and *Defined Benefit Plans.*

***Defined Contribution Plans* (DC Plans):** DC Plans are retirement Plans that provide for an "individual account" for each participant. The ultimate retirement benefit that each participant receives is dependent largely on two variables; the amount of employer contributions or forfeitures allocated to the account and the investment experience of the fund (earnings, gains/losses, expenses, etc.) There is no guaranteed retirement benefit (i.e. no "Defined Benefit"). DC Plans include the following:

A defined contribution Plan specifies what contribution the employee and employer will make to the employees' retirement or savings fund. It will provide a payout at retirement that is dependent upon the amount of money contributed and the performance of the investment vehicles utilized. There are many kinds of defined contribution plan. They are:

Deferred Profit Sharing and Employee Stock Ownership Plan

It is a defined contribution employee benefit that allows employees to become owners of stock in the company they work for. It is equity based deferred compensation plan. There are several features that make ESOPs unique as compared to other employee benefit plans. In an ESOP, the organization's distributes shares of stock to its employees by placing the stock into a trust managed on the employees' behalf. Employees receive regular reports on the value of their stock and when they leave the organization, they may sell the stock to the organization or (if it is a publicly traded company) on the open market. It is required by law to invest primarily in the securities of the sponsoring employer.

How does ESOP works?

(i) The ESOP operates through a trust, set up by the company that accepts tax deductible contributions from the company to purchase company stock.

(ii) The contributions made by the company are distributed to individual employee's accounts within the trust.

(iii) The amount of stock each individual received may vary according to pre-established formulas based on salary, service, or position.

(iv) The employees may cash out after vesting in the program or when they leave the company. The amount they may cash out may depend on the vesting requirements.

(v) When an ESOP employee who has at least ten years of participation in the ESOP reaches the age 55, he or she must be given the option of diversifying his/her ESOP account up to 25% of the value. This option continues until the age of sixty, at which time the employee has a one time option to diversify upto 50% of his/her account. This requirement is applicable to ESOP shares allocated to employees' accounts after December 31st, 1986.

(vi) Employees receive the vested portion of their accounts at termination, disability, death, or retirement. These distributions may be made in a lumpsum or in installments over a period of years. If employees become disabled or die, they or their beneficiaries receive the vested portion of their ESOP right away.

Advantages

(i) **Capital Appreciation:** Companies sell some or all of their equity to employees and by doing so, converts corporate and personal taxes into tax-free capital appreciation. This allows the owner to sell 100% of his or her company to get money out tax-free and still maintain control of the company.

(ii) **Incentive Based Retirement:** It provides a cost-effective plan to motivate employees.

(iii) **Tax Advantage:** It enables tax advantage purchasing of stock of a retiring company owner. With this purpose, a company owner may sell their shares to the ESOP and incur no taxable gain on the sale. A company owner can sell all or some of the company to the employees cost free. It has been found that owners who sell 30% or more of their company to an ESOP are allowed to "roll-over" and proceeds into their securities and defer taxation on the gain.

(iv) **Reduction of Tax Liability:** A company can reduce to corporate income taxes and increase its cash flow and networth by simply issuing treasury stock or newly issued stock to its ESOP.

Disadvantages

(i) **Defection:** If the ESOP is used to finance the companies' growth, the cash flow benefits must be weighed against the rate of dilution.

(ii) **Fiduciary liability:** The committee members of the plan are deemed to be fiduciaries and can be held liable if they knowingly participate in improper transactions.

(iii) **Liquidity:** If the value of the stock appreciates substantially, the ESOP and/or the company may not have sufficient funds to repurchase stock, upon employees' retirement.

(iv) **Stock Performance:** If the value of the company does not increase, the employees may feel that the ESOP is less attractive than a Profit sharing plan. In an extreme case, if the company fails, the employees will lose their benefits to the extent that the ESOP is not diversified in other investments.

(a) **Money Purchase Plan:** The employer specifies a level of annual contributions that are invested and when the employee retires, he or she is entitled to receive the amount of the contributions plus the investment earning.

(b) **401 (K) Plan:** It is a defined contribution plan in which employees may defer income upto a maximum amount allowed. Employees contribute a percentage of their earnings and employers may make matching contributions. The amount employees contribute is not taxed as part of their income until they receive it from the plan. Its matching feature makes it attractive to both employers and employees. Employees' benefit by accumulating tax-deferred retirement funds, employers benefit by reducing their risk, since there is no payment required when the employee leaves or retires. Usually, employees are free to decide individually how they wish to invest their funds.

(c) **Hybrid Plan:** It is a desired approach to retirement plan. It is a cash balance plan, with elements of both defined benefit and defined contribution plan that have notional balances in hypothetical accounts where, typically, each year the plan administrator will contribute an amount equal to a certain percentage of each participant's salary.

There is a switch from traditional benefit plans to cash balance plan, as it is more generous to young employees who will have many years ahead to earn interest.

Defined Benefit Plans **(DB Plans):** DB Plans are retirement Plans other than "individual account Plans" . In other words......any Plan that is not a Defined Contribution Plan usually is a Defined Benefit Plan. In a Defined Benefit Plan the ultimate retirement benefit is stated (i.e.: "definitely determinable".). The benefit is based on the Plan formula, your salary, and , in most cases, the number of years of service you work for your the employer. The ultimate benefit is called the "retirement benefit" and the amount/portion of that benefit that you have earned at any point in time is called your "accrued benefit". In most cases...you will only earn your full retirement benefit (i.e: "fully accrue your benefit) if you continue your employment until the "normal retirement age" stated in Plan document.

If a Plan is classified as a Defined Benefit Plan the following is true

(a) retirement benefits are geared to the Plan Formulas not to contributions

(b) it is not an individual account plan

(c) the annual employer contribution is actuarially determined

(d) some benefits may be insured by the PBGC.

A primary difference between the "Defined Contribution Plans" like the 401(k) Plan or Profit Sharing Plan and a "Defined Benefit Plan" is that the investment risk under a "Defined Contribution" Plan lies with the employee participant and the investment risk, under the "Defined Benefit Plan" lies with the employer sponsor.

The "Defined Benefit" Plan defines and promises a specific benefit at some point in the future. This defined benefit is provided typically at the retirement of the employee participant. For example, a typical benefit may be a monthly income starting at age 65 equal to 50% of the employee's average salary over the last three years of work.

The employer is required to contribute, and may deduct, whatever amount is actually necessary to assure the benefit is funded, which places the investment risk with the employer, not the participant. If the investments do not perform as projected, the employer may have more to contribute in the future.

Benefit accrual tends to reward long-term service, and because with older employees there is less time for assets to accumulate to fund the benefit, contributions for older employees generally are much higher than younger employees. Thus, older business owners, seeking large contributions often favour defined benefit plans.

For aging management groups who have little chance to save for retirement, a defined benefit plan is an excellent way to make up for lost time. A defined benefit plan provides the only way for companies to make annual tax-deductible contributions for their employees in excess of $41,000 or 100% of pay [the maximum for "defined contribution" plans].

For example, the following are the maximum contributions for 2004 that are tax deductible for defined benefit plans and defined contribution plans.

COMPARATIVE ANALYSIS **Defind Benefit Plan vs. Defined Contribution Plan**		
SCENARIO #1 Company owner is aged 50 and earns more than $205,000. Two other employees aged 25 and 30 earn $25,000 and $30,000 respectively.		
Age 50	$65,000	$41,000
Age 25	$1,800	$5,000
Age 30	$3,000	$6,000
SCENARIO #2 Company executives are aged 55 and 50 and earn more than $205,000 each. Two other employees aged 25 and 30 earn $25,000 and $30,000 respectively.		
Age 55	$117,000	$41,000
Age 50	$65,000	$41,000
Age 25	$1,800	$5,000
Age 30	$3,000	$6,000

However, because of the required funding costs, and potential growing funding liability for older employees, the number of defined benefit plans has dropped over the past decade. As the baby boom of employees is growing older and becoming more transitory in employment, larger employers have steered away from defined benefit plans to employee participatory plans such as 401(k) plans.

TYPES OF RETIREMENT PLAN

This chart provides quick details for each of the main types of employee retirement plans from traditional 401(k) plans to various kinds of Individual Retirement Accounts (IRA).

Table 9.1

Plan type	Summary	Annual plan limits*	Key feature	Notes
Traditional 401(k)	For any type or size company. Funded by employee elective deferrals and optional employer matching.	$15,000 in employee deferrals and up to $29,000 in optional matching funds; catch-up limit: $5,000.	Matching contributions can be vested over time.	Requires yearly discrimination testing to prevent investing primarily from highly-compensated staff members.
403b	For any non-profit business, government entity, or educational institution. Funded by employee elective deferrals and optional employer matching.	$15,000 in employee deferrals and up to $29,000 in optional matching funds; catch-up limit: $5,000.	"15-Year Rule": employees with 15 years service can contribute an additional $15,000 over five years.	Typically features fewer investment options than traditional 401(k) plans.
Safe Harbor 401(k)	For any size company. Funded by mandatory employer and optional employee contributions.	$44,000 (total employee and employer contributions); catch-up limit: $5,000.	Employer contributions 100% vested from day one. No discrimination testing required.	Employer must make contributions even when business is not doing well.
Simple 401(K)	For businesses with 100 employees or less and no other retirement plan.	$10,000 (total employee and employer contributions); catch-up limit: $5,000.	Employer contributions 100% vested from day one. No discrimination testing.	Considerably lower annual limits than traditional 401(k) plans.
Solo 401(k)	For self-employed, sole proprietors, partnerships, corporations, S-corporations. Covers owner and spouse only. Funded by salary and profit share contributions.	$44,000; catch-up limit: $5,000.	Features high contribution limits.	Must convert to traditional 401(k) or SIMPLE 401(k) once you add any non-spousal employees.

SEP-IRA	For self-employed and small businesses under 25 employees. Funded by employer contributions only.	$44,000 (based on years of service, performance, and employee salary)	Employer contributions 100% vested from day one.	Can supplement with another retirement plan.
SIMPLE IRA	For small businesses with 100 employees or fewer. Funded by mandatory employer and optional employee contributions.	$10,000 (matched or fixed contributions); catch-up limit: $2,500.	Employer contributions 100% vested from day one. Can reduce contributions when business is not doing well.	Considerably lower annual limits than traditional 401k plans.
KEOGH	For law partnerships, medical practices, and family businesses with 10 or fewer highly paid employees. Funded by employee and employer contributions.	$44,000 (defined contribution); $175,000 (defined benefit).	Defined contribution: Amount employees receive at retirement varies based on years of service, earnings, expenses, gains, and losses Defined benefit: Formula provides fixed monthly income upon retirement	Defined benefit is very complex; employer responsible for administration and investment choices. Defined contributions allow employees to make their own investment decisions.

FLEXIBLE COMPENSATION OR CAFETERIA STYLE OF COMPENSATION

It is a type of compensation which refers to compensation program that allows employees to choose what type and how much of each reward is desired during the coming year. It is also known as smorgasbord which allows employees to choose from a selection of employer provided benefits such as life insurance, health insurance, pension, unemployment compensation, and rest provided vacations etc. It was basically designed to enable senior executives, top professionals and managers to choose individually many of these benefits and services. The demands of services depend on their age, their educational and income levels, their life style and other forms of preferences. Recent studies suggest that flexible or cafeteria compensation programs are becoming increasingly popular among employees. It provides an opportunity to contain the costs of the benefit package and provides benefits on a more tax-effective basis. It also increases loyalty and motivation of employees, which in turn enhances productivity.

Benefits provided in a cafeteria compensation approach are:

- Accidental death, dismemberment insurance
- Bonus eligibility

- Business and professional membership
- Club membership
- Cash profit sharing
- Automobile allowance
- Medical assistance
- Housing allowance
- Deferred Bonus or Deferred Compensation Plan
- Dental and eye care insurance
- Education costs
- Free or subsidized lunches
- Group Life Insurance
- Health maintenance fees
- Interest-fee Loans
- Long-term disability benefit
- Recreational facilities
- Saving Plans
- Sabbatical leaves
- Sickness and accident insurance
- Stock bonus plan and stock purchase plan

Source: Robert M. Noe and R. Wayne Mondy, HRM. p.-346.

Features of Cafeteria Style Compensation

Under this programme, the employee is told that his total compensation mode is of, say Rs.2,000/- and than he can choose mix of salary life insurance, deferred compensation and other benefits that suit his particular needs. Each of the options carries a price and the employee can select up to Rs.2,000/- of salary – those items that he feels best suit his personal needs.

While adopting the programme, the management should remember that the most of younger employees are more concerned with "take home pay" than with "retirement benefits". On the other hand, older employees are more concerned about retirement and pension programmes.

Types of Cafeteria Plans

The two most popular types of cafeteria plan are:

(i) Pre-tax premium conversion plans

(ii) Flexible spending arrangements (FSA's)

(i) *Premium Conversion:* It is the simplest type of cafeteria plan which permits employees to pay their share of premiums for health coverage, life insurance and other qualified benefits such as disability insurance on a pre-tax basis. This plan converts what would otherwise be after-tax employee contributions to pre-tax contribution by means of an employee's election prior to the beginning of the year, to reduce pay and to have the company contribute the amount of the reduction to pay for the coverage selected by the employee.

(ii) *Flexible Spending Arrangements or flexible spending accounts:* It lets employees pay for certain benefit's expenses such as dental care, medical and dependent care expenses on a pre-tax basis periodically, employees can elect the amount of salary reduction dollars they wish to allocate to various elements in their plans. There are two types of FSA's –

(a) Health and

(b) Dependant care

In Health FSA employees may set aside money to pay for health plan deductibles and co-payments as well as other uninsured medical care expenses, such as dental or vision expenses, on a pre-tax basis.

In Dependent FSA, employees may be reimbursed for dependent care expenses that enable the employee and spouse to work. They are not subject to the uniform reimbursement requirement.

(i) The information regarding employee satisfaction with flexible compensation plans is limited. However, the employers hope that it will improve the understanding of the benefits provided.

(ii) These plans are very costly. The cost for development and administration exceeds those for traditional plans.

Advantages

(i) Employees can choose benefits that meet their individual needs and adjust those choices annually as needs change.

(ii) It help employers control costs by ensuring that money is not spent on benefits, that employees neither want nor need.

(iii) By offering more flexible cafeteria type benefits, employers gain an edge in attracting and retaining valuable employees.

(iv) It helps in improving employer-employee relationships, as giving employees control over their benefits promotes goodwill and creates a partnership in the benefit programs between both the parties.

(v) Cafeteria plans address the wide variation in benefit needs of diverse employees.

(vi) It helps in developing better understanding of the benefit package, as employees are actively involved in the selection process.

KEY TERMS

Flexible compensation	Defined benefit plan
Deferred benefits	Defined contribution plan
Qualified retirement plan	Dearness allowance
Hybrid plan	ESOP

SUMMERY

Benefits are considered to be the major factor in attracting and retaining employees. The provision of 'benefits and services' can be an important factor in maintaining the employees and reducing absenteeism and job turnover.

Various benefits provided to the employees may be classified on different basis.

U. S. Chamber of Commerce has classified employee benefits into four categories as follows:

(1) Legally required payments:

(i) Old age pension

(ii) Disability pension

(iii) Unemployment insurance

(iv) Worker's compensation.

(2) Contingent and deferred benefits:

(i) Pension plans

(ii) Group life insurance

(iii) Maternity leave.

(3) Payment for time not worked:

(i) Vacation

(ii) Holidays

(iii) Voting Pay Allowance

(4) Paid rest periods:

(i) Waste-up time

(ii) Lunch periods

(iii) Christmas Bonus

Qualified Retirement Plan Fall Into Two Categories: *Defined Contribution Plans and Defined Benefit Plans.*

DC Plans are retirement plans that provide for an "individual account" for each participant. It specifies what contribution the employee and employer will make to the employees, retirement or savings fund. There are many kinds of defined contribution plan. They are:

Deferred Profitt Sharing and Employee Stock ownership Plan:

DB Plans are retirement plans other than "individual account plans". In other words......any plan that is not a Defined Contribution Plan usually is a Defined Benefit Plan. In a Defined Benefit Plan, the ultimate retirement benefit is stated (i.e., "definitely determinable"). Flexible Compensation or Cafeteria Style of Compensation. It is a type of compensation which refers to compensation program that allows employees to choose what type and how much of each reward is desired during the coming year. It is also known as smorgasbord which allows employees to choose from a selection of employer provided benefits such as life insurance, health insurance, pension, unemployment compensation, and rest provide vacations etc.

REVIEW QUESTIONS

1. Research the current trends in defined contribution and defined benefit program. From the employee's perspective, what program is preferable and why?
2. Describe what you believe to be some of the more important employee benefits offered by an employee. Why?
3. What is cafeteria or flexible plan? What hurdles must be overcome before such plans will achieve greater acceptance and use?
4. Describe the operations and benefit of ESOP.
5. What are the various types of Qualified Retirement Plan? Explain their characteristics in detail.

References

Henderson, Richard I., *Compensation Management in a Knowledge-Based World.* 9th ed. Upper Saddle River, NJ: Prentice Hall, 2003.

Kleiman, Lawrence S., *Human Resource Management: A Tool for Competitive Advantage.* Cincinnati, OH: South-Western College Publishing, 2000.

Milkovich, George T., and Jerry M. Newman, *Compensation.* 8th ed. New York: McGraw-Hill/Irwin, 2005.

Warner, S. and Ward S.G., (2004) Recent Compensation Research: An Eclectic Review. *Human Resource Management Review,* 14: pp. 201-227.

Windhalm International and NFTC. (1999). *Global Relocation Trends,* 1999 Survey Report.

Armstrong, M. & Stephens, T. (2005). *Handbook of Employee Reward Management and Practice.* London and Sterling, VA: Kogan Page.

Balkin, D. B. & Gomez-Mejia, L. R., (1990). *Matching Compensation and Organizational Strategies.* Strategic Management Journal, 11: pp.153-169.

STATUTORY PROVISIONS RELATED TO COMPENSATION 10

LEARNING OBJECTIVES

After studying this chapter, you will be able to understand —

- ➯ Workmen's Compensation Act,1923
- ➯ Employee's State Insurance Act,1948
- ➯ The Employee's Provident Fund Act,1952
- ➯ The Payment of Gratuity Act, 1972.
- ➯ Maternity Benefit Act, 1961
- ➯ Payment of Bonus Act, 1965
- ➯ Law of Minimum Wages Act, 1948
- ➯ Payment of Wages Act, 1936
- ➯ Equal Remuneration Act, 1976

WORKMEN'S COMPENSATION ACT, 1923

The principle of Workmen's Compensation was formally adopted in India in 1923, it makes the employer liable to pay compensation for personal injury/caused by accident in course of employment. There were various amendments in this Act and finally came into force on July 1, 1923.

The provisions of the Workmen's Compensation Act, are following:

- It is the first social security measure undertaken in India which ensures relief for workmen and their dependants in case of accidents in course of employment and resulting in death or disablement of workmen.
- Claims under the Workmen's Compensation Act fall under the following categories:
  - (a) Accidents result in temporary disablement.
  - (b) Accidents results in permanent, partial or total disablement.
  - (c) Fatal accidents.

- Compensation for permanent total disablement and permanent partial disablement is payable on the scale prescribed. All claims for permanent disability must be recorded by a memorandum of agreement with the commission for workman's compensation.
- The Commissioner for Workmen's compensation must be notified of accident resulting in the death of an employer within 7 days of the date of accident. If the death of the workman was caused by an accident arising out of and in the course of his occupation or employment, compensation is payable and the amount of compensation must be deposited with the Commissioner within 30 days after receiving the notice of demand from the Commissioner.
- As amended, December 1972, this Act is applicable all over India to factories, mines, plantations, transport establishments, construction works, railway and other hazardous occupations.
- The amount of compensation is equal to 40% of the monthly wages of the deceased workman, multiplied by the relevant factor, or an amount of Rs. 20,000/- whichever is more, where death results from injury.
- At the time of total disablement an amount equal to 50% of the monthly wages of the deceased workman multiplied by the relevant factor or an amount of Rs. 24,000/- which ever is more, on the basis of enhanced rates, the minimum and maximum compensation payable in case of death is Rs.20,000 and 90,000 and in case of disablement is Rs. 24,000 and 11,400 respectively depending on the wages and age of the workman and the time of his death and disablement.
- Whether temporary disablement, whether total or partial, results from the injury, the workman will receive a half monthly payment equivalent to 25% of his monthly wages. This half monthly payment is payable from the date of disablement where such disablement lasts for a period of 28 days or more.
- Where permanent partial disablement result from the injury, compensation payable such a percentage of the compensation payable in the case of permanent total disablement, as is proportionate to the loss of earning capacity caused by the injury.
- If the employer does not pay the compensation within one month from the date it fell due, the Commissioner may order recovery of not only the amount of arrears but also a simple interest at the rate of six percent per annum on the amount due. If there is no justification for the delay in the opinion of the Commissioner, an additional sum not exceeding 50 percent of such amount may be recovered from the employer by way of penalty.
- Breach or violation of the provisions of the Act, is punishable.
- Returns, notices and statements to Commissioner must be sent correctly.

EMPLOYEE'S STATE INSURANCE ACT, 1948

- This is a social welfare legislation to help employees from the hardships arising from sickness, maternity, invalidity, accidents, occupational diseases, unemployment, old age and death.
- This Act covers smaller factories using power and employing 10 or more persons and those not using power but employing 20 or more people. They have also made the Act applicable to shops, hotels, cinemas including theatres, road transport, undertakings and newspaper establishments employing 20 or more persons with the approval of the Central Government.

- The scheme is administered by an autonomous corporation with the Minister of Labour at the centre assists Chairman, the Union Health Minister as the Vice-Chairman, the representatives of the state- Governments, employers and the medical profession nominated by the Central Government. This Act covers all employees whose monthly wages and salary (basic pay + D.A.) do not exceed Rs. 3,000 and who are employed either directly or through contractor, or whose services are hired or lent for the factory i.e., manufacturing process. The term "employee" as defined under the Act also includes persons connected with administration of the factory, purchase of raw material and distribution or sale or product of the factory or establishment. It also includes workers employed in a hospital maintained by a factory, persons who maintain buildings, watchman, gardener, employee of the head office of a factory, part-time workers and doctors. But it excludes apprentices engaged under the Apprentices Act of 1961 or under the standing orders of the establishment, casual workers, construction workers, any member of Indian Naval, Military or Air force.
- This scheme is financed by contribution from employers and employees, with the State Governments sharing one-eight of the cost of the medical care. The employer pays 4.7% of the wage bill, a maximum of Rs. 7.50 per week on the highest wage scale, and the insured person pays about 2.3% of his wage, around Rs. 4 per week. The maximum corresponding daily benefit rate for the insured person is Rs. 15. The State Government which implements the scheme is reimbursed to the extent of 7/8 of the expenses incurred on workers families and ¾ of the expenses incurred in the case of workers. In order to qualify for the benefit, the worker should have contributed to the scheme for a minimum period of 12 weeks.
- This Act has created a Fund known as Employee's State Insurance Fund, wherein the contribution, grants, donations are paid. This fund is utilized not only for the administration of the scheme, but also for giving cash and medical benefits to employers and their families, construction and maintenance of hospitals and dispensaries and other institutions and provision of medical and other ancillary services for the benefits of insured person. The benefits provided under the scheme includes:
  (a) Sickness and extended sickness benefit
  (b) Maternity benefit
  (c) Disablement benefit
  (d) Dependants benefit
  (e) Funeral benefit
  (f) Medical benefit.
- A special feature of the Act is that if an employee dies as a result of injuries sustained in the course of his employment, his dependants are entitled to receive the benefit. When a person is entitled to any of the benefits provided by the Employee State Insurance Act, he shall not be entitled to receive any similar benefit under any other enactment.

THE EMPLOYEE'S PROVIDENT FUND ACT, 1952

The Act was passed in 1952, with the objective of making some provisions for the future of the industrial worker after he retires, for the dependants in case of his early death and to cultivate a spirit of saving among the workers. It prescribes the obligation of the employers and employees and the authorities for the implementation of its provisions.

This Act applies to all factories and other establishments falling under any notified industry and employing 20 or more workers. Once the Act is applied, it does not cease to be applicable even if the number of employees falls below 20. In regard to employees, this Act is applicable to all persons who are employed directly or indirectly through contractor in any kind of work, manual or otherwise. The Employee's Provident fund scheme formulated under this Act covers all employers with monthly pay upto Rs. 3500/-.

- Worker's in establishments employing 20-50 persons pay 6.25 percent of their earnings and those with a larger strength pay 8 percent. Employers make an equal contribution.
- The Provident fund is refunded with interest in the event of death, permanent disability, superannuation, retrenchment, migration or on leaving service. On retirement, or after 15 years of service, a worker receives his own share and the employer's contribution varies according to the length of service.
- A member can withdraw to a certain extent from the fund account for any of the following purposes:
  - To pay insurance premium
  - To purchase or construct a property or house
  - To repay loans
  - To repair or make improvements or alterations of the house
  - To meet the expenses in case of illness, marriage of daughter, higher education of children, damage to property due to any natural calamity, unemployment on account of layoff or lockout.

PAYMENT OF GRATUITY ACT, 1972

Like the Employer's Provident Fund Act, the Payment of Gratuity Act of 1972 is a social security measure which the Government has undertaken to provide some protection to industrial workers against the risk of old age. This Act was passed in 1972, to provide a scheme for the payment of gratuity to persons employed on industrial and commercial establishments.

- This Act is applicable to all factories, mines, oilfields, plantations, ports, railways, shops or establishments in which 10 or more workers are employed.
- Every employee, irrespective of his remuneration, is entitled to receive gratuity if he has rendered service for 5 years or more. Gratuity is payable at the time of termination of service on account of retirement, resignation, death, or disablement due to accident or disease. The conditions of five years of continuous service is not applicable if the termination is due to death or permanent disablement.
- For calculating gratuity the rates of 15 days wages is to be based on the rate of wages last drawn by the employer concerned. In case of piece rated employee, daily wages are to be computed on the average of the total wages received by him for a period of three months

immediately preceding the termination of his employment. In the case of monthly related employee, the gratuity is to be calculated by dividing the monthly wage by 26 working days and multiplying the quotient by fifteen.

- For the payment of gratuity, the term "wages" includes all emoluments which are earned by an employee while on duty or on leave in accordance with his terms and conditions of employment and which are paid to him in cash and includes dearness allowance, house rent allowance, overtime wages and any other allowance. The Act extends to the whole of India and is applicable to employees in factories covered by the Factories Act and Shops and Establishments Act and all establishments, local bodies, etc.

MATERNITY BENEFIT ACT, 1961

- This Act regulates employment of women in certain establishments for certain periods before and after child birth and provides maternity and certain other benefits. The Act is not applicable to women employee covered by the Employer State Insurance Act.
- A women employee is entitled to a maximum of twelve weeks maternity leave, six weeks before and six weeks after her delivery. During the period of leave the employee is entitled to full wages/salary. The employee is also entitled to a medical bonus of Rs.25, if no prenatal confinement and post natal care has been provided by the employer free of charge. To avail of the leave and benefits, the employee should have put in 160 working days of service in the 12 months immediately preceding the date of expected delivery.
- In case of death of a woman employee, eligible for maternity benefits, the employer shall pay the amount of benefit to her nominee or legal representative as the case may be. In the case of miscarriage, a woman shall on production of prescribed proof, be entitled to leave with wages at the rate of the maternity benefit for the period of six weeks following the day of her miscarriage. If a woman allowed going on maternity leave, work in any other establishment for any period during the authorized leave, she forfeits the maternity benefit for such period.

PAYMENT OF BONUS ACT, 1965

This Act provides for the payment of bonus, linked with profit or productivity, to the employees in factories and establishments. The Supreme Court in *New Maneek Chowk Spinning and Weaving Company vs. Textile Labour Association* 1961 Guj. 521 at 526 suggested four types of bonus, namely–

(i) Production Bonus

(ii) Bonus as an implied term of contract between the parties.

(iii) Customary bonus in connection with some festival.

(iv) Profit Bonus.

Profit Bonus has given statutory recognition in the Payment of Bonus Act. Under this, the quantum of bonus depends on the extent of profit obtained in the relevant year.

- Bonus is payable to all categories of employees drawing wages up to Rs. 4,000/pm and engaged in any kind of work, whether skilled, unskilled, managerial, supervisory, manual, etc., except apprentices. An employees dismissed from services for fraud, riotous or violent behaviour, theft, misappropriation or sabotage of any property of the establishment is not eligible for bonus.

- The Act is designed
  (1) To impose statutory liability upon the employer of every establishment covered by the Act to pay bonus to employees in the establishment.
  (2) To define the principles of payment of bonus according to the prescribed formula.
  (3) To provide for payment of minimum and maximum bonus and linking payment of bonus with the scheme of set-off and set-on.
- This Act applies to every factory and every other establishment in which 20 or more persons are employed on any day of the accounting year. Bonus will be paid within 8 months from the closure of the accounting year.
- Bonus is regarded as deferred wages payable to employees. It is a right accrued to them by the Act and not a charity on the employer.
- The responsibility is imposed upon the Employer to calculate bonus and distribute it within 8 months from the closure of accounting year. If the provisions of Act 21 of 1965 are contravened, the punishment is imprisonment for a term which may extend to Rs. 1,000/- or with six months fine or both.
- Every employee is entitled to get a minimum bonus which shall be 8.33% of the salary or wage earned by him during the accounting year or Rs. 100/- whichever is higher.
- In case of employees having not completed 15 years of age at the beginning of accounting year, the minimum bonus is reduced to Rs. 65. It is well settled law that minimum bonus has to be paid even if the company is in loss.
- The Maximum bonus payable is not to exceed 20%.
- All the employees of General Insurance Companies, L.I.C., Central and State Government establishments, Indian Red Cross society, universities and educational institutions, hospitals, Chamber of Commerce, RBI, UTI, local bodies, etc., are also not entitled to bonus under the Act. If they are paid bonus, it is *ex-gratia* payment.

LAW OF MINIMUM WAGES ACT, 1948

It is an Act to provide fixing minimum rates of wages in certain employments. It is meant to help workmen to strike of fair bargain with their employers and ensure fair wages for them.

- This Act purports to achieve the prevention of exploitation of labour and for that purpose, authorize the appropriate government to take steps to prescribe minimum rates of wages in scheduled industries.
- The Act contemplates that minimum wages rate must ensure not the mere physical need of the worker which could keep him just only but also consider the following norms,

  The Norms for fixation of minimum wage are:

  (i) The standard working class family should be taken to consist of three consumption units for the one earner, the earnings of women, children and adolescents should be disregarded.

(ii) The minimum food requirement should be calculated on the basis of net intake of 2700 calories for an average Indian adult of moderate activity.

(iii) Clothing requirements should be estimated at capital consumption of 18 yards per annum which would for the average workers family of four, a total of 72 yards.

(iv) In respect of housing, the rent corresponding to the minimum area provided for under ground. Industrial Housing Scheme should be taken into consideration in fixing the minimum wage.

(v) Fuel, lighting and other miscellaneous items of expenditure should constitute 20% of the total minimum wages. Keeping in view, the socio-economic aspect of the wages structure, the Supreme Court added the following additional components as need for fixing the minimum wage in the industry:

(vi) Children education, medical requirement, minimum recreation including festivals, ceremonies and provision for old age, marriages etc., should further constitute 25% of the total minimum wages.

- The employees are entitled to the minimum wage at all times and under all times and under all circumstances. An employer who cannot pay the minimum wage has no right to engage labour and no justification to run the industry.
- The Act extends to the whole of India and applies to all establishments employing one or more persons in scheduled employment.

PAYMENT OF WAGES ACT, 1936

This is an Act to regulate the payment of wages, imposition of fines and deduction from wages to persons' employed in industry, drawing less than Rs.1,600/- per month. The main objections of this Act are:

(i) To pay the wages to the employees.

(ii) To pay the wages at proper time as specified in the Act.

(iii) To prevent unauthorized deductions.

- The Act is applicable to persons employed in any factory, railway and to such other establishments to which the State Government may, by notification, extend the provisions of the Act, after giving three months notice to that effect.
- The responsibility for the payment of wages under Sec. (3) of the Act is that of the employer or his representative. In the absence of an employeer, a person who employs the labourers and with whom they enter into a contract of employment will be regarded as an employer.
- No wage period shall exceed one month in any case. The main purpose of this provision is to ensure that immediate delay is not caused in the payment of wages and a long time does not elapse before wages are paid for which an employee has worked. Moreover, the Act is concerned merely with the fixation of wage periods and not with the fixation of wages.
- Where less than 1,000 persons are employed, wages shall be paid before the expiry of the 7th day and in other cases before the expiry of the 10th day, after the last day of the wage period.

- In case the employee terminates the services of an employee, he is entitled to receive the wage earned by him before the expiry of the 2nd working day from the day on which his employment is terminated Sec. 5 (2).
- Wages are to be paid to the employed person without deductions of any kind except those authorized by or under the Act, withholding of increment or promotion, reduction to a lower post or time scale or to a lower stage or time scale and suspension, are not to be deemed to be deductions from wages.
- Any contract or agreement whereby an employed person relinquishes any right conferred by this Act shall be null and void.

EQUAL REMUNERATION ACT, 1976

The Act provides for payment of equal remuneration to men and women workers for same work or work of a similar nature and for prevention of discrimination on ground of sex against women in the matter of employment.

- The Act prohibits an employer from reducing the rate of remuneration of any worker for the purpose of employing with the above provision relating to payment of equal remuneration to men and women workers for the same work or work of a similar nature.
- While making recruitment for the same work or work of a similar nature or in any condition of service subsequent to recruitment such as promotion, training or transfer, the employer is prohibited from making any discrimination against women except where the employment of women in such work is prohibited or restricted by or under any law in force. These provisions are effective on and from the commencement of the Act.
- For the purpose of providing increasing employment opportunities for women, the Central and State Governments are required to constitute one or more Advisory committees to advice them with regard to the extent to which women may be employed in such establishments or employments, as specified by the Central Government.
- The provision of the Act relating to requirement of equal treatment for men and women do not apply, if:
  (a) the terms and conditions of a woman's employment are, in any respect, affected by compliance with the law regulating the employment of women\;
  (b) any special treatment is accorded to women in connection with the birth, or expected birth of a child. In these cases, the requirement of equal treatment of men and women does not apply.

KEY TERMS	
Workmen's Compensation	Production Bonus
Employee State Insurance	Minimum Wage
Provident Fund	Equal Remuneration
Payment of Gratuity	

SUMMARY

The principle of Workmen's Compensation Act was formally adopted in India in 1923. It makes the employer liable to pay compensation for personal injury/caused by accident in course of employment. There were various amendments in this Act and finally came into force on July 1, 1923.

The principle of Employee's State Insurance Act, 1948: This is a social welfare legislation to help employees from various hardships. This Act has created a Fund known as Employee's State Insurance Fund, which is utilized not only for the administration of the scheme, but also for giving cash and medical benefits to employees and their families, construction and maintenance of hospitals and dispensaries and other institutions.

The Employee's Provident Fund Act , 1952:The objective is for making some provisions for the future of the industrial worker after he retires, for the dependants in case of his early death and to cultivate a spirit of saving among the workers.

The Payment of Gratuity Act, 1972. : It is a social security measure which the Government has undertaken to provide some protection to industrial workers against the risk of old age.

Maternity Benefit Act, 1961: This Act regulates employment of women in certain establishments for certain periods before and after childbirth and provides maternity and certain other benefits.

Payment of Bonus Act, 1965:This Act provides for the payment of bonus, linked with profit or productivity, to the employees in factories and establishments

Law of Minimum Wages Act, 1948: It is an Act to provide fixing minimum rates of wages in certain employments. It is meant to help workmen to strike off a fair bargain with their employers and ensure fair wages for them.

Payment of Wages Act, 1936: This is an Act to regulate the payment of wages, imposition of fines and deduction from wages to persons' employed in industry, drawing less than Rs.1, 600/- per month.

Equal Remuneration Act, 1976:The Act provides for payment of equal remuneration to men and women workers for same work or work of a similar nature and for prevention of discrimination on the ground of sex, against women in the matter of employment.

REVIEW QUESTIONS

1. Explain in detail salient features of Workmen's Compensation Act.
2. Explain in detail salient features of Employee's State Insurance Act.
3. What are the provisions provided under Employee's Provided Fund and Employee's Gratuity Act?
4. What are the salient features of Maternity Benefit Act.
5. Write short notes on:
   (i) Payment of Bonus Act
   (ii) Types of Bonus
   (iii) Payment of Wages Act

(iv) Minimum Wage Act

(v) Equal Remuneration Act

References

Beach D. S., *Human Resource Management/Personnel Management,* New York: Tata McGraw-Hill.

Dunn J. D. and Frank Rachel, " *Wages and Salary Administration*", 1972.

Dwidedi R. S., *Managing Human Resource,* Galgotia Publishing Company, New Delhi, 1999.

Mammoria C. B., *Dynamics of Industrial Relations,* Kalyani Publishers, 1995.

Milton L. Rock, *Handbook of Wages and Salary Administration.*

Subramaniam K. N., *"W ages in India",* Tata McGraw-Hills., New Delhi.

COMPENSATION OF SPECIAL GROUPS

11

LEARNING OBJECTIVES

After studying this chapter, you will be able to understand —

- ➪ Top executives
- ➪ Special features and components
- ➪ Compensation strategy for special groups
- ➪ Component of executive compensation
- ➪ Why executives are paid more
- ➪ Culture and pay
- ➪ Summary and conclusion
- ➪ Key terms
- ➪ Review questions

TOP EXECUTIVE

All organizations have specific goals and objectives that they strive to meet. Top executives devise strategies and formulate policies to ensure that these objectives are met. Although they have a wide range of titles such as chief executive officer, chief operating officer, board-chair president, vice-president, country administrator and formulate policies and direct the operation or business and corporation and other organizations.

A corporation's goals and policies are established by the chief executive officer in collaboration with other top executives, who are over seen by Board of Directors. In a large corporation, the chief executive officer meets frequently with subordinate executives to ensure that operations are conducted in accordance with these policies. The chief executive officer of corporation retains over-all accountability, however a chief operating officer may be delegated several responsibilities, including the authority to oversee executives who directs the activities of various departments and the organization policies on a day-to-day basis. In publicly held and no profit corporations, the Board of Directors ultimately is accountable for the success or failure of the enterprise and the chief executive officer reports to the Board.

In addition to being responsible for the operational success of a company, top executives also are increasingly being held accountable for the accuracy of their financial reporting particularly among publicly traded company.

Nature of the Work

The nature of the responsibilities of other high level executives depends on the size of the organization. In a small organization, such as independent retail stores or small manufactories, a partner, owner or general manager often is responsible for purchasing, hiring, training, quality control and day-to-day supervisory duties. In large organizations, the duties of executives are highly specialized. Some managers, for instance, are responsible for the overall working of the organization such as manufacturing, marketing, general operations, manager's plan, direct, or co-ordinate their operations of companies or public private sector organizations. Their duties include formulating policies, managing daily operations , planning the use of materials, human resources, but are to diverse and general in nature to be classified in any one area of management or administration, such as personnel, purchasing or administrative services.

Chief Executive Officers

Chief executives have overall responsibility for the operations of their organizations, working with executive staff, they set goals and arrange programs to attain these goals. Executives also appoint department heads, who manage the employees who carry out programs.Chief executive officers carry out a number of other important functions such as meeting with staff and board members to determine the level of support for proposed programs, sales purchasing, finance, personal training, administrative services, transportation or legal services.

Chief Financial Officers

He directs the organization financial goals, objectives and budgets. They oversee the investment of fund and manage associated risks, supervise cash management activities, executives, capital raising strategies to support a firm's expansion, and deal with merger and acquisitions.

Chief Information Officers

They are responsible for the overall technology direction of their organization. They are increasingly involved in the strategies business plan of a firm as a part of the executive team. These managers propose budgets for projects and programs and make decisions on staff training and equipment purchases. They supervise the work of these employees, review their output, and establish administrative procedures and policies. They also provide organizations with the vision to master information technology as a competitive tool. Have devised several strategies to attract workers into supervisory jobs. The most popular method is to key the base salary of supervisor to some amount exceeding the top-paid subordinate in the unit.

Executives

The CEO of a fortune 500 firm makes on average $ 10.6 million a year, an increase of 442 percent during the past decade. Some CEOs made more than $ 100 million in the early 2000s. CEOs earn approximately 240 times what the average employee makes, up from 42 times in 1980, far more than in any other industrialized nation both on absolute and relative ground. That is, U.S. CEOs make more money than CEOs in other countries and they earn more, compared to what the average worker does than CEOs from any other nation earns.

Employment of Top Executives

Employment of top executive including chief executives, general and operations managers, and legislators is expected to grow 2 percent from 2006 to 2016. Because the managers are essential to the success of any organization, their jobs are unlikely to be automated or offshore to other countries. Some top executives jobs may be eliminated through industry consolidation, as upper management is streamlined after merger and acquisitions.

Projected employment growth of top executives varies by industry, e.g., employment growth is expected to grow faster than average in professional, scientific and technical services and about as fast as the average in administrative support services.

COMPENSATION STRATEGY FOR SPECIAL GROUPS

Supervisor

The major challenge in compensating supervisors centres on equity. Previously, the supervisor's compensation was just like that of lower level managers. Due to which they make less money and little incentive. A typical board of directors comprises 10 outside the company and 3 inside directors, each having a term average of three years. But modern boards have changed considerably, approximately two thirds of boards now include more outside directors than inside directors (e.g., CEO, corporate officers) and this move to more outside directors comes with a price-higher compensation. The companies are planning to increase board pay because of competetion been found that total director's compensation ranges from $ 40,000 to the low $ 50,000. In addition to cash compensation, there is an increasing emphasis on directors rewards that attempt to link to corporate performance.Our survey sample of more than 75 proxies from fortune 500 companies gives us rich insight into the efforts boards are pursuing to secure and improve the appropriateness, fairness and effectiveness of compensation pay, for performance has been embraced by 100 percent of our sample group as the guiding philosophy for executive compensation.

- There is an undisputed escalation in CEO compensation i.e., the median cash compensation paid to S & P 500 CEOs has more than doubled since 1970 (in 1996 – constant dollars), and median total realized compensation (including gains from exercising stock options) has nearly quadrupled.

COMPONENTS OF EXECUTIVE COMPENSATION

Although there is substantial heterogeneity in pay practice across firms and industries, most executive pay packages contain 4 basic components: as base salary, an annual bonus tied to accounting performance, stock options and long terms incentive plans (including restricted stock plans and multi-year accounting based performance plans). In addition executives participate in "board based" employee benefits and Perks including life insurance and supplemental executive retirement plans (SERP's). In contrast to mid-level management "employment at will" arrangement, top executives increasingly negotiate formal employment contrast. These formal contrast typically last five years and specify minimum base salaries, target bonus payments with or without guarantee and severance arrangements in the event of separation or change in corporate control.

1. Base Salaries

Base salaries for CEOs are typically determined through competitive "benchmarking" based primarily on general industry surveys (except for utilities and financial institutions, which utilize industry specific surveys), and supplemented by detailed analysis of selected industry or market peers. The surveys, which report a variety of pay percentiles (e.g., 25th, 50th, 75th), typically adjust for company size either through size groupings or through simple log-linear regressions of log (salary) on log (size). Size is traditionally measured using company revenues, although market capitalization increasingly used especially in start ups with low revenues but high capitalization executives devote substantial attention to the salary – determined process, even through salaries comprise a declining percentage of total compensation. First base salaries are a key component of executive employment contrast (which typically guarantees minimum increase in base salaries for the subsequent five years.)

Second, since base salaries represent the "fixed component" in executive contracts, risk adverse executives will naturally prefer a dollar increase in base salary to a dollar increase in "target" bonus or variable compensation. Components of compensation are measured relative to base salary levels.

2. Annual Bonus Plans

Virtually, every profit company offers annual bonus plan covering its top executives and paid annually based on single year's performance. Inspite of their prevalence and importance, however most descriptions of executive bonus plans in the literature are a anecdotal non-representative, or gleaned from voluntary (and non-random) disclosures in company proxy statements. Inspite of substantial heterogeneity across companies and industries, executive bonus plan can be categorized in terms of 3 basic component.

These components are performance measure, performance standards, and the structure of pay performance relation. It has been found that annual bonus contracts are largely explicit with at the most a limited role for discretion. Discretion in annual bonuses shows up in a variety of possible ways. In some firms, boards can exercise discretion allocating a fixed bonus pool among participating executives, but the discretion in this case affords only individual allocation and not the overall amount of the payouts. In addition, the CEO (and other executives) will have some portion of their bonus that depends on "individual performance". Although there is a subjective flavor here, individual performance often includes, and performance relative to some predetermined objectives or strategic milestones, in any case, the weight on individual performance rarely exceeds about 25% of the executive's bonus.

3. Long Term incentive plans

In addition to bonus plans based on annual performance, many companies offer "Long term incentive plans (LTIP), typically based on rolling-average three or five years' cumulative performance.

Executive benefits since many benefits are tied to income level (e.g.,: life insurance, disability insurance, pension plans) executive typically receive higher benefits than most other employees.

In addition to ERISA – controlled defined benefit and defined contribution retirement plans, corporate executives are provided with an array of supplemental retirement programs that ensures that they receive equal, if not better, retirement programs than those offered to the remainder of the workforce.

4. Perquisites

Perquisites or perks enhance the quality of life of the executives and satisfy several of their needs. One type of perk is internal, i.e., providing a little something extra while the executive is inside the company, a luxury office, special parking, an executive dining room. A second category comprises perks that are also company related but are designed for business conducted externally such as company –paid–membership in clubs associations and payment of hotel, resorts, airplane, auto expenses etc. Another category is personal perks, which includes free home repairs, low cost loans, personal and legal counselling expenses for vacation homes, use of company property personally etc. Some of the commonly provide perks are company provided car, kidnap and ransom protection, attending professional meetings and conferences, spouse travel, club membership, season tickets to entertainment events, special relocation allowance, medical expense reimbursement, use of company credit card, no and low interest loans, college tuition reimbursement for children and most important is to provide loans at preferred rates of interest to assist them in exercising stock options (purchase stock options).

In addition to participating in company-wide retirement programs, top executives routinely participate in supplemental executive's retirement plans (SERPS). SERPS are non-qualified for tax purposes and can take a variety of different forms, including defined benefits based "credited" years of service which can deviate substantially from "actual" years of service or variable benefits based on inflation or company performance. A major goal of a SERP is to enable key officials to receive post retirement income that is commensurate with the compensation received by these top executives during active employment. It can be useful in standardizing retirement benefits in a multinational corporation or a divisionalized firm with different kinds of retirement plans.

Brief History of Executive Compensation

The Year	The Key Event
1974	Michael Bergerac cracks the $1 million mark when recruited to Revlon.
1979	Chrysler's Lee Lacocca takes $1 million plus 400,000 option shares.
1983	William Bendix becomes the first executive to collect a huge golden parachute (contract clause for payment in a takeover leading to termination) of $3.9 million over five years.
1984	Congress tries to limit exercise golden parachutes but gives rise to unintended consequences– the rules actually lead to larger amounts.
1986	New law gives favourable tax treatment to stock option awards. Sizes increase.
1987	Lee Lacocca receives first megagrant of stock options: 820,000 option shares worth 15.3 times his salary and bonus that year.
1987	Junk bond expert Michael Milkin explodes through the $5 million mark in salary and bonus.
1987	Leon Hirsch of US Surgical gets even larger megastock option award, worth 126 times his salary and bonus.
1992	Securities and Exchange Commission roles CEO salaries must be disclosed more often in proxy statements. Easier availability of peer compensation data service to drive up the standard.
1992	Michael of Walt Disney exercises low-cost stock options for pre-tax profit of $126 mollion.
1993	New tax law sets upper limit on tax-deductible executive compensation at $1 million but has unintended effect of raising bar to that level.
2000	Charles Wang, Computer Associates inti executive, cracks two-thirds of billion-dollar mark.
2003	Alfred Lerner, MBNA executive, is top-paid CEO, with $195 million, a drop from prior years, leading to speculation that furor over CEO pay is finally having an impact.

Source: Business Week, April 17, 2000, p. 100, April 23, 2003; and Wall Street Journal, April 11, 1996, p. R4.

Fig. 11.1

Long-term Incentive for Executives

Type	Description	Comments
Incentive stock options	Purchase of stock at a stipulated price, conforming with internal Revenue Code (Section 422A).	No tax at grants. Company may not deduct as expense.
Non-qualified stock options	Purchase of stock at a stipulated price, not conforming with internal Revenue Code.	Excess over fair market value taxed as ordinary income. Company may deduct.
Phantom stock plans	Cash or stock award determined by increase in stock price at a fixed future date.	Taxed as ordinary income. Does not require executive financing.
Stock appreciation rights	Cash or stock award determined by increase in stock price during any time chosen (by the executive) in the option period.	Taxed as ordinary income. Does not require executive financing.
Restricted stock plans	Grants of stock at a reduced price with the condition that it may not be sold before a specified date.	Excess over fair market value taxed as ordinary income.
Performance share/unit plans	Cash or stock award earned through achieving specific goals.	Taxed as ordinary income. Does not require executive financing.

Source: B. Ellig, The Complete Guide to Executive Compensation (New York: McGraw-Hill, 2002).

Fig. 11.2

CEO – SALARY

Who sets CEO's salary? There is no doubt, however, that CEOs and other top managers exert at least some influence on both the level and structure of their pay. Generally, there is a compensation committee consisting of two or more "outside" directors; although all major decisions related to top-level pay are passed through this committee, the committee rarely conducts market studies of complete pay levels or proposes new incentive plans, and only seldom retains its own compensation experts rather, initial recommendations for pay levels and new incentive plans typically emanate from the company's human resource department, often working in conjunction with outside accountants and compensation consultants. These recommendations are usually sent to top managers for approval and revision before being delivered to the compensation committee for consideration. The CEO typically participates in all committee deliberations, except for discussions specifically dealing with the level of the CEO's pay. The committee either accepts the recommendations or send them back for revisions. If accepted, the committee passes its recommendations for the approval of the full board of directors.

Top 5 Executives' Total Compensation (in millions)

	2002 Salary and Bonus	Long-Term Compensation	Total Pay
1. Alfred Lerner, MBNA	$9.0	$185.9	$194.9
2. Jeffrey Barbakow, Tenet Healthcare	$5.5	$111.1	$116.6
3. Millard Drexier, Gap	$2.5	$88.5	$91.0
4. Dennis Kozlowski, Tyco International	$4.0	$67.0	$71.0
5. Irwin lacobs, Qualcomm	$1.8	$61.6	$63.3

***Source*:** L. Lavelle, F. Jepersen, S. Ante and J. Kerstetter, "Executive Pay," Business Week, April 21, 2003.

Fig. 11.3

CULTURE AND PAY

Culture is defined as shared mental programming which is rooted in the value, benefits, and assumptions held in common by a group of people and which influence how information is processed. It is the complex mixture of assumptions, behaviours, stories, myths, metaphors and other ideas, but together it defines what it means to be a member of a particular society.

It is very critical for culture in managing international pay. The assumption that pay system must be designed to fit different national cultures is based in the belief that most of a country's inhabitants share a national character. Therefore, the job of the global manager is to define the national characteristics that influence pay system. It is widely affected by the Hoffstede cross cultural model who had proposed various attributes like power distance, uncertainty avoidance, individualism – collectivism and masculinity – feminity.

Advocates of this view believe that "it is crucial that companies adjust their compensation practices to the culture specifics of particular host country. The countries that have high power distance follows hierarchial pay structure (Malaysia and Mexico). In low power distance nation, egalitarianism is preferred (Australia and Netherlands) i.e., to place most of their employees in different but under the same compensation plan. This plan gives firms more flexibility to deploy employees in different areas without having to change their pay levels. It also reduces barriers between people who need to work closely together. Companies operating in nations with "collectivistic" cultures should use egalitarian pay structures, equal pay increases, and group–based rather than individual–based performance incentives. (Singapore, Japan, Israel, and Korea).Employers in the more "individualistic" national cultures, should use individual – based pay and performance based increases (United States, United Kingdom and Hong Kong).

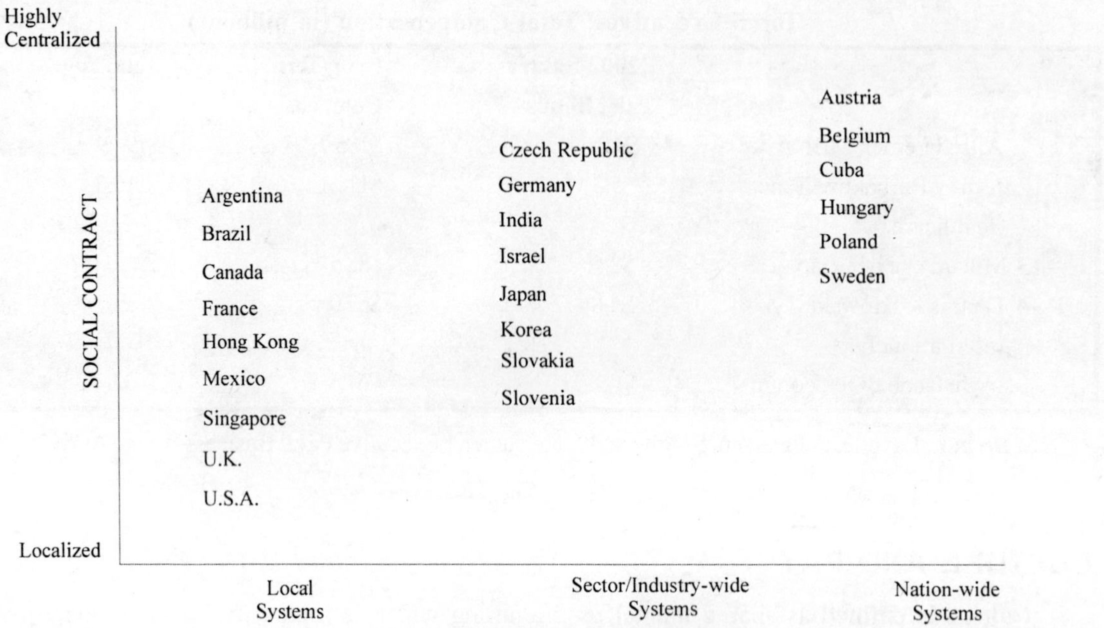

Fig. 11.4 Social Contracts and Pay

KEY TERMS

Base salary	Perks
Annual bonus plan	Long-term incentive
SERP's	

SUMMARY

Top executives devise strategies and formulate policies to ensure that these objectives are met although they have a wide range of titles such as chief executive officer, chief operating officer, board-chair president, vice-president, country administrator etc.

The chief executive officer of corporation retains overall accountability, however a chief operating officer may be delegated several responsibilities. The nature of the responsibilities of other high level executives depends on the size of the organization.

Chief Executive Officers have overall responsibility for the operations of their organizations, working with executive staff; they set goals and arrange programs to attain these goals. Chief Financial officers direct the organization's financial goals, objectives and budgets.

Chief Information Officers are responsible for the overall technology direction of their organization.

They are increasingly involved in the strategies business plan of a firm as a part of the executive team.

Employment of top executive including chief executives, general and operations managers, and legislators is expected to grow 2 percent from 2006 to 2016.

The components of Executive Compensation are as base salary, an annual bonus tied to accounting performance, stock options, and long-terms incentive plans (including restricted stock plans and multi-year accounting based performance plans). In addition, executives participate in "board based" employee benefits and also receive special benefits including life insurance and supplemental executive retirement plans (SERP's).

There is no doubt, however, that CEOs and other top managers exert at least some influence on both the level and structure of their pay. Generally, there is a compensation committee consisting of two or more "outside" directors; although all major decisions related to top-level pay are passed through this committee, the committee rarely conducts market studies of complete pay levels or proposes new incentive plans, and only seldom retains its own compensation experts rather, initial recommendations for pay levels.

Culture is defined as shared mental programming which is rooted in the value, benefits and assumptions held in common by a group of people and which influence how information is processed.

REVIEW QUESTIONS

1. What are the various components of an Executive compensation plan?
2. What are the duties and responsibilities of Top executives in the organisation?
3. Justify the galloping hike of CEOs' salary in the current scenario.
4. Comment on "Culture and pay of an expatriate in the global compensation
5. Identify and describe the components included within long term compensation.

References

Tosi, H. L., & Gomez-Mejia, Luis, R. (1989). The Decoupling of CEO Pay and Performance. An Agency Theory Perspective. *Administrative Science Quarterly,* 34: pp.169-189.

Windhalm International and NFTC.(1999). *Global Relocation Trends,* 1999. pp.Survey Report.

Hofstede, G.., (1984). *Culture's Consequences: International Differences in Work-related Values.* Thousand Oaks, CA: Sage Publications, Inc.

Gomez-Mejia, L. R., (1994). Executive Compensation: A Reassessment and a Future Research Agenda. *Research in Personnel and Human Resource Management,* 12: pp.161-222.

Towers Perrin, *"Worldwide Total Remuneration",* (1997).

Peter Dowling, Denice E. Welch and Randall S. Schuler, *"International Human Resource Management",* South Western College Publishing.

12 INTERNATIONAL COMPENSATION

LEARNING OBJECTIVES

After studying this chapter, you will be able to understand —

- Objectives of international compensation
- Responsibilities of an international manager
- Compensation plan for an expatriate
- Elements of compensation package of an expatriate
- Various approaches to international compensation
- Repatriation
- Managing global compensation
- Summary and conclusion
- Key terms
- Review questions

Meeting the challenge of recognizing and rewarding employees in the global economy will be the cornerstone of business success in the 21st century. While most organizations have not anticipated the resources required to meet this challenge, one thing is certain that globalization does not mean applying uniform human capital solutions in a diverse world. Globalization has increased the awareness of and concern for creating internationally equitable compensation systems in many companies. The complex nature of international compensation dictates that it receives special attention from organizations operating in a multinational environment. It is crucial that organizations understand the kind of employees employed by international firms, the elements that comprise an international compensation system and the special problems associated with returning citizens on overseas or employment to their home corporation for multinational firms. Successful management of compensation and benefits requires knowledge of the employment and taxation laws, customs, environment and employment practices of many foreign countries.

Also needed are familiarity with currency fluctuations and the effect of inflation on compensation and an understanding of why and when special allowances must be supplied and which allowances are necessary in what countries.

Most employers remain wedded to the traditional home-based method of expatriate pay. But it is found that 'one size fits all' approach to expatriate remuneration is not necessarily the most effective. There should be a wide gap between wages paid for comparable position in different countries due to difference in economic system, political, legal and cultural environment. Therefore, HR managers spend a great deal of time developing effective compensation and benefit programs for international employees and its importance gain tremendous success.

OBJECTIVES OF INTERNATIONAL COMPENSATION

- To utilize specific expertise possessed by the employer.
- To reduce risk of perceived inequities and simplifying the job by maintaining equitable wage-rate cross culturally.
- To enable the organization to attract and retain potential candidates, thereby matching local and regional standard.
- To stimulate performance and behaviour of an individual leading to organizations success.
- To understand the difference of compensation practice across organizations and to overcome the complexity in global design rewards.
- To enable the organization to optimize its total wage level.
- To broaden on employees or manager perspectives relative to the international operation.
- To facilitate the transfer and relation on international employees.
- To offer financial protection in terms of benefits, social security and living costs in the foreign location for employees.
- To raise the expectation of an employee in terms of career advancement and repatriation.

RESPONSIBILITIES OF AN INTERNATIONAL COMPENSATION MANAGER

- Partner closely with international HR, business managers, and executives to resolve grievances related to HR, compensation and systems.
- Work with HR generalists, HRIS, benefits and compensation to maintain consistent international approach and support.
- Evaluate design HR process and programs to support business results.
- Research, develop and administer appropriate international compensation plan.
- Develop monitor international data base by individual country.
- Develop people process to support entry into new global markets.
- Participate in and analyze results of compensation surveys for international management positions.

- Work with staffing to maintain expatriate administration and develop expatriate packages with our culture and philosophy.
- Maintain summaries of all international compensation plans by location.

Tools for Managing International Compensation

- Design an international compensation management grading system that corresponds identically to your domestic grading system.
- International salary ranges by country that allow you to smoothly expatriate a manager overseas, or from country to country and back home again without disruption.
- Reliable external compensation market data on competitive pay level for each major function.
- A standardized performance measurement system that weighs the contribution made by management in a consistent fashion regardless of where the executive is stationed.
- Salary increase guidelines that properly motivate and reward performance and are in line within your worldwide compensation strategic plan.
- A base delivery method that complies with local country laws and still remain integrated with your overall base pay systems.

Requirement of an Effective International Manager

- Strong analytical skills and ability to work will with matrices, numbers and trends.
- Proven ability to manage a growing organization.
- Ability to work in a fast paced, rapidly changing environment.
- Significant prior recruiting and management experience.
- Very bright and assertive with the ability to pick up new technologies and assess situation questions in existing international regions and entry into new countries.
- Great people skills at all levels of the company.
- Strong emphasis on team play rather than politics.
- Creative problem solver.

COMPONENTS OF INTERNATIONAL COMPENSATION

Establishing a compensation plan for a job in a foreign location begins with the determination of base pay. It is similar to the structure of domestic compensation program.The main components includes–

- Base salary and base pay
- Indirect monetary compensation (benefit)
  - (i) Fringe compensation including standard benefit
  - (ii) Relocation assistance

(iii) Education reimbursement for expatriate children
(iv) Home leave benefit and travel reimbursement
(v) Rest and relaxation leave and allowance.

- Equalization Benefit:
  (i) Cost of living allowance
  (ii) Education allowance for children
  (iii) Foreign service premium
  (iv) Emergency leave
  (v) Club membership
  (vi) Spousal employment
  (vii) Cross cultural training.
- Incentives:
  (i) Stock options
  (ii) Mobility premiums
  (iii) Perquisites
  (iv) Performance related rewards.

Base Salary

It is the amount of money that an expatriate normally receives in the home country. It is finally determined after establishing consistent compensation measures between countries that builds credibility both at home and abroad. Some multinational companies conduct their own local annual compensation survey which covers all forms of compensation including cash, short and long term incentives, retirement plans, medical benefit and perquisites.

There are various methods for setting base the pay. U.S companies use one of the three methods to calculate expatriates, base pay.

- Home country based method
- Host country based method
- Headquarters based method

(***Source***: Joseph Mertoechis).

In the United States, the rate of base pay was around $ 75,000 for upper middle managers in the late 1990's and this rate was similar to that paid to managers in both Japan and Germany.

The home country based pay method is often most appropriate for expatriates. The market or going rate of pay for a comparable job in the home country is normally used for setting this rate. This method of home country based pay is most suitable to an expatriates. The assignments are short in duration and local nationals performing comparable jobs receive substantially higher pay.

The host country based method compensation is based on the host country's pay scale and is suitable when assignments are of long duration. The expatriate's base pay will be competitive with other employees base pay in the host country rather than their counterparts at home.

The headquarter based method compensates all employees according to the pay scales used at the headquarter. This method is suitable for expatriate who move from one foreign assignment to another and rarely work in their home countries.

Indirect Monetry Compensation (Benefit)

The benefit package for expatriates is generally the same as the one provided in the home country.

- **Fringe compensation including standard benefits.** Benefits represent an important expatriate's compensation packages. It not only brings as sense of security among expatriates and their families but also makes their living more acceptable and enjoyable at the foreign site. Some of the fringe benefit include health benefits, company car, driver, domestic staff and child care, assistance to spouse in finding suitable and acceptable employment, medical, vacation, holidays, and emergency leave.
- **Relocation assistance:** This component covers expatriates expenses to relocate to foreign posts. It typically involves moving, shipping and storage charges that are associated with personal furniture, clothing, and other items that the expatriates and his or her family are taking to the new assignment. Some of the relocation assistance payment include:
- Temporary quarters prior to departure because the expatriate's house has been sold or rented.
- Transportation to the foreign post for employees and their families.
- Reasonable expenses incurred by the family during travel.
- Temporary quarters while waiting for delivery of household goods or while looking for suitable housing.
- Moving household goods to the foreign post.
- Storing household goods in the United States.

Source: Joseph J. Martocchio

- **Education reimbursement for expatriate's children:**

  It is also an integral part of the compensation package. These expenses cover costs such as tuition, transportation, enrollment fees, books' supplies, school uniform etc. Expatriate's typically place their children in private schools designed for English speaking students.

- **Home leave benefits & travel reimbursement:**

  This benefit enables an expatriate to make contact with his family either by calling or taking paid time off in the country. To avail this facility, an expatiate should serve in the foreign country for one year or six months. If time duration an expatriate is longer of, then he deserves a long leave and *vice versa*. In most companies, expatriates are even reimbursed for expenses associated with travel between the two destinated countries.

- **Rest and relaxation leave and allowance:**

  It has been found that an expatriate working in hardship locations may need some extra time away from the unpleasant conditions to get relaxed and recharge their energies. An expatriate may spend his time as designated by companies which also includes travel expense.

- **Equalization benefits:**

  These benefits are intended to keep expatriates in the same financial condition they were in, before accepting an overseas assignment and to reduce any negative aspects of living in a foreign country.

- **Cost of living allowance (COLA):**

  Cost of living allowance is the payment for differences between the home country and the overseas assignment. The difference is in terms of cost of food, other consumable items, services and housing in the home country and cost of those items in host country. The allowance is designed in such a manner so as to provide the expatriate with the same standard of living in both the countries. The provision of a housing allowance implies that employee's should be entitled to maintain their home country living standards or, in some cases, receive accommodation that is equivalent to that provided for similar foreign employees and peers.

- **Housing allowance:**

  Employers provide expatriate employees with housing and utility allowance to cover the difference between housing and utilities cost in the home and host country. Some firms provide the expatriate with a residence during the assignment and pay all associated expenses. Others give predetermined housing allotment each month and let expatriate choose their own residence.

- **Foreign service premium**:

  These are the monetary payments above and beyond regular base pay and typically range between 10% and 30% of base pay. FSPs are generally categorized as an incentive bonus for performing the assignment in the host country. These premiums generally apply to assignments that extend beyond one year. Some organizations are now granting expatriates lumpsum bonuses in lieu of FSPs which are made at the time of expatriation and repatriation.

- **Hardship allowance**:

  This allowance compensates expatriates for their hardships while working in hazardous areas or an area with a poor quality of life. Employers disperse hardship allowances in small amounts throughout the duration of expatriate's assignments. These allowances are offered at exceptionally severe locations such as Eastern Europe, China and some Middle-Eastern countries. It ranges from 10% to 25% of base pay, however increases with greater hardships. There are various criteria to identify hardship locations such as isolation, inadequate transportation facilities, inadequate housing, severe climate and lack of health facilities.

- **Emergency leave:**

  Paid leave for personal or family emergencies is a component of most expatriates' compensation package, such emergencies include critically ill family members or their deaths in the foreign post. Some companies also provide unpaid emergency leave of absence thereby bearing travel expenses between the destinated countries.

- **Club membership:**

  Country club memberships are provided to executives who use such facilities in the performance of their jobs.

- **Allowances for spouse assistance:**

  It helps to guard against or offset income lost by an expatriate's spouse as a result of relocating abroad. Some firms may pay an allowance to make up for a spouse's lost income. US firms are beginning to focus on providing spouses with employment opportunities abroad, either by offering job-search assistance or employment in the firm's foreign office.

- **Cross cultural training:**

  It helps in managing expatriate's expectation and creating learning. Which Provides more opportunities during their assignment. They can understand better what will be important to them in their assigned destination. They can also calibrate their expectations versus the experience of other expatriates in that destination. It also helps to achieve objectives that may be essentially unrealistic in their own context in their case, they may expect rewards that may never come.

- **Incentives:**

  In recent years, some MNC's have also been designing special incentive programmes for retaining expatriates.

Various Approaches to International Compensation

There are two main options in the area of international compensation:-

(a) The going rate approach (also referred to as the market rate approach).

(b) The balance sheet approach (also known as the build up approach).

The Going Rate Approach

The key characteristic of this approach are, the base salary for international transfer is linked to the salary structure on the host country. The multinational usually obtains information from local compensation surveys and must decide whether local national (MNC's) expatriates of the same nationality, or expatriates of all nationalities will be the reference point in terms of bench marking.

Advantages of Going Rate Approach

- This approach is simple and easy for expatriates to understand.
- Expatriates are able to identify with the host country, and there is often equality among expatriates of different nationalities.
- There is equality with local nationals which is very effective in attracting PCNs' or TCN's to a location that pays higher salaries than those received in the home country.

Disadvantages

- There can be variation between assignments for the same employees – most probably when we compare as assignment in an advanced economy with one in a developing country, and also between assignments in various advanced economies where difference in managerial salaries and the effect of local taxation can significantly influence an employee's compensation level using the going rate approach.
- There can also be variation between expatriates of the same nationality in different locations.
- A strict implementation can lead to rivalry for assignments to locations that are financially attractive and little interest in locations considered to be financially unattractive.
- The approach can also pose problem upon repatriation when the employee's salary reverts to a home country level that is below that of the host country.
- This approach not only creates problem for firms in developing countries, but also for firms from many countries where local managerial salaries are well below that of the United States, which is the world market leader in managerial salaries.

The Balance Sheet Approach

This is the most widely used approach for international compensation. The basic objective is to "keep the expatriate whole" i.e.,' maintaining relativity to PCN colleagues, and compensating for the costs of an international assignment through maintenance of home–country living standard, plus a financial inducement to make the package attractive. This approach links the base salary for PCN's and TCN's to the salary structure of the relevant home country. According to Reynolds, the balance sheet approach to international compensation is a system designed to equalize the purchasing power of employees at comparable position levels living abroad and in the home country, and to provide incentives to offset qualitative difference between assignment locations.

There are four major categories of outlays incurred by expatriates that are incorporated in the balance sheet approach.

1. **Goods and services:** Home country outlays for items such as food, personal care, clothing household furnishing, recreations, transportation and medical care.
2. **Housing:** Major costs associated with housing in the host country.
3. **Income taxes:** Parent–country and host country income taxes.
4. **Reserve:** Contributes to savings, payments for benefits, pension, social security taxes, and so on.

Where costs associated with the host–country assignment exceed equivalent costs in the parent country, these costs are met by both the firm and the expatriate to ensure that parent–country equivalent purchasing power is achieved.

Advantages of Balance Sheet Approach

- This approach provides equity between foreign assignments and between expatriates of the same nationality.

- Repatriation of expatriates is facilitated by the emphasis on equity with the parent country since expatriate compensation remains anchored to the compensation system in the parent country.
- This approach is easy to communicate to employees.

Disadvantages of Balance Sheet Approach

1. This approach results is considerable disparities – both between expatriates of different nationalities and between PCN's and HCN's.
2. There are chances of problem when international staffs are paid different amounts for performing the same job in the host location according to their different home base salary.
3. This approach can become quite complex to administer in the areas of taxation, living costs, and differentiating between PCN's and TCN's.

REPATRIATION

Repatriation is the activity of bringing the expatriate back to the home country. It has become more widely recognized by practitioners and academies that repatriation needs careful managing, although this increased attention is somewhat belated. It becomes a traumatic experience for some, even more than what was encountered in the foreign location.

From the multi-national perspective, repatriation is frequently considered as the final stage in the expatriation process but the multinational ability to attract future expatriates is effected by the manner in which it handles repatriation.

Typically, on completion of the foreign assignment, the multinational brings the expatriate back to the home country, although it should be noted that not all international assignments end with a transfer home: rather, the expatriate is reassigned to another international post.

Repatriation Process

1. **Preparation:**

   It involves developing plans for the future and gathering information about the new position. The firm may provide a checklist of items to be considered before the returning home or a thorough preparation of employees and family for the transfer home.

2. **Physical relocation:**

   It refers to removing personal effects, breaking ties with colleagues and friends, and travelling to the next posting, usually the home country. Most multinational use removal firms or relocation consultants to handle the physical relocation, both for the movement out and the return home of the employee and family, and this may be formalized in their HR policies.

3. **Transition:**

   It means settling into temporary accommodation where necessary, making arrangements for housing and schooling, and carrying out other administrative tasks e.g., renewing drivers license, applying for medical insurance, etc. Some companies hire relocation consultants to assist in this phase also.

Readjustments

It involves coping with reverse culture shock and career demands.The reentry phase may include a number of problems that are related directly to the repatriate's attitude about the effect that an international assignment has on future employment prospects. The lack of acceptance of repatriation programs among the survey respondents tends to illustrate the absence of organized efforts by large sophisticated multinationals to assist expatriated personnel.

One reason for this oversight may be that repatriation problems are not dramatic, or visible, or readily identifiable as expensive. However, some companies assign the expatriate a mentor (also referred to as a company contact, sponsor, or "godfather"). The mentor is usually in a more senior position than the expatriate, from the sending work unit, and knows the expatriate personally. A mentor should ensure that the expatriate is not forgotten when important decisions are made regarding positions, promotions and so on.

The Repatriation Program Include

(i) Preparation, physical relocation, and transition information (what the company will help with).

(ii) Financial and tax assistance (including benefit and tax changes, loss of overseas allowance).

(iii) Rentry position and career path assistance, reverse culture shock (including family disorientation).

(iv) School system and children's education (including adaptation) work place changes (such as corporate culture, structure and decentralization).

(v) Stress management, communication related training. Establishing networking opportunities and help in forming new social contacts.

It was found that an effective mentor is likely to alert the firm of the eminent return of the repatriate and thus affect the re-entry position, or the practice is part of a managed repatriation program.

MANAGING GLOBAL COMPENSATION AND BENEFITS

Key findings from the survey presented are:

- The most common structure for managing HR programs is partial centralization. More than half of all multinationals (56 percent), however, plan to shift to a more centralized structure over the next two years, up from 42 percent in 2004.
- Two-thirds of multinationals (66 percent) report they have adopted a globally consistent HR strategy. The strategies of financially high-performing companies tend to focus on outcomes –such as attracting and retaining key talent, linking rewards and results, and developing a common corporate culture – while the strategies of low performers focus on implementation.
- Half of multinational organizations (51 percent) have a formal or informal global total rewards strategy, and another 20 percent plan to develop a strategy within the next 12 to 24 months. Twenty-nine percent have no plans to do so. Of those companies that have a strategy, half also have a strategy for communicating it.

- High performing companies provide more opportunity for above-market compensation. For example, 25 percent of high-performing firms target total cash compensation at the 75th percentile or higher (versus no low-performing firms).

A bit more detail on the second point above, which addresses the top objectives or focal points of global HR strategies for high versus low performing companies (note that this distinction is based on self-reported, but validated, responses to a survey question regarding the organization's financial performance relative to peers). The top five objectives reported about high performing companies for their global HR strategies:

- Improving attraction and retention of key talent (50%)
- Ensuring a consistent link between rewards and results (50%)
- Developing a common corporate culture (39%)
- Adapting a global HR strategy to local culture (36%)
- Improving governance of compensation policies, implementation and administration (33%).

The top five objectives reported by low performing companies for their global HR strategies are:

- Implementing a consistent global HR philosophy (58%)
- Ensuring consistent link between rewards and results (46%)
- Improving attraction and retention of key talent (42%)
- Implementing streamlined and efficient processes (42%)
- Adapting a global HR strategy to local culture (27%).

KEY TERMS

Foreign service premium	Rest and relaxation leave benefits
Hardship allowance	Going rate approach
Relocation assistant payment	Balance sheet approach

SUMMARY

The objective of internal compensation manager is to stimulate performance and behaviour of an individual leading to organization's success.

The Components of international compensation are:

- Base salary and base pay.
- Indirect monetary compensation (benefit).
- Fringe compensation including standard benefit.
- Relocation assistance.

- Education reimbursement for expatriate's children.
- Home leave benefit and travel reimbursement.
- Rest and relaxation leave and allowance.

Equalization Benefit:

- Cost of living allowance.
- Education allowance for children.
- Foreign service premium.
- Emergency leave.
- Club membership.
- Spousal employment.
- Cross cultural training.

Incentives:

- Stock options.
- Mobility premiums.
- Perquisites.
- Performance related rewards.

There are two main options in the area of international compensation:-

(a) The going rate approach (also referred to as the market rate approach).

(b) The balance sheet approach (also known as the build up approach).

- The key characteristic of going rate approach are, the base salary for international transfer is linked to the salary structure on the host country.

The balance sheet approach: This is the most widely used approach for international compensation. The basic objective is to "keep the expatriate whole" i.e.,' maintaining relativity to PCN colleagues, and compensating for the costs of an international assignment through maintenance of home–country living standard, plus a financial inducement to make the package attractive.

Repatriation is the activity of bringing the expatriate back to the home country.

REVIEW QUESTIONS

1. What are the components of an executive compensation plan ?
2. Explain in detail the responsibilities of an international manager.
3. Differentiate among home country, host country and TCN employees.
4. What are the various approaches of the International compensation?

5. In the Balance Sheet approach to paying expariates, most of total compensation is linked to cost of living which resembles a traditional Japanese pay system. Evaluate this argument.
6. Discuss the strengths and weaknesses of the following methods for establishing base pay in international contexts : home-country based pay, headquarters based pay and host-country based pay.

References

"Managing Global Pay", Human Capital, New Delhi, No., 2000.

Suutari, V. & Tornikoski, C., (2000). *Determinants of Expatriate Compensation: Findings among Expatriate Members of SEFE.* Finnish Journal of Business Economics, 49(4): pp.517-539.

Suutari, V. and Tornikoski, C., (2001). *The Challenge of Expatriate Compensation: The Sources of Satisfaction and Dissatisfaction among Expatriates.* International Journal of Human Resource Management, 12(3): pp.1-16.

Bonache, J. & Z. Fernandez,. (1997). *Expatriate Compensation and its Links to Subsidiary Strategic Role: a Theoretical Analysis.* The International Journal of Human Resource Management, 4: pp.457-475.

Mathis, Robert L., and John H. Jackson. *Human Resource Management.* 11th ed. Mason, OH: Thomson/ South-Western, 2006.

Milkovich, George T., and Jerry M. Newman, *Compensation.* 8th ed. New York: McGraw-Hill/Irwin, 2005.

GLOSSARY

- **Absenteeism:** Any failure of an employee to report for or to remain at work as scheduled, regardless of reason.
- **Ability:** An individual's capability to engage in a specific behaviour.
- **Absolute judgment:** An appraisal format that asks supervisors to make judgment about an employee's performance based solely on performance standards.
- **Accountability:** A term used in job analysis to denote the end results to be achieved by the employee.
- **Across the board increase:** A general adjustment that provides equal increases to all employees.
- **Action learning:** A process in which participant's learn through experience.
- **Adjective checklist:** An individual or job rating technique or a performance appraisal instrument consisting of traits or behaviours demonstrated by an employee.
- **Adverse impact:** An unfavourable effect of employment practices with regard to minorities or women.
- **Adventure learning:** A team work and leadership training program based on the use of challenging activities.
- **Affirmative action:** Requirements of an employer to take positive steps to end discrimination (minorities and women).
- **Agency theory :** A theory of motivation that depicts exchange relationships in terms of two parties agents and principals. According to this theory, both sides of exchange will seek the most favourable exchange possible and will act opportunistically, if given a chance.
- **All salaried work force:** It not only exempts employees from provisions of the Fair Labour Standards Act, who traditionally are paid a salary rather than an hourly rate but also non-exempt employees receive a prescribed amount of money each pay period that does not primarily depend on the number of hours worked.
- **Alternatives dispute resolution (ADR):** Methods of solving a problem by bringing an impartial outsider but not using the court system.

- **Alternation ranking:** A job evaluation method that involves ordering the job description alternately at each extreme. All the jobs are considered and agreement is reached on, which is the most valuable and then the least valuable. Evaluators alternate between the next most valued and next least valued and so on until the jobs have been ordered.
- **Amortization:** Paying off an interest bearing liability through a series of installment payments.
- **Annuity problems:** The situation that exists when past merit payments, incorporated into an employees base pay, form an annuity allowing formerly productive employees to slack effective for several years while still earning high pay.
- **Appeals procedures:** Mechanisms are created to handle pay disagreements. They provide a forum for employees and managers to voice their complaints and receive a hearing.
- **Apprenticeship:** A work study learning method teaches job skills through a combination of on the job training and rated in behavioural terms and use critical incidents to describe various levels of performance.
- **Benchmark:** A standard with characteristics in detail that other classification can be compared as being above, below or comparable to it, refers to jobs used for making pay comparisons within or outside the organization.
- **Bonus:** A lumpsum payment to an employee in recognition of goal achievement.
- **Broadbanding:** A pay structure consisting of a few (four to eight) pay grades/ bands with each band having relatively wide range.
- **Business process reengineering (BPR):** A fundamental rethinking, a radical redesign of business processes to achieve dramatic improvements in cost quality, service and speed.
- **Business game:** A situational test in which candidates play themselves, not an assigned role and are evaluated within a group.
- **Cafeteria (Flexible) Benefit Plan:** A benefit plan in which employees have a choice as to the benefits they receive within some dollar limit.
- **Capital gains:** It is the difference between the company stock price at the time of purchase and the lower stock price at the time an executive receives the stock options.
- **Cash Balance Plan:** Retirement plan in which the employer sets up an individual account for each employee and contributes a percentage of the employee's salary; the account earns interest at a predefined rate.
- **Classes in compensation:** Grouping jobs based on asset of rule for each group or class, such as amount of independent judgment, skill, physical effort and so forth. Required classes usually contain similar jobs.
- **Cost of living adjustments (COLAs):** Represent periodic basic pay increase that is based on changes in prices, as indexed by the consumer price index (CPI).
- **Comparable worth:** The concept of measuring a job's value to the firm. This value is important to determine the rates of pay for jobs having dissimilar job content and making different requirements on the job holder.

- **Compensable factor:** Job attributes that provide the basis for evaluating the relative worth of jobs inside an organization. These include fundamental compensable element a job such as skills, effort responsibility and working conditions.
- **Competency:** Basic knowledge and abilities employees must acquire or demonstrate in a competency–based plan in order to successfully perform the work and to achieve business objectives.
- **Competency based pay:** Pay related directly to the kinds and levels of competencies (knowledge and skills) required in the performance of the work / job.
- **Competitiveness:** The ability of an organization to provide rates of pay comparable to that of labour market competitors.
- **Congruency:** The degree of consistency or "Fit" between the compensation system and other organizational components such as strategy etc.
- **Debarment:** The act of barring a contractor or sub-contractor from any government contract work because of violations of equal employment opportunity and affirmative action requirements.
- **Deferred profit sharing plan:** A plan in which a certain amount of profit is credited to each employee's account, payable at retirement termination, or death.
- **Defined benefit plans:** Pension plan under which an employer promises to pay a retiree a stated pension fund.
- **Disparate (unequal) treatment standard:** Discrimination Theory that laws the application of different standards to different classes of employees unless the standards can be shown to be business related.
- **Distributive justice:** Fairness in the amount of reward distributed to employees.
- **Downsizing:** The planned elimination of large number of personnel with the goal of enhancing the organization's competitiveness.
- **Dual coverage:** In families in which both spouses work, the coverage of specific claims from each spouses employment benefit package. Employers cut costs by specifying payment limitations under such conditions.
- **Earnings:** Total wages or compensation received by an employee for time worked or services rendered (including all compensation, overtime and premium pay).
- **Early- retirement window:** A type of offering by which employees are encouraged to retire early, the incentive being liberal pension and benefits plus perhaps, a cash payment.
- **Employee benefits:** Tangible compensation given to employees.
- **Employee compensation:** All forms of pay or rewards going to employees from their employment.
- **Employees Stock Ownership Plan (ESOP):** A stock bonus plan that allows employer to take advantage of certain tax privileges, while encouraging employee ownership of the company by granting stock to employees.

- **Employees Retirement Income Security Act (ERISA):** Federal Law that increased the responsibility of pension plan trustees to protect retirees, established certain rights related to vesting and portability, and created the Pension Benefit Guarantee Corporation.
- **Equalization Component:** As a part of an expatriate compensation package, equalization is one form of equity designed to keep the worker whole which comes in the form of tax equalization having and other allowances and premiums.
- **Equity:** The fairness of a pay system assessed in terms of the relative worth of jobs to the organization, competitive market rates outside the organization and the pay received by others doing the same job.
- **Equal Employment Opportunity (EEO):** The condition in which all individuals have an equal chance for employment, regardless of their race, colour, religion, sex, age, disability, or national origin.
- **Executive compensation:** The special components of compensation provided to executives. Tax considerations are critical in the design of these plans.
- **Expatriates:** Employees assigned to work in another country.
- **External equity:** Fairness in relation to the amount paid in the relevant external market.
- **Extrinsic compensation:** It includes both monetary and non-monetary rewards.
- **Fact finder:** A neutral party who studies the issues in a dispute and makes a public recommendation for a reasonable settlement.
- **Factor scales:** Measures that reflect different degrees within each compensable factor. Most commonly 5 to 7 degrees are defined.
- **Fiduciaries:** Pension Trustees.
- **Flat rate:** A single rate for all individuals performing a certain job ignoring seniority.
- **Flexible spending accounts:** Accounts into which employees can deposit pre-tax dollars (Upto a specified amount) to pay for additional benefits.
- **Flexible Benefits/Cafetaria Benefit Plan:** Individualized plans allowed by employers to accommodate employee preferences for benefits.
- **Flexible compensation:** The allocation of employees compensation in a variety of forms tailored to organization pay objectives or the needs of individuals employees.
- **Foreign service employee:** Any one working outside her or his home country with a planned return to that or a third country; also known as an expatriate.
- **Foreign service premium:** A percentage addition to base pay provided to compensate on expatriate for foreign environment factors.
- **401(K) Plan:** A defined contribution pension plan in which an employee can deduct a certain amount of his or her income from taxes and place the money into a personal retirement account; if the employer adds matching funds, the combined sums grow tax free until they are withdrawn, usually at retirement.

- **Functional job analysis:** A method of classifying job taking into account the extent to which instructions, reasoning, judgement, mathematical and verbal ability are necessary for performing job tasks.
- **Gain sharing:** An organization-wide incentive program in which employee co-operation leads to information sharing and employee involvement, which in turn lead to new behaviour that improve organizational productivity; the increase in productivity results in a financial bonus (based on the amount of increase), which is distributed monthly or quarterly.
- **Gantt Plan:** Individual incentive plan that provides for variable incentives as a function of a standard expressed as time period per unit of production. Under this plan, a standard time for a task is purposely set at a level requiring high effort to complete.
- **Globalization:** The interdependence of business operations internationally; commerce without borders.
- **Going rate:** An employer's best estimate of the rate of pay of the labour market to acquire needed personnel.
- **Golden parachute:** A kind of executive deferred compensation providing pay and benefits to executives following their termination resulting from a change in ownership or corporate take over.
- **Guaranteed wage rate:** The rate of pay an employer guarantees to his employees on incentive work.
- **Hardship allowance:** It is the compensation of expatriates for their sacrifices while on assignment.
- **Halsey 50-50 method:** Individual incentive method that provides for variable incentives as a function of a standard expressed as time period per unit of production. This plan derives its name from the shared split between worker and employer of any savings in direct costs.
- **Health Maintenance Organization (HMO):** A non-traditional health care delivery system. HMO's offer comprehensive benefits and out-patient services ; as well as hospital coverage, for a fixed monthly prepaid fee.
- **Home country based pay method:** It compensates expatriate the amount they would like to receive if they were performing similar work in the home country.
- **Host country based methods:** It compensates expatriates based on the host country's pay scales.
- **Housing allowances:** A differential paid to adjust for differences between housing costs at foreign work site and costs for similar housing at the home base.
- **Human resource strategies:** It specifies the particular use of HR practices to be consistent with competitive strategy.
- **Implicit contract:** The unwritten implied agreements; or patterns of reciprocal obligations and returns, between employers and employees. This includes reciprocal understanding about the nature of risks involved in wages, benefits and employability.

- **Improshare (IMproved PROductivity through SHAring):** A gain sharing plan in which a standard is developed to identify the expected hours required to produce an acceptable level of output. Any savings arising from production of agreed upon output in fewer than expected hours are shared by the firm and the worker.
- **Incentive:** It is defined as compensation, other than base wage or salaries, that fluctuates according to employees attainment of some standard, such as pre-established formula, individual or group goals, or company earnings.
- **Incentive Stock Options (ISOs):** A form of deferred compensation designed to influence long term performance. Gives an executive the right to pay today's market price for a block of share in company at future time. No tax is due until the shares are sold.
- **Individual Incentive Plans:** The reward to employees for meeting work related performance standards such as quality, productivity, customer satisfaction, safety and attendance. Any one or a combination of these standard may be used.
- **Individual Retirement Accounts (IRAs):** Tax favoured retirement savings plan that individuals can establish themselves.
- **Indirect compensation:** Compensation components normally included with an employee's benefits package.
- **Internal consistency:** Refers to the pay relationship among job or skill level within a single organization and focuses attention on employee and management acceptance of those relationships. It involves establishing equal pay for jobs for equal worth and acceptable pay differentials for jobs of unequal worth.
- **Internal equity:** The ranking of all jobs to each other relative to their value to the organization.
- **International alliance:** A collaboration between two or more multinational companies that allows them jointly to pursue a common goal.
- **International compensation:** Compensation practices related to employees in foreign work sites.
- **Job analysis:** A systematic process of collecting information related to the nature of a specific job. It provides the knowledge needed to define jobs and conduct job evaluation.
- **Job description:** A written summary of task requirements for a particular job design. The process of determining and specifying the contents, methods, and relationships of a job in order to satisfy, in the most effective and efficient manner, the technological and human considerations within organizational constraints.
- **Job evaluation:** It systematically recognize differences in the relative worth among a set of jobs and establishes pay differentials accordingly.
- **Job pricing:** The assignment of a rate of pay to a job or to job grades, the practice of establishing rates of pay by making judgment that combine internal equity and market value data.
- **Job satisfaction:** Normally, that part of the job description that includes the requisite qualifications of the job holder.

- **Job structure:** Relationship among jobs inside an organization, based on work content and each job's relative contribution to achieving the organization's objectives.
- **Key jobs (Benchmark jobs):** Selected jobs about which data may be gathered from other employers to provide the basis for setting pay.
- **Knowledge capital:** The value of the knowledge possessed by people at all levels of an organization.
- **Knowledge system:** Process that links pay to additional knowledge related to the same job (depth) or to a number of different jobs (breadth).
- **Labour market assessments:** It enables companies to determine the availability of qualified employees.
- **Localization:** The practice of paying expatriate on the same scale as local.
- **Living wage:** A term referring to wage rate that permits the employee to maintain a given standard of living in the face of inflation.
- **Long-term incentives:** Inducements offered in advance to influence longer rate (multi-year) results. Usually offered to top managers and professionals to get them to focus on long term organizational objectives.
- **Low and High:** Approach using the lowest and highest paid benchmark jobs in the external market to anchor an entire skill based structure.
- **Lumpsum:** Award payment of entire increase (typically merit based) at one time. Because amount is not factored into base pay, any benefits tied to base pay do not increase.
- **Management by Objectives:** A good oriented performance appraisal method, requires that supervisors and employees determine objectives for employees to meet during the rating period, and then employees approve how well they have achieved their objectives.
- **Marked based pay system:** A pay system that uses a direct market pricing approach for all of a firm's job.
- **Market pay lines:** Summary of the distribution of market rates for the benchmark jobs under consideration, several methods can be used to construct.
- **Minimum Wage:** The minimum wage level set under the Fair Labour Standards.
- **Merit Pay:** A reward that recognizes outstanding past performance. It can be given in the form of lumpsum payments or as increments to the base pay. Merit programs are commonly designed to pay different amounts (often at different times) depending on the level of performance.
- **Mobility premiums:** It is to reward an employee for moving from one assignment to another.
- **Mutual commitment compensation:** A pay strategy that combines high wages with an emphasis on quality, innovation and customer's service. Based on the belief that high wages are essential to reinforce co-operation and participation and will provide a better living standard for all employees.

- **National Electrical Manufacturing Association (NEMA):** The NEMA plan is a point factor job evaluation system that evolved into the National Position Evaluation among jobs across and within organizations and among individuals in the same job, in an organization plan sponsored by NMTA Associates.
- **Need theories:** Motivation theories that focus on internally generated needs, that induce behaviour designed to satisfy these needs.
- **Non-qualified Pension Plans:** They provide less favourable tax treatments for employers than qualified pension plans.
- **Non-qualified Stock Options:** A right given to an executive to purchase stock at a stipulated price; the excess over fair market value is taxed as ordinary income.
- **On call arrangements:** It is a method for employing temporary workers.
- **Organizational chart:** A diagram depicting an organization's structure including the names of the units, titles and names of individuals, their relative ranks and interrelationships as to authority and responsibility.
- **Organizational culture:** The composite of shared values, symbols and cognitive schemes that ties people together in the organization.
- **Outsourcing:** The practice of hiring outside vendors to perform functions that do not directly contribute to business objectives and in which the organization does not have a comparative advantage.
- **Package:** A term frequently used to describe a combination of pay and benefits received by workers as a result of collective bargaining.
- **Pay bands:** Pay approach in which separate job classifications are combined into a smaller number of divisions, called bands. Created to increase flexibility.
- **Pay differentials:** Differentials in pay.
- **Pay for knowledge plans:** The plan which reward managerial, service, or professional workers for successfully learning specific curricula.
- **Pay plan:** A schedule of pay rates or ranges and a list of showing the assignment of each class in the classification plan to one of the rates or ranges. May extend to rules of administration and the benefit package.
- **Pay range:** The range of pay rates from minimum to maximum set for a pay grade or class. It puts limits on the rates an employer will pay for a particular job.
- **Performance appraisal:** A system for rating the contributions of an employee with respect to his or her job. This rating serves as a basis for merit increases, promotions and or reassignment of work.
- **Pension plan:** A form of deferred compensation providing income to individuals throughout their retirement. Sometimes, companies use early retirement program to reduce workforce size and trim compensation expenditure.

- **Perquisites (perks):** The extras bestowed on top management, such as private dining rooms, company cars, airfare etc.
- **Phantom stock plan:** Stock plan in which an increase in stock price at a fixed future date determines the cash or stock award. It is called a phantom plan because the organization in question is not publicly traded. They are similar to restricted stock plans because executives must meet specific conditions before they can covert these phantom shares into real shares of company stock.
- **Piecework plan:** An individual incentive pay program, that rewards employees based on their individual hourly production against an objective output standard, determined by the pace at which manufacturing equipment operates. For each hour, workers receive piecework incentives for every item produced over the designated production standard worker and also receive a guaranteed hourly pay rate regardless of whether they meet the designated production standard.
- **Profit sharing plan:** It is the payment of a portion of company profits to employees, separate from base pay, cost of living adjustments, or permanent merit pay increases. Two basic kinds of profit sharing plans are used widely today; current profit sharing deferred profit sharing.
- **Present value:** The current worth of a series of amounts payable or receivable in the future after discounting each amount by an assumed rate of interest and adjusting for its probability of payment or receipt.
- **Purchasing power:** The ability to buy goods and services in a certain currency, determined by exchange rates and availability of goods. Companies must determine purchasing power when allocating allowances to expatriates.
- **Qualified benefit plan:** A benefit plan that meets IRS requirements. It can be either a defined benefit or a defined contribution plan. It must not discriminate in favour of officers, shareholders, supervisory personnel or highly compensated employees.
- **Qualified deferred compensation plan:** A deferred compensation program that qualifies for tax exemption. It must provide contributions or benefits for employees other than executives that are proportionate to contributions provided to executives.
- **Quartiles:** It allows compensation professionals to describe the distribution of data, usually annual base pay amount, based on four groupings.
- **Range spread:** It is the difference between the maximum and minimum pay rates of a given pay grade.
- **Range maximums:** The maximum values to be paid for a job grade, representing the top value the organization places on the output of the work.
- **Range minimum:** The minimum values to be paid for a job grade, representing the minimum value the organization places on the work, often rates below the minimum are used for trainees.

- **Red Circles:** These are the rates representing pay rates that are higher than the designated pay range maximums.
- **Relocation assistance:** Payments covering expatriates expenses to relocate to foreign posts.
- **Repatriation:** It is the process of making the transition from an international assignment and living abroad to a domestic assignment and living in the home country.
- **Restricted stock plan:** Plan that grants stock at a reduced price with the condition that it should not be sold before a specified date.
- **Rowan Plan:** Individual incentive plan that provides for variable incentives as a function of a standard expressed as time period per unit of production. It is similar to the Halsey Plan, but in this, a worker's bonus increases as the time required to compute the task decreases.
- **Rucker Plan:** It is a particular type of gain sharing program that emphasizes employee involvement. Gain sharing awards are based on the ratio between value added (less the costs of materials supplies and services rendered) and the total cost of employment.
- **Salary compression:** A salary inequity problem, generally caused by inflation, resulting in longer term employers in a position earning less than workers entering the firm today.
- **Salary continuation: plans** benefit options that provides some form of protection for disability. Some are legally required, such as worker's compensation provisions for work-related disability and social security disability income provisions for those who qualify.
- **Scanlon Plan:** A group cost saving plan designed to lower labour costs without lowering the level of a firm's activity. Incentives are derived as the ratio between labour costs and sales value of production (SVOP).
- **Short-term Incentives:** Inducements offered in advance to influence future short-range (annual) results. Usually, very specific performance standards are established.
- **Single rate system:** A compensation policy under which all employees in a given job are paid at the same rate.
- **Skill based pay system:** Links pay to the depth and/or breadth of the skills and knowledge a person acquires or demonstrat as that are relevant to the work. Typically applies to operators, technicians and office workers where the work is relatively specific and defined. The criterion chosen can influence employee behaviours by describing what is required to get higher pay.
- **Special groups:** Employee groups for whom compensation practices diverge from typical company procedures (e.g., supervisors, middle and upper management, non-supervisory professionals, sales and personnel in foreign subsidiaries).
- **Standard hour plan:** Individual incentive plan in which rate determination is based on time period per unit of production and wages vary directly as a constant function of product level. In this context, the incentive rate in standard hour plans is set based on completion of a task in some expected time period.
- **Statistical quality control:** A type of quality control that makes use of mathematical statistics in sampling inspections and in the analysis of quality control data.

- **Stock purchase plan:** A plan that allows employees to purchase stock.
- **Stock purchase plan (non-qualified):** A plan that is, in effect, a management stock purchase plan. It allows senior management or other key personnel to buy stock in the business. This plan has certain restrictions: (1) The stockholder must be employed for a certain period of time. (2) The business has the right to buy back the stock, and (3) stockholders cannot sell the stock for a defined period.
- **Stock purchase plan (qualified):** A program under which employers buy shares in the company's stock, with the company contributing a specific amount for each unit of employee's contribution. Also, stock may be offered at a fixed price (usually below market) and paid for in full by the employees.
- **Supplemental retirement plans:** These are plans offered to executives and are designed to restore benefit restricted under qualified plans.
- **Surplus value:** The difference between labour's use and exchange values. According to Marx, under capitalism wages are based on labour's exchange value – which is lower than its use value and thus provide only a subsistence wage.
- **Task:** Identifiable human efforts exerted for a specific purpose and completed within a prescribed period of time.
- **Tax Equalization:** A method whereby an expatriate pays neither more nor less tax than assumed home country tax on base pay.
- **Team Incentive:** Group incentives restricted to team members with payout usually based on improvements in productivity, customer satisfaction, financial performance or quality of goods and services directly attributable to the team.
- **Third Country Nationals (TCNs):** Employees of a US foreign subsidiary who maintain citizenship in a country other than the United States or the host country. TCNs compensation is tied to comparative wages in the local country, the United States, or the country of citizenship.
- **Total compensation:** The complete pay package for employees, including all forms of money, bonuses, benefits, services and stock.
- **Two-tier pay plans:** Wage structure that differentiates pay for the same jobs based on hiring date. A contract is negotiated that specifies that employers hired after a stated day will receive lower wages than their higher seniority peers working on the same or similar jobs.
- **Uncertainty avoidance:** A dimension of national culture representing the method by which society deals with risk and instability for its members.
- **Universal compensable factor:** Certain qualities that might be considered common to all jobs, such as mental, physical and skill requirements.
- **Universal job factors:** Factors that could theoretically be used to evaluate all jobs in all organizations.

- **Validity:** The quality that defines how well device measures what it is supposed to measure.
- **Variable pay:** Tying pay to productivity or some measure that can vary with the firms.
- **Vertical knowledge:** It refers to knowledge traditionally associated with supervisory activities – for example performance appraisal and grievance review procedures.
- **Voluntary termination:** They are initiated by employees, who do so to work for other companies or to begin their retirements.
- **Wage contour:** A stable group of wage determining units that have common wage making characteristics used for identifying market pay relationships.
- **Wage curve:** A series of wage rates shown graphically.
- **Wage rate:** The money rate expressed in dollars and cents paid to the employee per hour profitability.
- **Wages:** Compensation paid to hourly workers (including those on incentive pay) for services rendered.
- **Zones:** Ranges of pay used as controls or guidelines within pay bands that can keep the system more structurally intact. Maximums, midpoints and minimums provide guide to appropriate pay for certain levels of work without zones; employees may float to the maximum pay which for many jobs in the band is higher than market value.